For Ken, Jerry and Mr Morris,

Congratulations on the 40th Anniversary of the Band Room! And many more!!

Charles S. Gabriel
Col USAF

THE FORCE OF DESTINY

The Life and Times of Colonel Arnald D. Gabriel

MICHAEL A. GABRIEL

Foreword by Dr. Tim Lautzenheiser

THE FORCE OF DESTINY
THE LIFE AND TIMES OF COLONEL ARNALD D. GABRIEL

Copyright © 2016 Michael Gabriel.

All rights reserved. No part of this book may be used or reproduced by any means, graphic, electronic, or mechanical, including photocopying, recording, taping or by any information storage retrieval system without the written permission of the author except in the case of brief quotations embodied in critical articles and reviews.

Book cover design by Stilson Greene Graphic Design & Illustration, stilsongreene.com

Author photograph and interior photo processing by Jeanette Galie Burkle, Galie Photography, galiephotography.com

iUniverse books may be ordered through booksellers or by contacting:

iUniverse
1663 Liberty Drive
Bloomington, IN 47403
www.iuniverse.com
1-800-Authors (1-800-288-4677)

Because of the dynamic nature of the Internet, any web addresses or links contained in this book may have changed since publication and may no longer be valid. The views expressed in this work are solely those of the author and do not necessarily reflect the views of the publisher, and the publisher hereby disclaims any responsibility for them.

Any people depicted in stock imagery provided by Thinkstock are models, and such images are being used for illustrative purposes only.
Certain stock imagery © Thinkstock.

ISBN: 978-1-4917-8848-6 (sc)
ISBN: 978-1-4917-8849-3 (hc)
ISBN: 978-1-4917-8850-9 (e)

Library of Congress Control Number: 2016901639

Print information available on the last page.

iUniverse rev. date: 3/16/2016

CONTENTS

Foreword..ix
Preface and Acknowledgements xi
Prologue..xvii

Section I–The Early Years

    Chapter 1   High School 3
    Chapter 2   Induction 15
    Chapter 3   The Twenty-Ninth Infantry 25
    Chapter 4   D-day and Beyond 35
    Chapter 5   Holland and Germany 53
    Chapter 6   Aftermath and the Final Months Across Germany 63
    Chapter 7   Army of the Occupation 73
    Chapter 8   Home 83
    Chapter 9   Ithaca College 89

Section II–The Air Force

    Chapter 10 Air Force Bandsman 97
    Chapter 11 Sampson Air Force Base 101
    Chapter 12 Langley Air Force Base 109
    Chapter 13 Wiesbaden Air Force Base 117
    Chapter 14 The Air Force Academy 159
    Chapter 15 Bolling Air Force Base 167
    Chapter 16 The 1970s 235
    Chapter 17 Innovation 261

Chapter 18 The Guest Artist Series..275
Chapter 19 Retirement 297

Section III–Academia and Guest Conducting

Chapter 20 George Mason University and the McLean
            Symphony Orchestra...307
Chapter 21 Legacy 319

For Trish

FOREWORD

By definition, the word *hero* means: An individual of distinguished courage or ability, admired for his/her brave deeds and noble qualities. Colonel Arnald D. Gabriel is a *hero* to many of us, and he undeniably is the ultimate *hero* to everyone who is part of the music profession.

In the spring of 1970, I was working on my graduate degree at the University of Alabama. As part of my assistantship duties, I was in charge of the University Bands' exhibit during the all-state event. Colonel Gabriel was directing one of the three select bands. I left my post to watch an already-legendary conductor in action. For the next three hours, I was mesmerized as I witnessed musical magic guided by this remarkable man on the podium. Some five decades later, I am still captivated when Colonel Gabriel is in front of an ensemble—in fact, I'm more captivated now than ever.

Many years later, I had the privilege of working alongside him at several music festivals, and I quickly discovered Colonel Gabriel to convey his signature leadership style with or without his baton in hand; the maestro is truly a master of each and every facet of his being, absolutely first class. My hero embraced me as a colleague and as a friend. What greater gift could there be?

Fast-forward to today, and now yet another landmark gift has been given to all of us. You have in your hands a gripping biography penned by Colonel Gabriel's son, Michael A. Gabriel. *The Force of Destiny* is, in itself, a force of destiny. It takes the reader from the onset of Colonel Gabriel's boyhood as the son of immigrant parents seeking a better life in America and through his service as a combat infantryman who was part of the D-day invasion of Omaha Beach; all this is wrapped in heartfelt memories of the impact World War II had on his personal character and his professional future, pointing to more evidence of *why* the man is *a hero*. Following the war, the next stop was Ithaca College—a magnificent and heartrending story highlighting the importance of his relationship with his high school band director, Professor Stanley—and then an enlistment in the US Air Force, and the beginning of an eventual, never-to-be-rivaled tenure as the commander/conductor of the United States Air Force Band. The script is compelling; the writing is poetic.

The book's title, *The Force of Destiny*, is taken from Giuseppe Verdi's opera: *La Forza del Destino*. Translated, it means: The Power of Fate, The Force of Destiny. It is ever-apparent why the overture is a favorite in the colonel's vast conducting repertoire. It is, in great part, a reflection of his life's journey. From the very beginning, Arnald D. Gabriel was *destined* to become a *hero* at the hand of *fate*.

Several years ago Colonel Gabriel invited me to serve as his interviewer during a special session at the Midwest Clinic. He asked me to come to his home to prepare for this one-of-a-kind presentation. The four-hour exchange of information was equal to a rigorous PhD curriculum being delivered in one class setting. I laughed and I cried in reaction to the many shared stories while riding copilot through the introspective flight mirroring his life; once again, his hero status catapulted to new heights of admiration.

To this day, I eagerly look forward to every occasion when our paths cross at this-or-that workshop, convention, or concert. It is impossible *not* to find myself in the same state of awe watching the colonel in action ... much like that young graduate student in Tuscaloosa, Alabama. Being near the colonel, I know I'm in the presence of a *hero, my hero*, a man I truly love, not only for what he has unselfishly given to so many, but for his ongoing quest for excellence in every aspect of his life.

Kudos to Michael A. Gabriel for beautifully capturing the trademark spirit of his father and for his commitment and dedication to the creation of a manuscript reflecting Pulitzer-level artistry. Thank you!

And to Col. Arnald D. Gabriel, *thank you*. Thank you for redefining the word *hero*.

Dr. Tim Lautzenheiser

PREFACE AND ACKNOWLEDGEMENTS

The impetus for this book came from a series of family get-togethers where my siblings and I heard the first of my dad's war stories. These never-before-heard tales astounded each of us. He was in his eighties, and most of what he related those evenings had been kept private for more than sixty years. My initial desire was simply to document his journey to preserve family history and to provide some knowledge for his grandchildren and great-grandchildren. The interviews came from both face-to-face and phone conversations but mostly e-mail. The process for him has been cathartic and for me, revelatory. I have learned that most of us don't know our parents; their professional lives differ vastly from their parental lives. I have a good friend whose father passed away a couple of years ago, and he lamented to me, "I've spent the last two years trying to figure out who that guy was." I count myself as incredibly fortunate to have figured out who my dad was.

Although writing is a solitary endeavor, many people have contributed to this effort through the sharing of their recollections, stories, and heartfelt tributes of Arnald D. Gabriel. The danger of such a list is that I've left someone off, and if (when) I have, my apologies. To say that my father has an incredible memory is to understate the obvious yet it is, humanly, fallible. The conversations with dozens of people, both electronic and verbal, have been fascinating and enlightening and have added immensely to his story. Without exception, each of these shared stories or recollections has triggered further memories in him and layered the narrative beyond description. Errors in any work of this size and complexity are inevitable and are mine alone.

Current and former Air Force Band members have made the biggest contribution simply because the Air Force Band is Arnald's[1] crowning achievement and is at the heart of the story. First, I thank the current commander and conductor of the US Air Force Band, Col. Larry Lang. Colonel Lang has allowed me unfettered access to the band's library and archives and has taken time from his busy schedule to answer some pretty basic questions about rank, advancement, and military awards. My knowledge of the military comes from proximity and osmosis; I am an Air Force brat but a lifelong civilian. By extension, I want to thank the hardworking airmen who allowed me to interrupt their duties in the library by explaining the operation of the moving file system (and their assurances that I wouldn't be crushed between the massive panels—I'm not convinced), allowing a virtual takeover of a copy machine for a few hours ("Where can I find more paper for this?"), and disrupting someone doing actual work for the Air Force: Senior M.Sgt. Brian McCurdy, NCOIC (the guy in charge), and M.Sgt. Jennifer Tersero, historian (and who is married to Joe Tersero—see below).

The list of former band members must begin with Albert Bader; thanks for talking to me about the old days and the band's impression of the new guy. James "Mike" Bankhead and Craig Jessop gave me insights into not only Arnald's leadership style, but the care and concern he has for those with whom he works. Dr. Anthony Maiello certainly falls into the above category, and although not a member of the Air Force Band, his professional relationship with Arnald at George Mason University is second only to their close personal friendship. Each of the above has said, "Your father changed my life." As remarkable a statement as that is, I heard it many times over the past eight years.

Norval "Sandy" Jones, bagpipes, and John Bosworth, drums, gave me the incredible story of one of the most unique units in military bands: the Air Force Pipe Band. Thanks for allowing me to tell it.

---

[1] Throughout the book, I have referred to my dad as Arnald simply because it is his name. No one calls him that. He is called, Sir, Colonel, Gabe, Pop, Daddy, Grandpa, Great-Grandpa, Uncle Gabe, and, because most of his childhood contemporaries are gone, almost no one calls him Scratch anymore.

Johnny Woody, trumpet, Shannon W. Jones, clarinet, and Jimmie Nolan, percussion, all added their personal touch, and I thank you for taking the time to help me. The incomparable Lawrence Odom—piano, oboe, bassoon, trombone, harp, organ (I've probably missed something), and arranger—has a shared past with "Dominico" that dates back to 1958 and Wiesbaden. I suspect your insatiable desire for excellence is what you two share, and I thank you for your precious time. During my search through the band's archives, I discovered travelogues of the South American and European tours. These two typewritten documents were the personal impressions of a young vocalist with the Singing Sergeants, and without his generous permission to use them, most of what I wrote about the tours could not have been known to me; thank you, Ron Oltmanns.

Several years ago, my wife, Trish, and I traced Arnald's route through Europe during World War II. After leaving Normandy Beach, we headed north into Belgium and Holland where we were hosted by Harrie and Hellie Reumkens who graciously housed and fed us for three days. Harrie is the artistic director for the World Music Contest Kerkrade, the world's largest festival for wind music, and possesses a depth of knowledge about history that is astounding. Thank you for bringing my father's journey alive for me and for providing a powerfully emotional moment by pointing out a field outside the small village of Bourheim, Germany. I can express no greater thanks to Frances Arrowsmith, Harry Aschoff Jr., and Janis Blackburn for sharing their family history and deeply personal feelings about their fathers than by welcoming them into our family.

The following people have added to the book in a myriad of small yet important ways, and I thank you: Dale Underwood, saxophone virtuoso, University of Miami; Judy Shellenberger, band manager, Williamsport, Pennsylvania; Donald Carlson, Director, Twenty-Ninth Infantry Band; Bruce Moss, Bowling Green State University; and Mitch Bassman, George Mason University. Thanks to Dr. Tim Lautzenheiser for taking time out of a very busy schedule to pen the foreword to this book. (I'm told it was written somewhere over the North Pacific en route to Japan.)

Retired Chief M.Sgt. Harry Gleeson spent twenty years with the Air Force Band as a member of the Singing Sergeants, director of Public Affairs, was the voice of the Air Force Band as the band's announcer, and is the unofficial historian emeritus of the US Air Force Band; he possesses probably the largest collection of documents relating to their history,[2] and as such, has endured countless inquiries from me with regard to long-forgotten discussions, concert programs, and official documents, and has provided several of the stories contained within these pages. I cannot overstate his contribution, and I am eternally grateful.

Chief M.Sgt. Joe Tersero retired after twenty-one years with the Air Force Band as an instrumentalist (he played the bassoon). He was the chief music librarian, archivist, and historian[3] and was kind enough to do an initial edit of the book. He corrected countless errors of my horrible punctuation and spelling (no, spell-checker doesn't catch them all), and his fact-checking has saved me from, at best, embarrassment and, at worst, damaged credibility. He spent hours of his own valuable time pouring over my words, refusing any compensation save this inadequate paragraph. Thanks, Joe.

Joe's research led him to his contacts at the other service bands in the Washington, DC, area and include: the Marine Band Library: Chief Librarian Master Gunnery Sgt. Jane Cross; Gunnery Sgt. Kira Wharton; S.Sgt. Nishana Dobbeck; Gunnery Sgt. Jennifer Mills; S.Sgt. Tilden Olsen; and S.Sgt. Charles Paul. The US Army Band Library: Sgt. Maj. Kim S. Newlen and M.Sgt. Laura J. Lineberger. The US Navy Band Library: Chief Musician Amy M. Smith.

My mother-in-law, Carolyn Tate, was an early fan of my writing, and after sending her a few (truly awful) false starts, she encouraged me to keep at it. Although she is much too kind to say how bad the first attempts were, Carolyn's encouragement gave me the confidence to continue. Thanks, Mom.

No one has been a bigger supporter of mine than my wife, Trish. From listening to my early musings about the idea that, "Someone needs to write this stuff down," to removing every excuse I may have

---

2 He has taken on the daunting task of writing the *History of the Air Force Band*.
3 As a civilian, he now works for the US Marine Band in the same capacity.

had and allowing me to retire early from my airline career, she has been there encouraging, prodding, and cajoling. ("You know, none of us are getting any younger!") I have spent many thousands of hours with her flying multiengine jet airliners and probably an equal number of hours with her in sports venues across the country, and I am always amazed at her easygoing nature and positive attitude. I have a lot to learn from her. Thanks, Kiki.

Finally, I would like to thank the subject of this book. Pop, your willingness to dig up some very powerful and painful memories took remarkable strength, not a particularly surprising quality considering what I know now of your life, yet, still impressive. I am proud to have learned the details of your many accomplishments and am incredibly grateful and humbled by the trust you've placed in me to tell the remarkable story of your life. I love you.

The success of our operas rests most of the
time in the hands of the conductor.
This person is as necessary as a tenor or a prima donna.

—Giuseppe Verdi

PROLOGUE

The conductor strides confidently onstage to an enthusiastic applause, turns to the packed house, and humbly bows at the waist. The ovation crescendo reaches a climax, and as he straightens, he raises his hand in heartfelt thanks. His air force blue uniform shines electric in the spotlight, and as he turns and steps onto the elevated podium, the applause tapers and the audience returns to their seats.

There is a moment before the conductor's arms are raised—a moment before the music begins—where, with the band's attention fully on the leader, a small, intimate moment may take place between them. Through a look, a smile, even a whispered word unheard by all but the musicians, the conductor may convey his confidence to them, his faith in them. Tonight, however, the moment is simply a wordless, mutual acknowledgement of the others' professionalism; it is the easy rapport that old friends enjoy.

From the first downbeat and throughout the deeply emotional piece of music, the assembled patrons are transfixed. The colonel coaxes the best from the United States Air Force Band as the haunting strains of John William's "Hymn to the Fallen" fill the concert hall. Although written for the movie *Saving Private Ryan*, it is a largely unrecognized piece because it plays behind the final credits at the end of the film. It was written for and dedicated to those who lost their lives on battlefields around the world, and there are few pieces of music more stirring or evocative.

The music ends quietly, reverently. Woodwinds softly repeat the plaintive melody as the snare drum rolls a cadence reminiscent of a military funeral, and in a striking piece of genius, the choir is directed to hum the final chorus. The effect is breathtaking. After the final downbeat, all is quiet as hands rise, at first not to applaud, but to wipe away tears. The colonel is still, his hands clasped in front, and his head bowed. Slowly, the ovation begins and quickly fills the auditorium. Before he turns to the audience, he unabashedly wipes his eyes, regains his composure, and now facing them, bows deeply to the cheering throng, all on their feet.

The thunderous applause roils the hall in appreciation of not only the deeply emotional performance, but also as heartfelt thanks for the commander's return. Col. Arnald D. Gabriel spent more than twenty-one years as commander and conductor of the United States Air Force Band, molding the organization into world-class status largely through his innovative leadership. Now, some twenty years later, he returns as guest conductor and conductor emeritus for this Memorial Day concert at the Daughters of the American Revolution (DAR) Constitution Hall in Washington, DC, in solemn tribute to the men and women who have paid for our freedom with their lives. The concert also commemorates the upcoming sixtieth anniversary of D-day. The colonel's tribute and emotion is deeper than most know and is hidden in plain sight in the collection of medals and ribbons displayed on his uniform.

Even to the uninitiated there is recognition of the overarching success in his more than thirty-year military career. There is, however, a jarring incongruity that even a rudimentary knowledge of military awards reveals: set atop the five or so rows of ribbons and medals is one that is rectangular in shape. A 1795 Springfield musket lies on a blue field trimmed in silver and backed by an elliptical laurel wreath: the Combat Infantryman's Badge (CIB). The CIB is awarded to "personnel with an infantry specialty who have satisfactorily performed duty while ... engaged in active ground combat." Set lower in the resplendent display is the Bronze Star Medal with Oak Leaf Cluster. *Two* Bronze Stars. The Bronze Star is awarded for "heroic or meritorious service." When it is awarded for bravery, it is the fourth-highest combat award this nation may bestow. Combat awards on the chest of a retired air force musician and full-bird colonel. There is also the French *Croix de Guerre* and the Legion of Merit with two Oak Leaf Clusters. The medals only hint at events nearly a lifetime ago, and like most of his generation, he is reticent to discuss his role and quick to deflect praise.

Colonel Gabriel exits the stage to a standing ovation no amount of bowing, waving, or deference to the band can quiet. He returns and prodded into two encores, performs each with an energy and passion that belie his age.

Today is his seventy-ninth birthday.

SECTION ONE
The Early Years

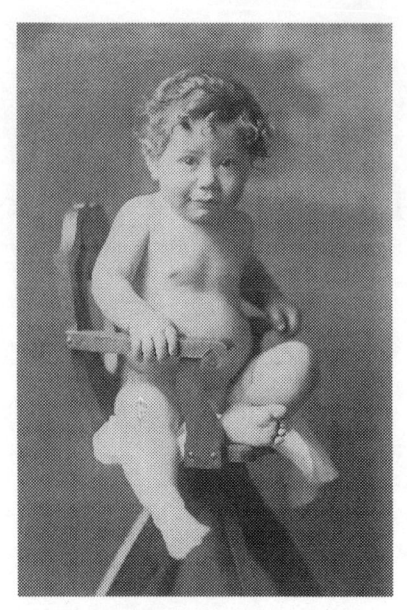

Baby Arnald

Left Tackle

Cortland High School
Senior Picture

CHAPTER ONE

High School

The train steamed out of the Cortland, New York, station, billowed an impossible cloud of smoke into the mild December morning, and slowly gathered speed. Arnald was certain his fellow passengers could hear his pounding heart, for he was off on quite an adventure. Sure, he'd been to Uncle Tony's house in Brooklyn with his family a few times, but that was nothing compared to this: at age seventeen, a train trip to Washington, DC, by himself. He even had to change trains in Philadelphia, another place he'd never been.

In December 1942 the entire country seemed to be on the move. With the attack on Pearl Harbor just over a year earlier, Americans readied themselves for President Roosevelt's prediction that, "This generation of Americans has a rendezvous with destiny." The Battle of Midway, the turning point in the Pacific theater, had been just six months earlier, and Operation Torch, the Allied invasion of North Africa, had begun only a month prior.

The manifestation of America's commitment to the war effort was no more evident than in the train stations and aboard the rolling stock of its primary mode of transportation: passenger trains. Uniformed personnel outnumbered other passengers and, if on official business, took priority. Arnald's train was no different. The mood aboard was necessarily somber and businesslike, but he was far too excited to notice.

The anticipation of the trip was almost too much to bear. Ever since hearing the United States Navy Band in concert at Cortland High

School, he'd wanted to play music with them and had taken it upon himself to write and ask for an audition. They had agreed to hear him and scheduled the audition in Washington, DC, over the Christmas break. He was now clattering through the Pennsylvania countryside filled with purpose, just hours from meeting his brother Armand (also known as "Min").

A couple of years older, Armand had gotten a job with the Government Printing Office and had moved to Washington the year before. Arnold looked up to Min and missed his big brother. Although slightly smaller than the stocky and stronger Arnold, Min was tough. The two had played many years of sandlot football in the neighborhood and were a fearsome pair as they anchored the offensive and defensive lines. Min was a better student and had a knack for details that had been recognized and put to good use by the Government Printing Office. He was one of thousands of young men and women who were pouring into the city as the government war effort swelled the population of the formerly sleepy southern city on the Potomac River.

The mood of the country in 1942 dictated that all able-bodied young men enter military service, and Ferdinand and Filomena were no different in their feelings. As Italian immigrants, Arnold's parents personified the American dream. Ferdinand spent two years in the US Army through two separate enlistments of a year each and was fiercely proud to be a naturalized American citizen. It was that large measure of unspoken pride with which he put Arnold on the train that morning.

As Arnold stepped off the train at Union Station in Washington, DC, he was in awe. The building was cavernous. Hundreds and maybe thousands of people moved purposely through the echoing marble terminal, and the sound of arriving and departing trains was deafening. He followed the flow of passengers toward the exit, somehow met Min, and was shepherded out onto the busy streets of the nation's capital. They then boarded a streetcar and rode to Min's rented room on Decatur Street, Northwest.

The audition was set for the following day, and while Min was at work, Arnold hopped a streetcar to the Navy Yard. Nestled against the northern shore of the Anacostia River, just upriver from its confluence with the Potomac River, the Navy Yard was just like every other military installation at the time. The fortress burst with officialdom and regiment, and though it should have been somewhat intimidating to a seventeen-year-old upstate New York boy, it was instead immediately appealing. Any trepidation he may have harbored on the trip down evaporated, and he entered the audition with a confidence and certainty that shone through his performance.

His acceptance came immediately. Arnald had passed the audition and was given a letter that he was to show to the draft induction board after he graduated from high school in June. It allowed him to bypass the draft and enter the navy as a musician. The desire to serve his country would now dovetail perfectly with his aspirations to play music. He left the Navy Yard and boarded the evening streetcar back to Decatur Street buoyed by the prospect of a bright future.

As he traveled through the busy streets of Washington, he looked at the city through new eyes. Arnald was now more than just a visitor; he would soon be a resident of the rapidly growing city and a member of the United States Navy Band program. He was about to fulfill a dream he'd had since the night he'd heard the band on one of their tour stops at Cortland High School. It had been an evening of sheer perfection. The sharp resplendence of the uniforms lent an air of precision to the performance, but the music was heaven-sent. Arnald had never heard music played as beautifully or as professionally. He wanted nothing more than to play music with them, and the fulfillment of that dream was now at hand.

Arnald wandered the streets of his soon-to-be new home, anxious to tell his big brother the exciting news. Min had the late shift at the Government Printing Office and didn't get off until midnight. At around eleven o'clock, Arnald found himself perched on the parapet of the Post Office Building, wondering what his future in this city held and reflecting on his life to this point.

Early Years

Arnald's parents, Ferdinando Gabriele and Filomena Guadagno, emigrated from Italy separately, but as most immigrants of the time did, both came through Ellis Island. His father, Ferdinando, was born in 1890 in Dogliola, a small farming village in the Abruzzi region near the Aegean Sea. It was a poor village nestled in the foothills of the Apennine Mountains where formal education rarely continued past the seventh or eighth grade. In later years, Ferdinando was often heard to say that his father, Dominico, was so illiterate that, "he couldn't write an O in the sand with a drinking glass."

The family struggled to eke out an existence in the rocky soil, and Ferdinando worked in the local vineyard and olive groves and even tended a few sheep. Their small house had dirt floors and no running water; a shared village well was the only source of water. Italy's decision to attack the Ottoman Empire and wrest control of what later came to be known as Libya resulted in Ferdinando being drafted in 1912 at age twenty-two. The war lasted only about a year, and he served in the Italian Army until the end. The economic cost of the war caused further hardship throughout the country, and with the money he had garnered from his service, Ferdinando decided to follow millions of émigrés to new opportunities in America. He secured passage aboard the *Principe Di Piemonte*, a ship departing the Port of Napoli bound for the United States of America. Ferdinando survived the squalid conditions aboard the ship, arrived in New York, and was processed through Ellis Island on May 2, 1913.

Ferdinand worked for a few years as a waiter in Manhattan before moving to upstate New York where he joined the US Army in Syracuse. After a one-year enlistment, he then returned to Manhattan and to his job as a waiter, where, in late 1920, he met Filomena Guadagno. She had come into the restaurant with her brother, and both had just arrived from Italy. Ferdinando had become a naturalized citizen that year and, presumably in an effort to plan for his future with Filomena, rejoined the army for another one-year enlistment.

Little is known about Filomena Guadagno's life in Italy, for she spoke little of it. She was born and raised in the small town of Ascoli

The Force of Destiny

Satriano near the city of Foggia on the east coast. After her mother died, she was raised by a stepmother who favored her own daughter over Filomena. At the age of eighteen, she and her older brother Antonio boarded the *Duca D. Aosta* from the port of Napoli and arrived on Ellis Island on September 20, 1920. The chance meeting at the Manhattan restaurant led to her marriage to Ferdinando on March 27, 1922.

Following Italian custom (and over her brother Tony's violent objections), the couple were married in a civil ceremony in Manhattan and had a Catholic ceremony a month later. They moved upstate to Cortland, New York, and Ferdinando worked for a time in the Wickwire Brothers factory. The factory produced wire cloth and nails and was Cortland County's largest employer. With the money he saved from his army enlistment, Ferdinando then bought a small grocery store through a loan foreclosure at 122 Elm Street in Cortland, New York, and settled down to raise a family.

Arnaldo Dominico Gabriele was born in the second floor bedroom, just above the newly acquired family grocery store at 6:15 a.m. on May 31, 1925. Armando had been born a little more than two years prior and been named after Armando Diaz, Ferdinando's commanding officer and a general in the Italian army. Arnaldo was named because it sounded similar to Armando. The entire neighborhood celebrated Arnaldo's arrival that day, because Filomena had given birth to a stillborn baby girl the year before. Eight years later, Ricardo arrived and, like his two brothers before him, was born in the living quarters above the small grocery store.

It was a tough upbringing for Arnaldo and his brothers, as the family suffered the hardships of most newly arrived ethnic immigrants. Their difficulties were exacerbated by the deepening effects of the Great Depression which, by the time Arnaldo reached grade school, had spread worldwide. They lived in the east end of Cortland in an Italian enclave that was, both literally and figuratively, on the other side of the railroad tracks. Italian was the spoken language in the neighborhood to the extent that when Arnaldo[4] started school at age five, he spoke virtually no English.

Most days in early childhood were filled with attendance at school and work in the store. The work consisted of restocking, cleaning and other chores, and delivering groceries to neighbors. During the darkest days of the Great Depression, both parents supplemented their meager income from the grocery store; Ma worked in a garment factory, and Pa worked part-time in Sardo's bar, a local watering hole. At those times, the two older boys worked behind the counter at the store. Although there are many tragic memories of the time, Arnald remembers one particular evening when the family split a can of beans for dinner. "It seems like we were always hungry," he says. During the summer months, the Hallstead Canning Company hired the boys for work in the fields. Arnald worked for several summers in the stifling heat picking beans for eight cents a basket.

Arnald spent most of his free time with a close-knit circle of friends from the east end, a gang who referred to themselves as the Rinkydinks. The origin of the name and each of their nicknames are lost to memory, but their shared ethnic backgrounds and low social status in Cortland bound them together for life. The members included brother Min; Arnald, nicknamed "Scratch"; the four Doloisio brothers, including Albert "Dub," Tony "Gallagher," Nick, and Ernie "Himp"; Tony Delnero "Spirky"; the two Giamichael brothers, Mike and Louie, aka "Cherokee" (or "Cheróke"); Chet Gigluto; and finally, Benny Mastronardi. Their mischief in the neighborhood amounted to a largely harmless series of pranks not unknown to most kids. They became so adept at sneaking into the local theater, for example, that the owner finally relented and allowed them free access.

Music had always been a part of Ferdinand's life. During his second enlistment in the US Army, he took clarinet lessons from Nick Dadamio, the neighborhood barber, and tried to play in the army

---

4 When Ferdinando registered his son for school, he listed his name as Arnald Domenic Gabriel, dropping the vowels at the end of the names in an apparent effort to assimilate into American life and reduce the ethnic flavor of his name. The official transcript of his New York State birth certificate still reads Arnaldo Domenico Gabriele.

band at his base. He was, unfortunately, a man of great drive and little musical talent; he ended his enlistment playing the cymbals. He did, however, play the bugle in the Cortland American Legion Drum and Bugle Corps and remained active in the local music scene. Arnald's earliest exposure to music came in the Saturday afternoon Texaco broadcasts of the Metropolitan Opera that Ferdinand listened to in the grocery store. The magical sounds coming from the radio fascinated the young boy and provided a respite from his unrelenting work schedule.

Although their upbringing was tough, Arnald was a bright child with an artistic flair. When he was about eight years old, he participated in the annual Play Day program sponsored by the Elks Club and the town of Cortland. He joined hundreds of other children on the beautiful August afternoon and garnered first prize for "best decorated dog" by dressing Jip, his Pomeranian, with a fancy blue ribbon that Ma had fashioned for him.

At about the same time, a touring company held a concert around the corner from the family store in the basement of St. Anthony's Church on Pomeroy Street. The group staged a production of *Cavalleria Rusticana*, a one-act opera by Pietro Mascagni. Despite the primitive sets and tiny orchestra consisting of a piano, a couple of stringed instruments, and a handful of woodwinds, young Arnald was captivated. The opera is a story filled with intrigue, adultery, murder, and passion, and near the end, the *Intermezzo Symphonica*. The subtle and yet overwhelming instrumental interlude is of such sheer soaring beauty that it captured the heart of this little boy. The piece left such a profound impression that, to this day, it is his favorite piece of music. Mascgani's opera also instilled a passion and interest in music to the extent that when the Sons of the American Legion formed a fife and drum corps, he joined. He took to the fife and, without lessons, began to play in the group. He became so accomplished that he taught newcomers the instrument.

At age twelve, Arnald entered junior high school and joined the band. He naturally gravitated toward the flute and played in the junior/senior high school band. In an effort to foster Arnald's obvious talent and interest in music, Ferdinand hired Mr. Graham to teach Arnald the flute. The weekly lessons cost fifty cents, an astronomical amount of money in 1937 in the depths of the Depression. Ferdinand drove him to the first lesson perhaps a half a dozen blocks to Lincoln Avenue, and as they sat in the car, in a gesture to emphasize his commitment to music, Ferdinand had Arnald make the sign of the cross with the fifty-cent piece. He also related the story of the dying words of one of Italy's most revered musicians, Giuseppe Verdi: "I have but one regret having to die at this time. I was just beginning to learn something about music." The obvious lesson of dedicating oneself to a lifetime of learning was not lost on Arnald.

When he entered his freshman year of high school, the band director, George Light, was replaced by Burton E. Stanley, a strict disciplinarian who demanded excellence from his young musicians. Professor Stanley also saw the raw talent and great potential of one of his flute players, and so he began to give Arnald private lessons. In a remarkable act of charity, he charged the family nothing. He also asked Ferdinand to replace the fifty-dollar flute Arnald played because he felt the poor quality instrument was limiting his development as a musician. Somehow, Ferdinand scraped together $328 and bought a silver Haynes flute. It is a classic instrument that is still in Arnald's possession today, and though it's worth thousands of dollars, it is also filled with priceless memories.

Arnald also played a year of junior varsity football and played two years on the varsity squad. He was on the wrestling team and intramural basketball throughout the winter months and continued to play in the band and take private flute lessons. It was a delicate balancing act that didn't always please Professor Stanley. Arnald's challenge was to hide the occasional split lip or bruised finger or at least convince the director that it wouldn't affect his music. Although he was allowed to continue to play contact sports and remain in the band, Arnald was the last student permitted to do so at the school.

Beginning in the summer following his freshman year, Arnald and brother Min joined the Cortland Civic Band. Min played the bassoon and Arnald the flute, and the experience not only allowed them to continue to play throughout the summer, but helped broaden their musical knowledge and expertise. Programs were largely the music of

Italian composers: Verdi, Puccini, Rossini, Mascagni, and others whose seminal influence formed the bedrock of their community. The rest of their time was split between helping out at the grocery store and summer jobs.

During the school year, his day began at four in the morning when Arnald woke and left the house for his job at John Tucci's bakery. He took the bread out of the oven, sliced it, loaded it on the delivery truck, and delivered to customers in Cortland and neighboring Homer, New York. A couple of hours were spent driving around in the predawn darkness of rural upstate New York before heading to high school classes and afterschool football, wrestling, basketball, or band practice. He maintained that schedule for two years without the apparent benefit of a driver's license.

Senior Year

After considerable reflection about not only his own life but that of his family, Arnald now felt his years of hard work were about to pay off. The lofty view from the roof of the Post Office building allowed him to see a rough sketch of his future. The letter he had gotten from the audition that afternoon allowed him to bypass the draft and provided him acceptance into the Navy School of Music. The school was located in Anacostia, a section of the city just up the Potomac River from National Airport. The new, modern airport had opened only a year and a half earlier and seemed to be a symbol of the bright future of not only Washington, DC, and this country, but of Arnald's future as well.

After returning to Cortland, the remaining months of his senior year of high school seemed to pass in a blur. Intramural basketball, playing with the Cortland Civic Band, early mornings at Tucci Bakery, and a part-time job as a pinsetter in the bowling alley all served to fill his life. Despite the busy schedule, he also managed to spend time with the Rinkydinks, his east-end buddies, and hang out at the Varsity pool room on Main Street; it was the natural alternative to the high school fraternities that "none of my ethnic group were ever invited to join."

He also dated Mary Peters,[5] a pretty brunette who played bassoon in the band and was drum majorette in the marching band. She was accepted to the Crane School of Music in Potsdam, New York, after high school, and with Arnald heading to the Navy School of Music in Washington, they relished their last few months together. The busy but fulfilling life rounded out his last days of adolescence as a certain settled confidence came over Arnald that spring. Although that confidence was tinged with a measure of anxiety about the challenges that lay ahead, the prospect of playing with some of the world's best musicians while fulfilling his military commitment helped inspire Arnald to work even harder at school and work. In late May, he was featured in a flute solo at the weekly meeting of the Kiwanis Club. He joined a quartet of handpicked musicians led by Burton E. Stanley at the Hotel Cortland in a performance that garnered special attention in a newspaper article covering the event. He approached his music with a new sense of professionalism for, as the caption next to his senior yearbook picture stated, he was "Navy Bound."

Six days after he graduated from Cortland High on June 22, 1943, Arnald reported to the recruiting station in Binghamton, New York. There, he proudly presented the acceptance papers he'd received from the Navy Band in December that allowed him to bypass the draft and report to the navy for induction. In a shocking turn of events, he was told that all those bypass letters were invalid, and that all recruits were going into the army. All his effort over the years, and especially the past few months, now seemed in vain. He would have to walk away from the focus of his life and set aside his dreams. Arnald was stunned, but with his strong desire to serve his country, he took the induction physical and joined the army. He went home to say his good-byes, and a week later, he boarded a train to army boot camp. Although not evident at the time, it is apparent now that the US troop buildup for the war effort had begun.

---

5 Pseudonym.

Ft. Eustis, Virginia

Flight training at the University of Buffalo

Tony Doloisio, Min, and Arnald, December 1943

CHAPTER TWO

Induction

After World War I, the United States reduced her interest in other nations' conflicts and drastically downsized the military. Although up from its low point in 1933, the US Army still ranked eighteenth in the world in 1939. Even after two decades of entrenched isolationism and an almost irrational fear of militarists, there was a growing realization that events in Europe and China would be increasingly hard to ignore. The remaining isolationist feelings that had blanketed the country in the late 1930s were abruptly swept away on December 7, 1941, after the Japanese surprise attack on Pearl Harbor.

The US military buildup following Pearl Harbor became more focused in June 1943. Success in the six-month-old invasion of Africa, it was suspected, would lead to an attack of Europe but would require many more infantry troops. The rejection of Arnald's bypass letter from the navy was part of that effort. Still reeling from the surprising turn of events and in a near state of shock, he reported to Camp Upton, New York.

The camp was an induction center near Patchogue, New York. The Long Island camp occupied the site of what is now Brookhaven National Laboratory and had recently been reactivated after a twenty-year dormancy. An infantry training camp during World War I, it was home to recruits that formed the bulk of the Seventy-Seventh Division who gained fame during pivotal fighting at the Argonne Forest in August 1918. Camp Upton's reactivation as an induction center provided Arnald and the rest of the new inductees with a brief glimpse of army life. Aside from getting their immunizations, uniforms, and other routine provisions, the week was filled with make-busy time. One exercise involved restacking blankets from one end of a warehouse to the other.

In early July, Arnald reported to Fort Eustis, Virginia, for basic training. Fort Eustis was another World War I installation that had subsequently closed and reopened as a result of the United States' rapidly expanding effort in the war. It was officially reopened as the Coast Artillery Replacement Center in August 1940 and served as basic training for an antiaircraft battalion. Arnald and the rest of the green recruits settled in for four long months of army boot camp.

Several weeks of training passed without a break. Because only a limited number of recruits could be allowed time off, a contest was held. It was decided that the unit with the cleanest barracks would get a highly sought after weekend pass off the post. After a furious effort, Arnald's barracks tied with another and had to answer one question that would constitute the tiebreaker. Arnald was selected from his barracks to answer, and with flip-of-the-coin luck, he guessed correctly the answer to, "What color are a general's stars?" Elated, he and four of his homesick, upstate New York buddies hired a cab for eight dollars apiece and were driven to Binghamton. Arnald hitchhiked the rest of the way home to Cortland and spent a grand total of six hours visiting his girlfriend and his family before returning to camp. Their hard-earned leave had lasted from Saturday at noon until Monday morning at seven o'clock.

At Fort Eustis, he was assigned to a unit where recruits were trained to fire .50 caliber machine guns mounted on half-tracks. The vehicle was designated as the M16, and its guns were mounted in multiples of up to four. Although used primarily as an antiaircraft gun, the meat chopper, as it was known, was an effective weapon that could destroy almost any ground target. Because the half-track was originally built as a vehicle simply to move soldiers during combat, any effort to add protective armor plating resulted in handling problems. There was also a sense of exposure to the soldiers firing the .50 calibers, and at that stage of the weapon's evolution, it was obvious to even this green recruit: "We would be vulnerable to ground and air fire, and it was an assignment we all hated." Those feelings and that sense of frustration are certainly common to most boot camp soldiers, but Arnald's perception of the weapon's shortfalls led directly to a change in his young career's trajectory.

After little more than three months of training, Arnald learned from his buddy and fellow recruit Wally Stolarcik from neighboring Binghamton, New York, of an opportunity that would allow him to escape the drudgery at Fort Eustis. Two programs were available to those recruits deemed bright enough: the Army Air Corps and the Army Specialized Training Program (ASTP). The ASTP promised a four-year degree in three years' time with majors in mathematics, engineering, agriculture, and other fields of study that the army anticipated it would need during the war. They also paid for room, board, and a $50 per month private's salary. Arnald's brother Armand, who had joined the army at the same time and had become a military policeman (MP), opted for ASTP at Brooklyn College. Arnald chose the excitement of flying airplanes and eagerly joined the Army Air Corps.

In September, to assess his basic skills prior to becoming a pilot, Arnald was sent by train to Keesler Field in Biloxi, Mississippi. Keesler was built primarily as a training facility for pilots and aircraft mechanics in 1941 at a cost of $10 million. Thousands of workers built what would later become the largest military technical training installation in the world. In 1943 assessment to become a pilot consisted of a series of rudimentary psychomotor tests. Depth perception was measured by aligning, at some distance, two parallel dowel rods. Another test measured hand-eye coordination by using a stylus to follow a serpentine line around a spinning turntable.

The oppressive Mississippi heat was another new experience for Arnald, but one particular oddity in the regimen at Keesler is more memorable. Due to the eccentricity of their commanding officer, and presumably to raise morale, recruits were required to sing as they went from one class to the next. There is something unforgettable about the peculiar sight of sweating recruits singing "Let the Sun Shine, Nelly" in the sweltering midday Mississippi sun.

The three weeks in Mississippi went quickly, and after passing the pilot assessment tests, Arnald took a train to Buffalo, New York, to attend initial pilot training at the University of Buffalo. Three to four hundred recruits and he were now part of the College Training Detachment (CTD). It was an atmosphere more reminiscent of college than of the army.

Although classes were held at the university, the soldiers were housed in the Grover Cleveland Country Club (now called the Country Club of Buffalo). Their meals, which included steak three times a week, were served on linen-draped tables by an all-female wait staff. Here, there were no contests to get off post. Arnald and the rest of the pilot recruits were free from Saturday noon till Monday morning. The City of Buffalo was very generous in giving the cadets passes to sporting events and concerts.

Due to the fact that most of the eligible young men of Buffalo were away in various branches of the service, finding accompaniment on dates as wide-ranging as a concert of the Russian Cossack Choir in Kleinhan's Music Hall or a simple trolley ride to the Glass Bar was never a problem. There was even an occasional evening at the burlesque theater, but mostly Arnald dated a "pretty blonde girl named Debbie Light[6] from just across Main Street." Even on evenings deemed too cold to go out, women of the community would bring cookies and milk to the cadets' dorm at the country club.

The training was challenging, but satisfying. Weekdays began with predawn classes arrived at, oftentimes, by trudging through two to three feet of snow. Arnald attended ground school for about ten weeks and then began flying. Beginning in November, he flew the Piper J-3 Cub and Aeronca Chief about once a week at the Cheektowaga Airport (now the Buffalo International Airport). Both airplanes were single-engine, two-seat trainers, and the unique challenges of learning how to fly were exacerbated by the brutally gusty winds that blew off Lake Erie during the winter months and by the fact that training was accomplished in unheated cockpits. He was also required to attend physical training (PT) in the gym for three hours a day and to take a three-mile run down Bailey Avenue and Main Street on Saturday.

---

6 Pseudonym.

The Force of Destiny

The cadets were training for pilot positions in the Army Air Corps in airplanes with roles as diverse as fighters, bombers, transport, and observation. Because the most sought after slot was in a fighter squadron, only the top-ranked students were selected for advanced fighter training. Arnald worked hard to position himself at the top of his class; his goal was to fly the North American P-51 Mustang. A number of improvements had been made to the airplane during the past few years, and it was now the premier fighter/escort airplane employed by the Allies. Unexpectedly, the idyllic, albeit cold, lifestyle at the Grover Cleveland Country Club was about to come to an abrupt end.

With air superiority established over Europe in a surprisingly short amount of time, commander of the US Army Air Forces, Gen. Henry "Hap" Arnold, responded to the sharply reduced estimates for pilots. In March 1944 he canceled the CTD pilot training program, and seventy-one thousand pilot recruits became army infantry soldiers "at the convenience of the government." Arnold's short military career as a pilot was about to take another drastic turn; this time, he was assigned to the Seventy-Eighth Infantry Division and received orders for Camp Pickett, Virginia.

Camp Pickett was carved out of four rural Virginia counties that became a more than forty-five thousand–acre training facility. Built to accommodate the training of one infantry division, demand became so great by mid-1943 that the army simultaneously conducted the training of two divisions at Pickett. The Seventy-Eighth Infantry Division, "The Lightning Division," was the last wartime division to be trained there.

Now army private first class (PFC), Arnald Gabriel reported to Camp Pickett in March 1944 and was taught to fire the Browning automatic rifle (BAR). He was assigned to the Seventy-Eighth in training that was slated for six weeks. The culture shock from country club living to life in a wartime army barracks was jarring. Additionally, "We 'college guys' were resented by the infantry cadre," and it took little to draw the ire of his superiors resulting in KP (kitchen police) or guard duty. There was also an awareness of his musical background by at least one instructor sergeant. In a training class of enemy defenses that included a discussion about a coiled barbed wire called concertina wire, the sergeant pointedly remarked: "Gabriel! Concertina wire don't play music. It plays hell!"

Due to regular PT in Buffalo, Arnald arrived at Camp Pickett a fit young man. Ever the athlete, he joined the boxing squad and fought with the 311th Regimental boxing team, winning eleven of twelve bouts, four by knockout. His one loss was an exhibition match against a fighter five years his senior and vastly more experienced. "Tampa" Tommy Gomez was a bruising heavyweight who, by March 1944, had won forty-six of his forty-nine professional bouts, most by knockout. "That exhibition bout against Gomez convinced me that boxing as a career was not for me." Arnald had little to be ashamed about.

A look into the future would reveal that following a distinguished army career where Tommy was awarded the Purple Heart for wounds sustained during the Battle of the Bulge, he would return home and continue as a heavyweight boxer. "Tampa" Tommy fought more than eighty times, most famously against "Jersey" Joe Wolcott. He was also ranked number seventy-three in *Ring Magazine*'s all-time greatest punchers. Private First Class Gabriel felt fortunate to have escaped the bout with only two chipped front teeth; it seems unlikely that he could have faced a more formidable opponent in the entire US Army.

Weeks of training at Pickett did little to improve Arnald's sense of displacement. The harsh difference in lifestyle between his college days in Buffalo and the strict training regimen of the Seventy-Eighth forced a decision. In an effort to escape the unpleasantness of Camp Pickett, and with perfect eighteen-year-old logic, he volunteered for overseas duty.

The decision to volunteer is a tough one to reconcile. It took him out of a stateside unit, albeit one actively training for combat, and made him available for just about anything overseas. In March 1944 US forces were heavily engaged in a bloody march across the Pacific in an island-by-island effort to push the Japanese back to Japan. The invasion of Iwo Jima was still a year away. The Allied invasion of Italy on the bloody beachhead at Anzio was only a month prior, and a German counteroffensive there had just been turned back. Troop buildup continued in England for the upcoming invasion of Hitler's fortress Europe. Obviously, Operation Overlord and Eisenhower's plan for the liberation of the continent could not have been known, especially to an eighteen-year-old PFC in boot camp, but to cast one's fate to the wind in such an uncertain time as he did seems rash, even caviler. His explanation is simple: "My intention was not to get into combat but just to get out of the Seventy-Eighth. I didn't know D-day was so imminent." Regardless of the reasoning, Arnald left training with the Seventy-Eighth Division.

Camp Pickett also served as a Replacement Depot, more commonly referred to as a Repple Depple. Its purpose was to assign individual soldiers as replacements in units overseas, primarily replacing those lost in combat. The army devised the system after a study of the problem during the Civil War and World War I. It was, academically, sound policy. Units could be kept at full strength and at the front line by infusing fresh troops as needed. These replacement soldiers, however, were little more than the army's orphans. They usually arrived at the Repple Depple alone and uncertain of their fate. Any friends made were quickly forgotten, as each was shipped out to different units. Upon arrival at the new posting, the replacement soldier joined a unit that had not only been training together, sometimes for years, but also, in the case of many units, were lifelong friends. The army had ignored one of the most important concepts in combat warfare—that of unit cohesion and morale—and had replaced it with expediency. Arnald found himself just such an orphan and after enduring days of uncertainty at Pickett finally received his orders and was put on a train to New York City where he boarded a troopship bound for England. He was about to enter the European Theater of Operations (ETO).

PFC Arnald Gabriel boarded the *Ile de France* at pier 86 in New York on April 7, 1944, with ten thousand other infantry troops. The ship was a French ocean liner that was commissioned and had completed her maiden voyage in 1927. Due to her reputation for service and her unique art deco styling, she had carried a record number of first-class passengers across the Atlantic by 1935. The outbreak of war on the continent had laid her up in 1939, and in 1940 she was requisitioned by the British Admiralty, stripped of her art deco finery, and outfitted as a troop transport. Due to their speed, ocean liners of the day required no military escort. It was felt that the relatively slow speed of the German U-Boat (seven knots when submerged) posed little danger to the much faster ships.

One tactic used to further confound the U-boats was to sail in a zigzag pattern. The technique was effective against U-boat attacks but caused much consternation to troops who had to endure periodic abrupt course changes. It also lengthened the crossing to about ten days' time. Further, the ten thousand troops on board were far more than the approximately thirteen hundred paying cruise line passengers the ship normally carried. To accommodate the number, about five thousand troops spent twelve hours above deck before switching with the other five thousand to bunks below for twelve hours. Beyond the meals and "rack time" in the crowded bunks, there was little to do. Life above deck meant enduring the cold, gray North Atlantic weather, and, as Arnald remembers, "We were all bored to death."

At long last on about April 16, 1944, the *Ile de France* docked at Glasgow, Scotland, and Private First Class Gabriel reported to yet another Repple Depple. Some days later, he was posted to his new unit and sent to Slapton Sands, near Lands' End, England. Arnald had just left the frying pan of the Seventy-Eighth Division and landed in the fire of the Twenty-Ninth Division.

Twenty-Ninth Infantry Division Symbol

CHAPTER THREE

The Twenty-Ninth Infantry

The Twenty-Ninth Infantry Division was organized in July 1917, three months after the United States' entry into The Great War. The division brought together National Guard units from Virginia, Maryland, New Jersey, and Delaware. Early fears of bringing together Yankee and Confederate boys into one unit quickly subsided as pride in the new Blue and Gray Division overrode even the deep-seated feelings of the Civil War. The division patch echoed their commitment to unity with a circular blue and gray yin-and-yang symbol.

Private First Class Gabriel was joining a military unit whose roots, as with the Fifth Maryland, predate the Revolutionary War. The proud lineage of the 116th of Virginia includes service with Stonewall Jackson in the Second Virginia during the Civil War. The legacy was so ingrained that many still refer to the soldiers of the Twenty-Ninth Infantry as the Stonewallers. Each individual guard unit was recruited locally and was composed not only of men from the same community, but close, lifelong friends who shared much more than a division patch. National Guard service was more than a military commitment; it was a social center where friends and family gathered for regimental polo matches in the horse country of rural Maryland and Virginia.

When Arnald joined the Twenty-Ninth in 1944, it was made up of National Guard units from Virginia, Maryland, and Delaware and had been mobilized for the war effort in 1941. They had been training in England since October 1942. They had been there so long, and with little to convince the locals that they were going anywhere soon, that they were jokingly referred to as England's own. Their commanding officer was Maj. Gen. Charles Gerhardt, a West Pointer and a tough career man who demanded as near to perfection as was possible. An unhooked chinstrap or unwashed jeep, even in the midst of war games, was inexcusable and would elicit a profane dressing down by the general himself. He was responsible for instilling a measure of pride and of boosting morale as well. Gerhardt supplied the Twenty-Ninth with its battle cry—Twenty-Nine Let's Go!—and required it on all signage and official correspondence.

It was into this tight-knit family that Arnald reported. He was now the ultimate outsider; he had ties to no one in the unit, knew nothing of the Twenty-Ninth Infantry, and still carried the label of college-boy. Additionally, in 1943 there was still a certain amount of prejudice toward his ethnic, Italian heritage. Isolated and thousands of miles from home, he daily battled his vertiginous sense of detachment.

Arnald was assigned to the 116th regiment, E (Easy) company and began training as an ammo carrier for the .30 caliber light machine gun. In pecking order, the ammo carrier was the bottom man in a three-man machine gun squad. It was like moving to a new town and knowing no one. The other soldiers of the 116th weren't aloof or unapproachable, but with the intense training at Land's End, England, there was not a lot of time for social interaction. Resigned to his plight, Arnald concentrated on learning his new job.

In addition to the infantry-wide training, Arnald had the added burden of mastering his new weapon. The M1919 .30 caliber light machine gun was the modified version of a much heavier and less portable water-cooled machine gun from World War I. With either a central tripod arrangement or a barrel-mounted bipod, it was versatile both on point while dug into a foxhole or while pushing through city streets on the move.

His selection as ammo carrier, he suspects, was due to his strength and broad-shouldered physique that was honed from years as an interior lineman on the football team, as a high school wrestler, and lately, a boxer. The job was simply, as the name suggests—to be nearby and to supply the assistant gunner and gunner ammo when needed. The training, however, required Arnald to know the .30 caliber light

The Force of Destiny

machine gun as well as any man in the squad. The implication was obvious: in combat, any soldier is required to assume the duties of another due to incapacitation or death.

Part of the training was to fieldstrip the weapon. Arnald had to disassemble the machine gun into its component parts and reassemble it, all while blindfolded. It was an exercise designed to simulate the very real possibility of having to clean the weapon while on a pitch-black battlefield. The training was so ingrained that more than sixty years later, when describing the drill, his eyes close involuntarily, and decades' old muscle memory forces his hands into a ballet of precision movements.

Proximity to the coast of occupied France presented a very real danger as well. At about the time of Arnald's arrival in April 1944, the Twenty-Ninth Division began Operation Fox. It was an amphibious training exercise utilizing the carefully selected beaches of Slapton Sands. They were similar to the beaches on the Cotentin Peninsula across the English Channel in the Normandy Region of France. These were war games in name only; live artillery and mortars were used in a simulated invasion using thousands of troops and hundreds of boats. The training was intense and deadly serious, and they were not without casualties. Toward the end of the month in a similar exercise, VII Corps soldiers were attacked by a group of German E-boats that had infiltrated the area. The E-boat was actually the German *Schnellboot* (literally, fast boat), a torpedo boat used to harass shipping interests in the channel; in the attack, more than seven hundred men were lost and more than three hundred wounded.

Because most of the soldiers in the Twenty-Ninth had been in England for more than eighteen months, many recognized the ratcheting up of the training and especially the more frequent visits by high-ranking officers. Gen. Dwight Eisenhower, Supreme Commander of Allied Forces, and Gen. "Monty" Montgomery, British ranking officer, visited the Twenty-Ninth at the beginning of 1944. The increased activity may have been obvious to many, but not to Arnald. He was simply overwhelmed with the whirlwind nature of his new assignment, awash in new duties and responsibilities and not just a little apprehensive about what the future held. Larger events taking place around him didn't register.

Military training is designed to instill a sense of brotherhood and *esprit de corps* among the troops, especially within a given platoon or particular machine gun squad. Although they trained together and certainly established the degree of trust required of soldiers heading into combat, his status as a replacement never allowed Arnald to achieve the level of camaraderie as did the other members of the squad. Their lifelong friendships naturally bound them together and added to the sense of isolation he felt. It was simply a matter of taking one day at a time and accomplishing the next task required of him. To this day, when asked the names of the other members of the three-man squad with whom he trained for two months and entered battle, he doesn't remember.

For a short time, Arnald and the rest of the 116th regiment were quartered in Tidworth Barracks, some thirty miles north of Portsmouth. Despite the sense of detachment he felt throughout April and the beginning of May 1944, there was no mistaking the feeling that something was different about the move in mid-May. The Twenty-Ninth Division moved west along the coast to marshaling areas near Plymouth and Falmouth. These areas were called sausages by the soldiers because of their long, narrow appearance on maps.

Because most troop movements were at night to avoid detection, the soldiers knew what their destination was only after they arrived. Security was as it had never been before: the soldiers were confined to the sausages, and the areas were surrounded by coiled barbed wire. Special attention was given to camouflage. No fires were allowed, and the men were required to stay on the established gravel paths rather than make new ones through the fields that would be visible to German reconnaissance planes. Throughout southern England, there were almost 175,000 men in sausages, waiting.

Arriving in mid-May, life in the sausages became another example of the army's penchant to hurry up and wait. Although the men recognized that they were on the verge of something big, boredom easily set in. In an attempt to entertain the troops, music was broadcast over speakers scattered around the encampment, and movies were shown that were memorable only because, "We had to sit on our helmets to watch them." On May 31, Arnald's birthday passed as just another day waiting for orders to move out. He was now nineteen years old.

Finally, in early June he and the rest of the regiment boarded trucks and were transported to Portsmouth on the coast. Before dawn on June 4, Arnald's battalion boarded the transport *Thomas Jefferson* under overcast and rain-streaked skies. They set out across the English Channel, but high winds and a driving downpour caused very rough seas. After some time on the pitching boat, they returned to shore and waited for orders. They spent another miserable day on board with little let up in the weather. The next morning, June 6, 1944, the orders came. They set off in the predawn darkness and joined the largest invasion force in human history. There were more than fifty-three hundred ships of all sizes from twelve nations and 175,000 soldiers set to cross the English Channel. The invasion of Hitler's Fortress Europe had begun.

Due to the sheer scale of the plan, General Eisenhower's Operation Overlord was necessarily complex. The invasion was targeted at the north-facing coast of France in a province called Normandy. The infantry were to be preceded by an aerial bombardment using B-17s to destroy fortifications on the beach and along the bluffs and cliffs just inland. Next, the navy was to follow up with shelling from offshore to hit anything the B-17s missed. On a section of the beach the Allies called Omaha Beach, the 743rd Tank Battalion was to precede the first infantry units ashore with their amphibious force; this initial assault was designed to clear the way for forty thousand soldiers and thirty-five hundred vehicles scheduled to come ashore at Omaha Beach on that day alone. At the forefront of the massive assault, and among the first infantry soldiers steaming across the channel to lead the attack, was Arnald and the rest of the 116th regiment of the Twenty-Ninth division.

About midway across the channel, they transferred to Higgins boats.[7] The flat-bottomed boats pitched violently in the rolling seas, and among the thirty-five or so men standing shoulder to shoulder on the boats, the fear was palpable. As they closed in on the shore, the constant drone of hundreds of Allied aircraft overhead slowly faded and was replaced almost immediately by the thunderous shelling of the navy battleships. They were firing directly over the heads of the flotilla of army infantry in an effort to soften the beach. The deafening roar of the massive guns were augmented by return fire from the Germans onshore and resulted in an unimaginable cacophony. The men shivered not only from the cold waves breaking over the bow and sides of the boat, but from trepidation about what they were to face on the beach. As the boat was tossed in the misty, gray morning, Arnald remembers: "Guys were throwing up not only from seasickness, but from fear. Almost everybody got sick—or wanted to." As they were to find out, much of the carefully plotted strategy to soften the beach didn't work nearly as well as planned.

    The failure was clearly one of faulty intelligence. The expectation was that the Allies would face the German 716th Division, a second-rate unit composed of war-weary veterans of the Russian Front; one division was even composed of ex-Soviet prisoners of war. About nine months prior, in the fall of 1943, Hitler replaced the commander in western France with Field Marshal Erwin Rommel, the "Desert Fox." Rommel immediately moved the crack 352nd Division into the western sector and deployed much of them along the coast in heavily fortified pillboxes and trenches that were scattered in perfectly defensive positions along the cliffs and bluffs of Normandy. The general in charge of this reinforced sector had spent much of his time practicing

---

7 Higgins boats were the LCVP (Landing Craft, Vehicle, Personnel). Built by Higgins Industries in New Orleans, they were the brainchild of its founder, Andrew Higgins, and were a derivative of his Eureka boat that he developed in the swamps of Southern Louisiana. Made of wood, it allowed the delivery and off-loading of a platoon of as many as thirty-six men by using the entire forward bulkhead as a ramp. It then had the ability to extract itself and return for more men.

The Force of Destiny

for the possibility of an Allied attack there. His intent was to crush any invasion while still on the beach.

The B-17 bombing of those fortifications that morning never happened. A delay in the bomb release was planned so as not to hit Allied troopships just offshore, and because of the wind and cloud cover, the bombs landed as much as two miles inland. While virtually destroying towns like St. Laurent and Vierville, they did little to the defenses on the coast. The naval shelling was accurate, but also failed to knock out enemy guns. Credit in this case goes more to the design of the German fortifications than blame to the Allied navies.

Arnald and the rest of the 116th were facing more than the heavily fortified pillboxes and well dug-in positions along the coastal bluffs. Springtime tides along the Normandy coast show a greater variation than any other time of year. The low tide exposes more than five hundred yards of beach, and with high tide, just a few yards of sand is exposed. From that point, a ten-yard band of shingle (small smooth stones that were tossed up by the tidal action) lead to a seawall. With the expectation that the Allies would attack at high tide to take advantage of the shorter beach, the Germans had constructed several layers of crude but effective barriers in hopes of slowing an assault. Large wire gates, known as Belgian barn doors, and wooden stakes pointed to sea were both tipped with mines that would explode on impact. Closer in, hedgehogs were steel rails welded together at odd angles set to rip the hull of any unsuspecting boat pilot who tried for the beach at high tide. Because General Eisenhower and the other D-day planners decided to launch the attack at low tide, most of these obstacles were visible. It therefore meant having to cross many yards of heavily defended beach to get to the relative safety of the seawall. The plan was to have engineer battalions behind the initial assault destroy the obstacles before the tide rose and the second and third waves came ashore.

Each company of the 116th regiment was split among six landing craft carrying about thirty-five men. Four companies formed the first wave of infantry on the beach: A, F, G, and E; Arnald was assigned to E Company and was therefore part of the first wave ashore. The plan was to land opposite one of several draws—shallow, sloped inclines naturally formed by water runoff from the higher terrain to the south. There were either dirt or hard surface roads built along their wide faces, and because of the steep bluffs and sheer cliffs along most of the beach, the draws were the only way for vehicles to get off the beach and were therefore strategically vital. The Germans also recognized their importance and concentrated their firepower along them.

As the first wave motored toward the beach, massive shells from the navy thundered overhead. Seasickness caused by many hours on board the larger transports and now by the pitching Higgins boats affected nearly everyone. Some of the Higgins boats struck mines or were hit by enemy shells fired from hidden positions along the bluffs, and snipers fired at the vulnerable men huddled together on the boats. Still, the coxswains steered the boats onward and closed the distance to shore.

Landing in France

CHAPTER FOUR

D-day and Beyond

One hour after low tide and a half hour after sunrise, the first four companies of the 116th Regiment, Twenty-Ninth Infantry came ashore on Omaha Beach. It did not begin well. Two of the A Company boats struck mines or were shelled and never made it to shore. The others landed right where they planned, opposite a draw that led to the small village of Vierville, but because G Company boats scheduled to land next to them were blown by the wind farther east, all the fire along the bluffs was concentrated on the remaining A Company boats.

As the forward ramps of the four Higgins boats dropped, the bullets and mortars rained down in a concentrated fire. Many never made it off the boats. The rest struggled through neck-deep water and attempted to hide behind the barriers on shore. Scores were cut down before reaching the seawall. Many of the young men were from a small Virginia town called Bedford, and none had much of a chance. Only a couple of dozen of the more than two hundred soldiers survived, and virtually all of them were wounded.

F Company also landed where they were supposed to and fared somewhat better. They landed opposite the next draw to the east, called the Les Moulins draw, but as they splashed off the boats, the smoke from a vigorous brush fire upwind of their position obscured them. It allowed most of them to make it to the seawall in position at the mouth of the draw. G Company landed just east of F and enjoyed a similar fate due to the fortunate smoke cover.

Arnald and the rest of E Company came ashore much farther east than planned. Because of the strong tidal current and winds, none of their boats landed within a half a mile of its assigned sector. He remembers that, "In our practice landings, the ramp normally dropped pretty close to shore, so there was little or no wading." Today would be different. "Our LCI[8] [sic] dropped its ramp about thirty or forty yards from shore. The water was up to our thighs, and since it was choppy, even higher." Struggling through the rising tide and carrying from sixty to eighty pounds of equipment under heavy fire proved to be too much for some of the soldiers. "Many guys just couldn't carry their equipment, so they dropped their rifles, field packs, and helmets and fought their way to shore. Many were killed or wounded." One of the E Company boats took a direct hit from an artillery shell and never made it to the beach.

The scene was chaos, and with the German artillery, MG 34s, "burp" guns, and mortars, the noise was continuous and deafening. In the midst of it all, Arnald called on nearly a year's worth of military basic training, as well as his boxing and football conditioning, and with a combination of courage and self-preservation, he managed to muscle two containers of ammo to shore through the frigid rising tide and deadly rain of bullets and mortars. Once there, "It was total disorientation, confusion, fear, and too many other emotions to recount. Guys on the beach and in the water were terribly wounded or dead; many of the wounded crying out for their mamas." The shore was horribly littered with the dead and dying, the men with whom he'd trained shoulder to shoulder fell and splashed into the wind-whipped surf. He fought a rising sense of helplessness at both the unseen enemy gun emplacements and the inability to help his fallen brothers.

The German defenses proved to be ideally suited to their task. The pillboxes and trenches were aligned along the bluffs and pointed not to sea, but along the beach. The gently curving shore at Omaha lent further efficiency to the gunfire aimed at the troops wading ashore,

---

8 Arnald referred to any troop-carrying amphibious boat as an LCI; it was actually the LCVP Higgins boat.

The Force of Destiny

because each gun placement had full view of the beach and the ability to blanket the entire landing zone.

"We landed so far left of where we were supposed to that some of our guys ended up with different units." In fact, they had landed so far east that they were mixed with units from the First Division (the Big Red One). In his heroic effort to get to shore, Arnald had been separated from his machine gun squad, and, "I managed to team up with a .30 caliber machine gunner that I did not know and gave him ammo." He noticed the soldier's Twenty-Ninth Division patch, so he was probably the second machine gunner in E Company. (Each company had two machine gun squads.) With others making it to the seawall and his fortunate rendezvous with the .30 caliber machine gunner, Arnald began to feel a sense of purpose and fell back on his training.

The grass fire helped to obscure their position along the seawall, but the mortars continued to fall. It became apparent that, in the words of Col. George A. Taylor, "Two kinds of people are staying on this beach, the dead and those who are going to die. Now let's get the hell out of here!" Very slowly, and with the help from the second wave troops coming ashore behind them, they fought their way up the bluff.

After the seawall, the first obstacle was a string of coiled barbed wire. They were able to advance, "thanks to the guys with Bangalore torpedoes[9] who blew holes in the barbed wire." Those guys were the engineer battalions who continued to lead the way by clearing the path of mines. "Mines were everywhere, and our engineer units suffered from them. I really admired those guys." Even though "we were fortunate to have a draw to help us," it took more than four hours to reach the top of the bluff. They were under constant fire from well-hidden enemy guns and mortars, and the causalities continued to mount.

The scene on the beach was staggering. One colonel estimated thirty-five to fifty corpses per one hundred yards of beach. Close to one-third of the 116th Regiment had been killed or wounded, almost one thousand men. Some entire companies were reduced to a few men.

---

9 Bangalore torpedoes are a high explosive set at the end of a metal tube used to clear barbed wire and mines at a safe distance.

Arnald said it best: "You can read about the carnage in books and by watching movies, but nothing can instill the horror, anguish, fear, desperation, and helplessness as witnessing it firsthand."

"By dark we were probably one hundred to one hundred and fifty yards inland, which was a good toehold but not as good as our plan." Nearly twelve hours of constant fighting, and their progress was barely the length of a football field. They dug into their foxholes, but darkness brought little rest as the gunfire, shelling, and mortars continued through the night. They had advanced to the outskirts of the small village of St. Laurent. Because of their drastically reduced strength, Arnald's E Company and some other elements of the Second Battalion were held in reserve outside the village. The next morning they were sent back down the Les Moulins draw in a mopping-up exercise and, surprisingly, found pockets of stiff resistance.

From there, they headed west to the town of Vierville. The tiny village was nearly destroyed. "I wish our air forces and naval bombardment had done as much damage to the costal defenses as they did to those villages inland. They were flattened." In this part of France, there were very few French civilians to be seen; most had fled due either to the German occupation or the prior night's Allied Naval shelling.

The 175th Regiment

About midday on June 7, D plus one, the 175th regiment of the Twenty-Ninth Division came ashore on Omaha Beach. Although the Allies had been fighting for nearly a day and a half, the 175th still encountered scattered enemy gunfire, though much less than the day before. They also lost two landing craft to mines. Once inland, they gathered near the small town of Gruchy that night and received their orders:

> The 175th Infantry will advance from designated assembly area, seize and defend Isigny with the least possible delay.

The Force of Destiny

They were to move about nine miles inland along a very heavily defended road to capture the town of Isigny and, more importantly, the bridge over the Aure River. Because the Germans had flooded the Aure Valley, the bridge was vital to the advance of the entire division out of the Normandy Region. To keep the 175th as near to full strength as possible, men from some of the depleted units of the 116th were assigned to fill the ranks. An E Company communications corporal used his EE-8 field phone to contact Arnald's company commander (to preclude the possibility of his being reported KIA or MIA), and the process was complete. While the rest of his company was designated as "division reserve" and went to the town of Grandcamp for a day's rest, Arnald joined I (Item) Company of the 175th Division and moved up to the assistant machine gunner position.

On the morning of June 8 and with little or no rest in the past few days, Arnald and his new unit began their march down the road to Isigny. Led by a battalion of Sherman tanks, the column was nearly two miles long. The column suffered sporadic attacks from the Germans in an effort to delay their progress and had to contend with a new storm that moved over the area. The winds and heavy rain persisted throughout most of the afternoon and made travel down the country road much more difficult. A brief respite in the weather allowed some relief, but in a classic friendly-fire incident, they were attacked by British Typhoon fighter-bombers. For several minutes the Typhoons strafed and bombed the troops mistakenly, thinking they were German soldiers. The mistake cost six American lives and eighteen wounded.

They continued to march overnight, driven by the urgency to capture Isigny, and as they approached, the three battalions of the 175th split up to engage the enemy on three different fronts. Arnald, with I Company, and the rest of the Third Battalion captured the village of St. Germain-du-Pert and rejoined the other two battalions on the outskirts of Isigny as the first American soldiers to enter the town. After advancing nervously over a bridge first thought to be strung with explosives, they took the town with little resistance. Isigny was in complete ruin. In the predawn darkness, fires burned from most of the buildings that remained standing, and there were very few French civilians left.

Each day brought another town and the sight of more devastation, but as with most combat soldiers, a shell began to form. "As a private in the army, you know two things: the guy to your right and the guy to your left." He was acting on instinct and training; you do what you're told and try to stay alive. There is little regard for or interest in the larger picture. The concerns of generals and heads of state mean little to the foot soldier whose needs are more basic: keep your weapon clean, listen to your sergeant, and, because they were on the front lines, keep your eyes open.

They continued to move forward, and the villages and towns they went through would soon become distant memories with the passing days. The road signs were the only clue as to their position: la Herennerie, Lison, les Buteaux, and others long forgotten. As soldiers nearby fell in small skirmishes and larger battles, they were replaced with new faces. "Somewhere between Isigny and Saint-Lô, I remember a couple of guys in the section named Murphy and Davis who were casualties before we got to Saint-Lô." It just didn't pay to try to remember names.

Moving forward was more than simply marching from one town to the next. Advancing inland from the coast, the terrain changes dramatically. The area was dominated by a patchwork of fields bordered by a thick tangle of hedgerows. Not only was the foliage nearly impassable, the hedgerows sat on mounds of earth almost four feet high and nearly as thick. Country lanes edged the fields but were claustrophobically narrow due to the earthen walls and overhanging shrubs. There was only one small entrance to each field, and the Germans had set up deadly crossing fire and presited mortar positions to prevent access. The fighting through these fields was "back and forth, back and forth," Arnald remembers. As time went on, the soldiers learned to use tanks with battering rams welded to the front to blast through the hedges.[10] It was just another adjustment the

---

10 The steel used was, ironically, taken from the German "hedgehogs" in the tidal flats off Omaha Beach.

army had to make in the field due to the fact that aerial reconnaissance photos didn't show the true nature of the hedgerows.

The early June temperatures warmed up quickly, and, "It was hot and smelly with dead bodies and dead animals everywhere." Their olive drab uniforms were stiff and hung heavily due to being impregnated with a waterproof solution prior to the invasion. Even in these seemingly unbearable conditions, Arnald found time to shave almost every day. Their commanding officer, Maj. Gen. Charles Gerhardt, had instilled such discipline in his troops that squatting down in his foxhole to "find a little dirty water" with which to shave was just another part of being a soldier.

In the days following D-day, one of the objectives was to have units that had come ashore on Sword, Juno, Gold, and Utah (the other landing beaches used for the invasion), link up with each other, and then with the Eighty-Second and 101st Airborne. In the early morning darkness of June 6, the Airborne units had parachuted miles inland in an attempt to secure the flanks of those soldiers landing on the beaches. High winds scattered many and prevented the paratroopers from fully completing their mission to capture several key bridges, but they were able to gather in sufficient numbers to divert enemy attention from the beach. Most continued to fight until joining forces with the infantry but some were overwhelmed by dropping too close to German positions and were captured quickly.

Today, Nazi atrocities are well-known and universally despised. Their depravity is no more fully illustrated by what Arnald and his platoon encountered "a number of days after D-day when we met up with the Eighty-Second Airborne, or what was left of them." The Nazis had captured and killed a group of the American soldiers. They then strung up the men by their feet, spread-eagle; their genitals had been cut off and stuffed into their mouths. It was a calculated form of psychological warfare, cruel in the extreme. What inures a man to these images? Here is a sight unimaginable in its callousness that even more than sixty years later, Arnald remembers as "a horrible scene to witness."

Another form of what must be considered psychological warfare was a specially designed mine referred to as the Bouncing Betty. It was a small mine that when stepped on, sprung out of the ground to the crotch area and exploded. It was not often fatal, but "you can imagine not only the impact on the guys who were maimed by these, but also on those of us who witnessed it." Another tactic involved leaving a Luger in plain sight; the Germans knew that most GIs desired the pistol as a war trophy. To ensure the pistol was not booby-trapped, a guy would tie a string around the handle and jump into a foxhole to pull it to him only to discover the foxhole was mined.

The advance of Arnald and the 175th and other infantry units from the Twenty-Ninth Division continued steadily southward toward the strategic city of Saint-Lô. It was an important communication center and crossroads of east-west traffic for the Germans. The relative ease with which the Twenty-Ninth had moved thus far was due to the retreat of the German 352nd Division; their retreat was designed to give them time for reinforcements to arrive.

About June 14, those troops arrived in the form of the German Third FJ Division, an elite, highly trained and motivated group of former paratroopers that were now fighting as infantrymen. One significant battle took place, on a hill designated simply as Hill 108. It was a hill in name only; standing on this subtle rise in terrain afforded no visual advantage due to the surrounding hedgerow country. The First Battalion of the 175th had taken the hill, and the Germans, strengthened by the Third FJ Division, counterattacked on June 18. The ferocity of the fighting was tremendous with both sides suffering many casualties. The next day, Arnald and the rest of the Third Battalion relieved the battered First on what came to be known as Purple Heart Hill. The First Battalion lost more than 40 percent of its strength. The Germans were similarly affected and a very brief period of stagnation began that enabled both sides to recover and strengthen.

Despite the lull in the fighting and due to their being on the front line, the casualties continued to mount and near the beginning of July, Arnald was elevated to machine gunner in the squad. In combat, the machine gun squads were deployed on the flanks of the riflemen to provide enfilading and covering fire. It was said that the life expectancy of a machine gunner was only three days because of the fact that every fifth round he fired was a tracer to help with the sighting of his target. Of course, the enemy also knew that and learned to aim at the source of the tracer. Arnald's answer to the dilemma was to "dig a lot of foxholes and keep moving. You can't hit a moving target!" Due to the command structure and abundance of men of higher rank in the support personnel coming ashore behind him, no promotion was offered; he was still a PFC, a private first class.

The Battle for St. Lô

The days leading up to the taking of Saint-Lô were a series of slow, costly advances answered by German counterattacks. The final thrust into the city was made by an all-out attack that was preceded by a relentless bombing campaign. The first troops were led into the city by a mechanized force of trucks, tanks, and other artillery. The 175th Division with Arnald and the Third Battalion was held on the east side of the city as reinforcements; they entered the city in the days that followed, still under heavy enemy counterattacks and bombing.

The afternoon prior to the final push into Saint-Lô, in the relative calm on the flank of the city, Arnald was sent by his sergeant back to the company command post for supplies armed with just his sidearm. He came across a US Sherman tank and one of its severely wounded crewmembers lying, in obvious pain, beside the twisted, burning hulk. The soldier was crying for his mama, and as Arnald neared in an attempt to offer help, the mortally injured man beseeched Arnald to "hold me." As he slipped his arm around the man's shoulders, the man came apart at the waist. He had been horrifically wounded across his midsection, and the slight movement caused the separation. The soldier died in Arnald's arms, and, "I will never know how he had the strength to cry out for his mama." It was another horrific memory he needed to set aside and deal with later; the job to which he was entrusted was paramount. Doing it properly meant his survival and the survival of his brothers on the battlefield, and although an experience beyond imagination, Arnald still had not witnessed the worst of combat.

In the days that followed, the units in St. Lo were relieved by other troops streaming into the area, and for the first time since landing on Omaha Beach forty-five days earlier, Arnald and the rest of the Twenty-Ninth Division stepped back from the front lines. Although only three miles to the rear now, and still in the hedgerows, they were able to regroup, clean up, and take stock.

For the first time in six weeks of frontline combat, Arnald and his squad enjoyed a hot shower, a hot meal, a good shave, and a new issue of clothes. They had arrived, however, in the middle of the night, and while still dirty, unshaven, and unfed, Arnald, while trudging through the camp, was stopped by a lieutenant who was fresh off the boat as a replacement and was new to the war. "Shape up, Soldier, you look awful!" the lieutenant barked. Arnald informed the green officer that he'd come ashore six weeks ago, been on the front lines since then, and had just now arrived in camp, "Sir!" The lieutenant took stock of the haggard GI in front of him, turned on his heel, and said nothing more.

For a few days, the soldiers settled into their foxholes, and the fighting became more defensive. The relative safety of life just behind the front lines allowed the troops to rest and, to the consternation of most, to train. Training was held daily on hedgerow defenses, battle drills, calisthenics, and instruction concerning mines and booby traps. It seemed there was literally no rest for the weary. Arnald was also able to write letters to his girlfriend and to Ma and Pa. They were necessarily general in nature due to imposed censorship that was designed to preclude inadvertently divulging vital troop movement and position. It was, however, his only tenuous connection with home.

When the men were in a static position for a day or more, slit trenches were dug as latrines away from the tents and foxholes. They were about six feet long and narrow enough to straddle. Prior to moving out, soldiers would backfill the trenches and post a sign for the troops coming up that read: "CLOSED LATRINE," and under that, the date. In one of the many bittersweet ironies that is war, the French civilians, upon finding the trenches and thinking they were graves, reverently placed fresh flowers on them.

Replacements continued to be assigned to the units to fill the ranks as the battle to take Saint-Lô was the costliest in the history of the Twenty-Ninth Division. In the six weeks since D-day more than seven thousand men had been killed or wounded in the division. Having lost both his squad members, Arnald was joined by two new replacements: Johnny Arrowsmith as assistant gunner and Harry Aschoff as ammo carrier.

After the fall of the strategic city of Saint-Lô, Arnald and the rest of the Twenty-Ninth Infantry's role was one of pursuit. The Germans' retreat consisted of sporadic, heavy fighting followed by a steady withdrawal. Arnald's division deployed east and became an important element in what became known as the Falaise Pocket. Surrounded on three sides, the trapped Germans had only two choices: retreat east to escape the advancing Allied troops or surrender. Hundreds of German soldiers in the rearward units were forced to give up and were captured. Although the fighting was not nearly as intense as the days immediately following D-day, it took nearly a month of steady effort to collapse the Falaise Pocket. As the pocket was pinched shut, the Twenty-Ninth found itself turned from a frontline unit to rear echelon. They were moved farther back to a point about four miles behind the front and for the first time since D-day became nonoperational. A short period of resupply, training, and recovery began.

Brest

Now, on the entire Brittany Peninsula, the only area controlled by the Germans was the important port city of Brest. Life in the rear ended quickly as orders were received to head west, back to the coast, to secure this vital port.

Brest was the second largest port in France, and although now isolated from the rest of their army, it was strongly held by the Germans. Attention turned toward this strategic city as Arnald's 175th Regiment and other units of the Twenty-Ninth Infantry were sent west for the attack. A massive convoy of trucks carried them back across France through dozens of small villages and towns now filled with throngs of jubilant and grateful French citizens.

To the men, the most remarkable aspect of the trip to the coast was how untouched by war the region seemed to be. The late August weather was spectacular as the countryside burst with color. They passed endless fields of farmland nearing the harvest. The newly liberated populous lined the roads, and when Arnald and the men passed through the many villages and towns, the ecstatic, often crying citizens enthusiastically waved French and American flags at the bewildered soldiers. For men who had spent more than two months on the front lines in combat and faced nothing but utter destruction and death, the scenes were surreal.

As the convoys inevitably had to slow through the crowds, the delirious French threw flowers to their conquering heroes, and when the trucks stopped, the men were hugged by the sobbing, grateful crowd. "They gave us eggs, onions, and whatever else they grew on their farms. And Calvados. I don't know what it was made of, but it was potent. We called it Buzz-Bomb Fluid." (What Arnald remembers is a distilled apple brandy that comes only from the lower Normandy region they were traversing.)

Arnald and the 175th were tasked with taking the town of Recouvrance on the western edge of the city of Brest. As a U-boat base, Brest was vital to the Germans and was thus heavily fortified. For months they had poured thousands of yards of concrete and hardened many of the structures in town. The steel-enforced pillboxes were surrounded by antitank ditches, road barriers, and minefields. Huge 280mm guns normally pointed to sea as a critical defense of the city were swiveled inland toward the Twenty-Ninth. The fighting was as fierce as they'd experienced since they'd come ashore in June but with a critical difference: other units of the Twenty-Ninth were able to rotate periodically to the front and allow a day or so rest.

Although Arnald, Harry, and Johnny had only fought together as a machine gun squad for a few weeks now, it was the longest Arnald had served with the same two men. A solid friendship formed between the young men, and a bond forged by combat solidified the union. Early in the battle for Brest, Harry was hit by shrapnel from a German mortar and was taken to an aid station to recover. Arnald's assistant gunner promised to return to his buddies and, true to his word, joined them for the march into the center of the city by mid-September. PFC Harry Aschoff was awarded the Purple Heart for his wound.

Hitler had instructed the German command defending the city to hold Brest for three months' time, but the relentless attack by the Allies, including a massive aerial assault, allowed them to take the city by the middle of September. "We were told there were fourteen thousand Germans holding Brest, but there were probably twice that number," Arnald remembers. The actual number of enemy in the city was closer to fifty thousand. Among the thousands of captured soldiers were kids as young as fourteen or fifteen. Although they were only a few years younger than Arnald and many of his Twenty-Ninth division brothers, they appeared to be mere children.

The battle for Brest was among the costliest for the Twenty-Ninth division since arriving in France. The 175th regiment alone lost nearly two thousand men in fierce fighting; in Arnald's weapons platoon of twenty-two men, there were eleven casualties. The resistance, however, ended abruptly in mid-September as the Germans unexpectedly surrendered. The jubilant troops were allowed a much needed R&R, or rest and relaxation, and spirits were buoyed as plans were made to give as many as 15 percent of the division furloughs to England. After more than three and a half months at or near the front lines, the nearest fighting was now several days travel to the east. A relaxed mien overtook the young fighting men as they were allowed to enjoy the late September weather in southwestern France. As is typical in wartime, their early autumn respite ended suddenly as orders were received that canceled all planned furloughs.

Belgium and Holland

By this time, the Allied front had swept across France and into Germany through the Rhineland. In order to rejoin the distant fighting, the troops of the Twenty-Ninth Division were split into two groups with the first boarding a truck convoy. Arnald and his group made their way back to the front courtesy of the 40-and-8 railway; a sign that adorned each boxcar doorway said, *"Hommes 40 Chevaux 8."*

Used by troops in the First World War, the narrow-gauge railroad was so named because the cramped boxcars would hold forty men or eight horses. Their four-day, four-night trip to the northern front was an uncomfortable ordeal of endless countryside with little to do to pass the time. When the train slowed through the villages along the route, however, the air was filled with cheers by the same delirious citizens of France, and now Belgium, yelling, "*Vive les Américains*," and waving French and American flags.

Many replacements joined the ranks of the 175th after the battle at Brest. The trip allowed conversation and the opportunity to get to know some of the new guys. Among the new soldiers was a tall Texan from Ft. Worth with a "John Wayne saunter." He was assigned to the other machine gun squad in Arnald's section, previously having served with the Eighty-Second Airborne. He continued to wear his jump boots instead of the standard issue combat boot all the others wore. When asked the reason for his requested transfer to a weapons squad in a combat unit, he related how his brother had lost one of his boots during the invasion on D-day. The problem, he said, was that his foot was still in it. The remark was typical of the gallows humor employed by the soldiers to mask the fear they all had.

Harry, Johnny, and Arnald spend much of the time talking about their lives before their enlistment and, of course, their families. It was a time unavailable during combat, a time unencumbered by the constant threat of the enemy just over the hedgerow, just around the next corner. Harry was the oldest at thirty-four and talked of his wife and two-year-old son in New Jersey, Harry Jr. He'd worked as a vacuum cleaner salesman door-to-door and, more recently, worked with his father in a house-moving venture actually relocating homes on a flatbed truck.

Johnny was from Thompsonville, Connecticut (now called Enfield), and was four years older than Arnald. Although he didn't graduate high school, he'd taken a job with Pratt and Whitney and also worked with his father in a landscaping business. He was the eldest of six children, five boys and one girl, and his family called him Sonny. The left-hander was a talented athlete and played a lot of baseball when he wasn't working. Arnald and he became close. "We did everything together; we were probably best friends." Johnny was married just after high school, had recently become a father, and had yet to see his newborn daughter, Francis. They talked little about their aspirations after the war, however, due largely to the uncertainty of it all.

As their conversation continued over the days, in a flash of inspiration, they decided to name their machine gun. Their weapon, the M1919 .30 light machine gun around which the squad was formed and the obvious focus of their lives became: Hellzapoppin. The reference was taken from a popular Vaudeville comedy team called "Olsen and Johnson" whose tagline was, "Anything can happen and probably will!" It seemed appropriate. They requisitioned a bit of white paint from one of the supply guys and were able to paint the new name on the stock of the weapon.

Because the cramped space was barely twenty by eight feet, nighttime aboard the clattering boxcars was another story; it was a sleepless affair of jostling with the tangle of men for enough room to stretch out. In the rapidly cooling autumn evenings, what little warmth was generated from body heat was swept away in the drafty cars, and the constant noise prevented any good rest. The exhausted troops gratefully disembarked after four long days at the assembly area just south of the city of Maastricht, Holland.

The units of the Twenty-Ninth resumed their familiar positions on the front lines, but with an important difference. For nearly three and a half months, they had been fighting along the claustrophobically narrow lanes bordered by the boscage in summertime France. The battlefield now could not have been more different. Late fall in southern Holland brought intermittent rains to a gray, wide-open, and rolling patchwork of farmland interspersed with small towns and larger cities. They were on the move eastward, and the month of October found Arnald and his unit involved in a series of minor skirmishes as they pushed toward the German border.

In early November, during a lull in the fighting and dug into a foxhole, Johnny and Harry went back to the rear kitchen area to get dinner for the group. Arnald remained on watch and manned the machine gun, but as time grew longer waiting for their return, he had to deal with a growing urgency. Use of the latrine was simply a matter of the nearest tree, because, "I wasn't going to go in my foxhole!" He bounded out of the safety of the foxhole and stole behind the nearest tree the same moment as a randomly fired mortar exploded in the foxhole, obliterating Hellzapoppin. There was little time to ponder the seemingly random nature of war. The close calls of nearby explosions or bullets whistling by your head or sidestepping a trip wire or a land mine had become what was expected of these front-line soldiers. That the war, or certainly their lives, could have ended at that moment was given no further thought; they had neither the luxury of time nor the inclination to dwell on the possible consequences. The three-man machine gun squad was resupplied within hours and prepared to move out with the newly christened, Hellzapoppin II.

Johnny Arrowsmith and Arnald, Bourheim, Germany

CHAPTER FIVE

Holland and Germany

The steady march through southern Holland was made much more difficult due to the weather. Rains blew in off the North Sea nearly every day, much more than average for the area, and with the armored divisions and trucks chewing up the roads, mud was everywhere. Their foxholes filled with water, and keeping dry became impossible. The push eastward slowed, awaiting better weather. The plan to resume the eastern movement was to have begun November 11, Armistice Day, but the poor weather prevented air reconnaissance and support. Finally, the weather improved, and on November 16, a massive push began that would come to be known as the November Offensive.

Arnald and the rest of the 175th crossed southern Holland and across the Siegfried Line[11] into Germany, fighting from one small town to the next. Once they crossed the German border, the resistance stiffened, and the fighting became much more intense. Each village had a system of trenches that had been dug by the German civilians, and all were filled with water and mud. The towns were meant as lines of defense for the city of Jülich, the Allies' ultimate goal on the Roer River.

Several days after beginning the offensive, Arnald and his squad were tasked with taking a series of three farmhouses, each separated

---

11 The Siegfried Line was a nearly four-hundred-mile-long system of concrete pillboxes and antitank fortifications known as the "dragon's teeth," built by Hitler along the western border of Germany. Today, less than 2 percent of the structures remain.

by trees and hedges. They crawled carefully through the mud and secured the first two, finding both abandoned. Arnald took the lead in approaching the third house and, creeping to a stand of trees, carefully pulled aside branches to allow a better look. As he peered through the hedge, he came face-to-face with a German 88mm gun. The massive antitank, antiaircraft weapon had been abandoned, probably due to the softening-up efforts of the aerial and artillery bombardment, and once again, Arnald was confronted with the chance nature of his life in war. There was little doubt as to what his fate would have been had the gun been manned.

Their advance through the countryside was typical of the frontline units of any advancing army. There are times when the movement of individual squads outpaced their supply lines, and because the enemy was just over the next hill or around the next corner, food, in the form of K rations, were slow in coming forward. During a particularly long stretch where Harry, Johnny, and Arnald had run low on K rations, their hunger grew and forced action. The farms they passed were abandoned and largely stripped of anything useful, but after days of nibbling on the last of their food, a lone, scrawny chicken popped out of hiding and fortuitously into their waiting hands. Fires were prohibited, so the three men sliced it up with their trench knives, stripped as many of the feathers as possible, and dined. The raw, meager meal sustained them for the few days it took the kitchen to get supplies forward.

The final resistance prior to the Roer River and Jülich was the village of Bourheim. It was hardly a village at all but more a collection of farmhouses—a tiny rural community a kilometer or so from the river. Initial reports from Bourheim were that the enemy had retreated and left the village unprotected. It was the last line of defense before the Roer River and the city of Jülich. As they approached the buildings, the fighting intensified, and causalities mounted. One of the members of the other machine gun squad (there are two in each company) was a former navy pilot named Rutherford. He had washed out of flight school because of his penchant for buzzing cows. Nearing Bourheim in intense fighting, Rutherford was seen running in a crouch toward the rear, holding his badly wounded shoulder, his left arm hanging

The Force of Destiny

limp by his side. As he spotted Arnald, he yelled, "I'll see ya later, Gabe!" Rutherford was obviously headed home due to his million-dollar wound,[12] and in a perverse twist of logic, the shouted greeting sustained Arnald for months: "Well, I *can't* die. Rutherford said he'd see me later!"

On the outskirts of Bourheim and while Arnald and Johnny were dug into their muddy foxhole, the Germans began yet another counterattack. (Because Arnald had the .30 caliber machine gun outfitted with the assault mount that allowed portability, only two squad members were needed to man it.) The blitzkrieg-like attack began with a rain of mortars pinning the men down. Immediately following, tanks rolled toward them with infantry bringing up the rear. Clearly outnumbered and with nowhere to turn, Arnald, in a flash of inspiration and self-preservation, instructed his partner to "lie down and play dead!" The squad of soldiers and tanks swept by, placing the two briefly behind enemy lines. After the troops passed, Arnald and Johnny popped out of the muck and, firing furiously, dropped the Germans from the rear. The heroic scene was witnessed by Lieutenant Eamon (their commanding officer) and earned PFC Arnald Gabriel and PFC Johnny Arrowsmith the Bronze Star Medal. Due to the disjointed structure of front-line combat communications, however, they were not notified of or awarded the honor for nearly ten days.

A distinct difference compared to the fighting after D-day was the ability of the front-line soldier to rotate to the rear for short periods. About once a week they made their way back past the slag heaps to Heerlen, Holland, now deep in Allied territory, and to a working coal mine. Rows of showerheads installed for the Dutch coal miners sent hot water over cold, grateful bodies. "I could have stayed under those showers all day," Arnald remembers. There were even the luxury of hot meals and replacement pants for the mud-soaked uniforms. "I didn't even mind the itchy English wool pants with the rear patch pockets." Anything was better than what came out of the bottom of a cold, water-filled foxhole.

---

12 An infantryman's reference to an injury that was not too serious, but serious enough to go home.

One day when Arnald's buddy Johnny was back at the rear, Clyde "Spot" Collins moved up to fill in. "We called him Spot because he was never 'on the spot'!" In the "heat of battle" things move quickly. When changing the ammo belt on a .30 caliber machine gun, the gunner's hand is laid over the open breech of the gun for a split second. Arnald had performed the maneuver perhaps hundreds of times over many months, but as his hand passed the open breech, Spot slammed it shut. "My left middle finger blew up like a golf ball," Arnald painfully remembers. Harry urged him to have it looked at, and he headed back to the aid station.

The medic who attended to his hand was Gabriel Acosta from Santa Barbara, California. He'd seen quite a number of injuries during his time with the Twenty-Ninth and advised Arnald that this injury would qualify him for a Purple Heart Medal. Arnald's thoughts went back to D-day and the more than five months of horribly wounded comrades he'd seen on the battlefield, some with missing limbs, others barely alive. With little deliberation, he refused to consider the suggestion. Arnald had Acosta lance the rapidly swelling finger to relieve the pressure and bandage it; in two days, he returned to his foxhole on the front lines.

Spot was a country boy from South Carolina and nearly illiterate. After mail call, Spot would ask Arnald to read him the letters from his sister back home in Spartanburg. He would then help him answer, writing the letter Spot dictated. It usually required Arnald to fill in the blanks to Spot's request to, "Just tell her I'm doing fine."

Entering Bourheim, Arnald was once again the lead. The early reports of the village being abandoned were obviously false, and the troops were subjected to a massive aerial assault followed by an artillery barrage. As they entered the town, Arnald and his squad started up a dirt street that initially appeared empty. Turning a corner, they stepped into the path of a German King Tiger tank, the most powerful tank in World War II. The tanker fired his machine gun on the approaching troops, sending Arnald and the rest of the squad into the ditch that ran along each side of the road. Within minutes, an advancing American Sherman tank was able to fire on and repulse the Tiger. Emerging from the ditch, Arnald found several machine gun holes had ventilated his bloused pants.

In an eerily similar story on another street in town, another Tiger tank surprised a group of Twenty-Ninth infantrymen in their foxholes. Sweeping the massive gun toward the men, the tank was able to hold them until German soldiers came forward. The GIs had little choice but to surrender, but as they rose, their hands held high, the Germans fired on the defenseless Americans. "It was gut-wrenching to watch them machine gunned before our eyes."

For three days the Germans counterattacked. Massive mortar shelling was followed by the relentless tank squads and a swarm of infantry. "It was street to street, building to building, and sometimes room to room," Arnald says. Time was spent moving through the town, on perimeter watch, or trying to rest. There was very little of the latter. Standing watch was generally a four-hours-on, two-hours-off duty. Constant vigilance and lack of rest burned the eyes and, "When you go days like that, it's not hard to imagine the origin of the phrase 'the thousand-yard stare' when talking about the front-line soldier. Maybe you've seen that empty look in the eyes of combat men."

"When night fell, you never knew if Americans or Germans were in the next building," Arnald remembers. Bodies lay where they fell because the medics and graves registration personnel were unable to approach the intense fighting. The fog of war descended on the town as utter confusion and disorientation enveloped the men. The din of mortar explosions, machine gun, and small arms fire mixed with constant orders and other communications being yelled back and forth all though the thick smoke and haze made even the simplest task nearly impossible. The deafening sounds of grenades fired by launchers from M1 rifles, the shrill screech of the screaming mimis,[13] the horrible sound of the dying men all around, and the sight of the dead on the ground and hanging from windows or vehicles continued unabated for days. Arnald remembers thinking that, "with all the resources available to America, it comes down to this: man to man; men who have personally nothing against each other but who must

---

[13] The screaming mimi was a rocket-launched weapon whose explosive power was nearly as frightening as its terrifying howl prior to impact.

kill or be killed." It was a relentless, utterly exhausting ordeal that required constant vigilance in the face of unimaginable horror and mind-numbing fatigue.

After five days of attacks, fully seven determined counterattacks, and bloody back-and-forth fighting, the enemy attempted one final, massive thrust. With the help of US Air Corps P-47 fighter airplanes that swept over the small town, the attack was repulsed, the Germans withdrew, and Bourheim grew silent. Troops from the Twenty-Ninth Infantry streamed into what was left of the little village, took stock, and cast their eyes across the Roer River to the key city of Jülich, Germany.

On the Bank of the Roer River

The retreating enemy had left extensive and, to Arnald's mind, elaborate entrenchments throughout the town and along the river. They also, however, left a vast network of booby traps, land mines, and other hidden explosives that made the foxholes unusable and added to the rising casualty count.

In their static position near the banks of the Roer River, their newly dug foxholes became much more sophisticated. Slats of wood were procured to line the floor, and canvas provided a "roof" over all but the gun placements. Evenings found the machine gunners (Harry, Johnny, Smitty, Hoople, Flogey, and Spot) and the mortar guys (Foose, Rutherford, and Les Wheaton from Ithaca, New York) huddled together playing cards that were provided by Special Services while noshing on C rations that they'd garnished with local onions. The meals were supplemented by a few vegetables from the surrounding farms, but Arnald's favorite C ration was pork and beans. They also sliced and fried potatoes in fat that had been brought forward from the rear kitchen area.

Early December arrived with falling temperatures and snow. As the ever-present mud froze and was covered, staying warm became the next challenge. The Allied advance into Germany was halted, and for the northernmost American soldiers on the eastern front, training exercises became the priority. Farther north, in territory still held by the enemy, several dams held back an enormous amount of water that, if released at a strategically inopportune time, could either isolate troops who had crossed the river or wipe them out. The emphasis and thrust toward the dams north of the Jülich area was to either capture or destroy them prior to any river crossing. Training for Arnald and the rest of the 175th, however, involved deploying pontoon bridges and learning river-crossing techniques.

On December 16 the Germans began a massive offensive with thousands of troops and hundreds of Panzer tanks in a desperate push westward. The objective was to split the advancing Allied line; isolate the troops in the north, in Belgium, Holland, and western Germany; and negotiate a cease-fire. Although some sort of offensive was expected, the bold advance shocked the Allies and took the Germans deep into newly liberated territory before they were stopped. The resulting shift in the line of fighting and its general shape gave the offensive its now familiar name: the Battle of the Bulge.

Troops who had been fighting alongside Arnald's 175th Battalion were sent south to participate in the battle, and because of the intense fighting over the past couple of months, the 175th's unit strength was reduced by about 30 percent. It left a precariously thin line of defense with little hope for reinforcements. Fortunately, the Germans' main effort was to the south with their plan to divide, isolate, and force a conclusion to the war. Should the enemy succeed, it was clear to Arnald and those with whom he'd been fighting that they would be cut off from all Allied support.

Over the next few weeks, the men settled into a routine waiting for orders to cross the Roer River and attack Jülich. In the relative quiet that ensued, Arnald spent much of his time on reconnaissance patrols in the fields that sloped down to the river east of Bourheim, probing the enemy's position and strength. He carried the .30 caliber machine gun, not with the tripod used for stationary firing, but with the assault mount bipod designed for the purpose. Reconnaissance patrols quickly became combat patrols when they were discovered, and the bullets started flying. Because the patrols were done at night, the cover of darkness prevented many casualties.

Michael A. Gabriel

The Germans in Jülich set up loudspeakers aimed toward the 175th's command post (CP) and played broadcasts from Axis Sally, the German equivalent of Tokyo Rose. Popular American songs were played that were designed to make the men feel homesick. Between tunes, Sally would remind them of the danger they would be in when German General von Rundstedt closed the pincer movement in his march to the North Sea. She repeated the mantra of the Bulge German soldiers that promised, "Liége by Christmas and Paris by New Years." The propagandist also told the soldiers that their wives and girlfriends were, in fact, not waiting for them back home and were sleeping with other men. Arnald remembers that the lies were not particularly convincing but that the music was a nice diversion.

Christmas Day dawned on Arnald's bitter-cold watch at the forward outpost on the river. The quiet morning gave way to the strangely peaceful sound of their German counterparts over in Jülich singing Christmas carols. Normally there were very few German Air Force Luftwaffe aircraft in the skies over Allied troops; air superiority had long been established, and successes in bombing strategic fuel depots kept most Luftwaffe on the ground. On Christmas, after Arnald returned to the CP, a streaking Luftwaffe airplane rocketed overhead. It fired nothing and dropped no bombs, but the sight and sound of an enemy aircraft *without propellers* moving faster than anything they'd ever seen shook them. "It was the first time that we had seen a German jet, and it scared the hell out of us when it went by," he recalls. It's not surprising. That Christmas day they had witnessed the first successful jet fighter in aviation history. Germany's development of the Messerschmitt Me 262 had the potential to change the course of the war except that its production and insertion into the conflict came too late. The unusual day ended with a much appreciated treat: a traditional Christmas dinner with all the fixings was brought forward from the rear kitchen area.

The weeks dragged on, and the unrelenting cold and deepening snow made the weekly visits to the hot showers a treasured gift. New Year's Day 1945 was another day on forward watch trying to stay warm, but as with Christmas Day, a holiday dinner with turkey was served to troops weary of C rations. The measured routine provided

The Force of Destiny

a degree of comfort that had been missing in the nearly constant movement of the past six months and found Arnald, Johnny, and Harry in a closer friendship than each had developed in a lifetime.

January 8, 1945, was a day like most others. News that Hitler had ordered a withdrawal of his "bulge" troops had little immediate effect on the three soldiers as they trudged through the snow for yet another late-night watch at the river. A light snow fell as Arnald took the first two-hour shift while the others slept. The evening was unremarkable; there were few sounds and little movement from his counterparts across the frozen river in Jülich. When his time was up, Arnald was relieved by one of his buddies. He quietly shuffled to the rear of the foxhole, settled against the hard floor and frozen ground, and, surprisingly, dozed off.

Shortly after midnight, the mortar landed. There was no warning, no small arms fire, no organized attack, and no following fire. The explosion blasted the sanctity of the foxhole and sent the three men flying, their limp bodies landing in a sickening heap. Arnald woke hours later in a haze, his head pounding from the effects of a severe concussion, his body battered and sore. As he struggled to assess his whereabouts, his memory slowly returned, and a rising fear overtook him. He painfully cast his eyes around the room. He was in a supply station at his company CP in Bourheim, medic Gabriel Acosta standing by his side.

Arnald immediately asked about the condition of his two friends, and Acosta wordlessly looked across the small room. Two mattress covers served as makeshift body bags, a temporary accommodation awaiting the Graves Registration personnel. PFC Harry E. Aschoff and PFC John W. Arrowsmith Jr. had each been in the army for less than a year. Sudden realization thundered through Arnald, and the shock took his breath like a heavyweight punch to the gut. As a witness to more than seven months of indescribable carnage and bloodshed, the loss staggered him as he reeled on his cot. The nineteen-year-old boy broke down in uncontrollable shakes and violent heaves. He curled into a fetal position accompanied by his wracking sobs and searched for a way to go on.

PFC Foose, PFC Hoople and Arnald, Mönchen-Gladbach, Germany

CHAPTER SIX

Aftermath and the Final Months Across Germany

Physically, Arnald healed quickly. The headaches subsided, and the minor bumps and bruises were quickly forgotten. The first sergeant of I Company, Joe Staley, asked him to stay back at the CP, and Arnald was given what he considered busywork to occupy his time. He helped the supply sergeant prepare equipment for the line; he assisted Cpl. "Goldie" Goldberg sort mail in the mail room. The conditions in the rear echelon were certainly comfortable; the friendly and even cheerful attitude of those with whom he worked was pleasant enough. In stark contrast to his job on the front lines, the buildings were warm and dry, and he was near the mess hall. It was relatively safe duty, and given his commitment over the past seven months, he couldn't be faulted for wanting to stay where he was. But after less than a week, he asked to return to the machine gun squad. "I felt guilty and just wanted to get back to the line," he says simply.

Now a combat veteran, he returned to find fewer men with his experience on the forward lines. Although replacements were finally coming up to fill the depleted ranks, they were former truck drivers, administration clerks, and mail-room guys. Most experienced, combat-trained soldiers were being sent south to the fighting at the bulge.

New leadership was needed to help lead these green soldiers, and to that end, Arnald was offered a battlefield promotion. In recognition of his experience and leadership abilities, Lieutenant Butler approved his elevation in rank and appointed him section leader. He was given a manual and told to study and then report to the battalion commander. He memorized the procedures and protocols and a list of military definitions, including: "What is a map?" and "What is enfiladed fire?"

When Arnald headed to the rear, he found Major Ballard sitting behind a kitchen table in a house that had been designated as the battalion's CP. "Private Gabriel reporting as ordered, Sir!" he barked, snapping to attention.

The major had one question: "Gabriel, do you know what end of that machine gun the bullets come out of?" Arnald answered in the affirmative, and Major Ballard replied, "That is all, *Sergeant*."

His normal rise in rank should have been to corporal, but it's obvious that Arnald's reputation for leadership and his heroics on the battlefield had been made known to the major through positive reports from his immediate superiors. There was a certain gratification in the official acknowledgment of his efforts and his elevation in rank, but it did little to alter his reality. He was no closer to going home, and he was still terribly burdened with the loss of his two friends.

When he received the new stripes, he realized that he'd been promoted to an E-5 staff sergeant, leapfrogging Smitty, the ranking sergeant in the section. He was an E-4 buck sergeant, a high school dropout, and probably, Arnald surmised, lacking in leadership skills. When asked how the coal miner from Pennsylvania reacted, Arnald remembers that, "Smitty took it okay."

During the balance of January and into February, their mission changed little. They pushed through knee-deep snow to their watch at the river and the occasional patrol in enemy territory. Snow packs, a kind of heavy winter boot, were ordered but not yet received from supply.[14] The highlight of each week was still the trip back into Holland and the hot showers at the coal-mine building.

In Bourheim, the front-line men were housed in the second story of a bombed-out building overlooking the Roer River. In yet another grisly footnote that defined his life at the time, the basement of their building held the dead body of what appeared to be a teenage girl.

---

14 Because of the vagaries of army supply, they received them in April.

She remained in the basement for their three-month occupation of the village.

By now, the Red Cross and Salvation Army had moved up and became part of the weekly visits to the rear. Arnald patronized the Salvation Army because they charged the men nothing for coffee and donuts; the Red Cross charged them ten cents, and because he had his pay sent home to Ma and Pa, Arnald usually had no money. The USO shows had also moved into the rear areas and became a much-looked-forward-to event. The now-famous camp shows featured dozens of movie stars and the top entertainers of the day performing stage, musical, and comedy shows. Arnald never attended. Despite his lifelong love of music, the prospect of seeing the world's best musicians, actors, and comedians perform didn't interest him. His life and focus had changed.

Thankfully, the weather warmed, and the snow began to melt; unfortunately, heavy rains began, and the mud returned. The narrow lanes, foxholes, and trenches filled with water and sucking mud that seemed to cover everything. Their GI issue boots were not waterproof, and trench foot sent many back to the CP and the medics for treatment. They were resigned to being either knee-deep in snow or ankle-deep in mud.

About mid-February an unexpected break came Arnald's way. He and several other men were selected to go to Paris for five days R&R. "They must have thought I needed the days off," he surmised. The men boarded the canvas-covered duce-and-a-half truck and lumbered the more than three hundred miles to the City of Lights.

Quartered in a hotel near the Champs-Elysees with dozens of other GIs, the days and nights were spent in full revelry. The days passed quickly, however, and during his final evening, he was stopped by an MP who questioned his disorderly appearance. Eyeing Arnald, his tie askew, shirt and pants wrinkled, and needing a shave, the spit-and-polish MP barked, "Straighten up, GI!" Arnald's smart-ass reply that he was "heading back to the front tomorrow, what difference does it make?" must have struck a note of logic to the man, because the MP turned and walked away without another word.

Michael A. Gabriel

Crossing the Roer River

By the end of February, the slow Allied buildup behind Bourheim was complete. The battle plan was to have the engineer battalion string three pontoon bridges across the Roer River and, with the support of rear artillery, assault Jülich. At about three o'clock on the morning of February 23, the engineers got to work. Unfortunately, the Germans were ready for them and immediately destroyed two of the temporary bridges. The lone access to Jülich across the Roer in his southern sector was directly outside the second-story window Arnald and his men occupied.

The bridge was heavily defended by German mortar fire, small arms, and especially machine gun emplacements that were holding up the entire advance. Sergeant Gabriel had been using the .30 caliber machine gun, Hellzapoppin II, with the assault mount because the window sill in the crumbling building wasn't strong enough to support the tripod. He picked up the weapon and, firing from his hip, took out the enemy machine gun nests allowing the Twenty-Ninth Infantry troops to cross the river safely. His heroic action that morning was witnessed by Lt. Newt Butler and earned him a second Bronze Star Medal. Arnald was to later read the announcement of his two Bronze Star Medals in his hometown newspaper, the *Cortland Standard*:

> On November 26, 1944, at Bourheim, Germany, PFC Gabriel and another man held their position after enemy armor had over-run the forward defensive positions, and then delivered a murderous fire on the supporting enemy infantry. By standing fast in the face of superior enemy numbers, PFC Gabriel contributed materially to the repelling of the enemy counter-attack. On February 28, 1945, during the initial bridging operations prior to the crossing of the Roer River, PFC (sic)[15] Gabriel and another man by constant devotion to duty and fine teamwork, successfully fired

---

[15] Arnald had been promoted to sergeant by then.

upon and silenced every enemy machinegun that fired in their assigned sector.

"I don't know how many 'every' is, since I fired at the source of their tracer bullets," Arnald says, "probably three or four." Later that day, when his squad crossed the floating bridge under heavy enemy fire, a mortar exploded near Arnald, sprayed him with shrapnel, and nearly forced him into the swollen river. He continued across the bridge and made his way to the medic where Gabriel Acosta treated the wounds on his left arm with sulpha powder to prevent infection and covered it with a bandage. Again eligible for a Purple Heart, Arnald once more refused to consider applying for the honor. "I thought of buddies of mine with missing limbs or blown to bits," Arnald reasoned. He immediately rejoined the fighting with his machine gun squad and led the advance into Jülich.

Inching across Jülich was as tough as any battle he'd fought so far. Flamethrowers were used to rout the Germans from their dug-in positions, and eventually, the tide began to turn. For three days they fought, and as they gained the upper hand, the enemy started to surrender. The prisoners were sent back across the footbridge and, in a fit of retaliation, the engineers on the opposite shore shot them, upset that some of their buddies died putting up the bridges. The small village of Stetternich sat on a hill beyond Jülich, and the German soldiers there were witness to the shootings. It made it very difficult to take the village for that reason. "A lesson of combat the engineers did not know," Arnald mused.

Jülich was a key victory, because now the German army was in full retreat. Without letup, the Twenty-Ninth continued their march to the northeast to Müchen-Gladbach,[16] originally a city of about three hundred thousand, now housing around twenty thousand civilians. They had just spent the better part of four days of intense combat, and their commanders thought that the capture of the city was important enough to march overnight a distance of more than forty kilometers to begin the assault. Although resistance was much lighter than

---

16 The city would change its name to "Mönchen-Gladbach" in 1950 and "Mönchengladbach" in 1960.

expected, it still took several days to capture and secure the city. In a frightening moment of déjà vu, Arnald, while rounding a street corner as they advanced through the city one day, came face-to-face with another German King Tiger tank. This time, the shock of seeing the behemoth caused him to drop his .30 caliber machine gun and duck into an alleyway. He returned sometime later to discover that the tank had run over Hellzapoppin II and destroyed the weapon. Yet another was requisitioned from supply, and (naturally) Hellzapoppin III was christened.

From the time they left Bourheim and crossed into Jülich, Arnald had been tasked with carrying the machine gun. Constantly on the move through the city streets, the tripod mount the new men had been trained on was not used. "The new replacements had no idea about house-to-house fighting with the assault mount," he says.

The new replacements ... There was never a reference to the other men in his machine gun squad by name. In communicating with them, it was always, "hey, you," or, "you and the other guy." Since January 9, Arnald had stopped using names. He wasn't interested in who they were or where they were from; he didn't want to make new friends, because after Harry and Johnny, "losing a friend in combat just hurt too much."

Advancing through Mönchen-Gladbach was the first time Arnald and the soldiers of the Twenty-Ninth had seen German civilians in any number. Strangely enough, the Americans were welcomed as liberators. "I think they were as sick of the war as we were." Most of the captured German soldiers took on that same resigned attitude as well. The SS officers maintained a defiant tone, however. In their final days in the city, the Americans were rounding up many prisoners, and one day Arnald saw a haughty SS officer being led to a truck by a number of soldiers. He boldly walked up to the man and snatched the Iron Cross medal the man wore on his chest. The still-proud German snapped to attention and clicked his heels in a defiant gesture. "I thought he was going to give me a Heil Hitler salute too!"

München-Gladbach was now the largest city in Germany held by the Allied forces. For the Twenty-Ninth Infantry, the war was just about over. Leaving the city, their pursuit eastward across the plains of

The Force of Destiny

Germany was met with little resistance. The Twenty-Ninth was tasked with securing the industrial heart of the country in the Ruhr Valley as they moved east and captured the cities of Essen, Dortmund, and others. Travel along Hitler's *Autobahn*, a highway he'd built to quickly move his own troops, made the advance much quicker.

Due to the speed of the advancing army, there were times when the front line thinned, and Arnald found himself temporarily walking alone. During one such time, he came upon a farmhouse occupied by a young German *hausfrau* perhaps three to four months pregnant and all alone. As he approached, she broke down in tears and fell into his arms, sobbing. They stood quietly for several minutes, two lonely teenagers consoling each other amid the folly and utter confusion of war. Their starvation for a tender touch, a soft, human encounter overcame all else around them. The poignancy of the moment, though brief, transcended the simple fact that they spoke not a word of each other's language. Their chance meeting ended quietly, and now carefully pulling himself away, Arnald picked up his weapon and moved off to locate his men.

As they progressed deeper into the country, they also liberated hundreds of POWs in dozens of camps. One camp held a number of Italian prisoners, and although Arnald spoke the language in a distinct Abbrutzese dialect, he was asked to serve as interpreter to men who spoke in a Florentine tongue. In their first exchange, the prisoners asked, "Capito?" meaning, "Do you understand?" When he answered "yeah" in English, he was asked to avoid the word because it sounded too much like the German "Ja." Arnald remembers, "I guess they had had enough of the German language."

In asking what the obviously underfed men had been eating, the answer was, "la cavallo." He was led around to the rear of a rundown barn where he was shown the remains of a horse with most of its underside eaten away. The remaining flesh was rotting, putrid and alive with a mass of maggots and buzzing flies. The scene left Arnald wondering what health issues the men may have had when his unit pulled out the next day.

In the final push through the country, Arnald's Third Battalion was sent to clear a small forested area near Klotz. Although they were told it was only a mopping-up operation and to expect little resistance, the fighting was fierce with very few of the enemy willing to surrender. Additionally, the trees offered yet another unique battlefield experience to the combat veterans for which they had little formal training, truly a baptism under fire.

They were now at the banks of the Elbe River, and due to the tenets of the Yalta Convention, they were not permitted to advance any farther. The Russians were pushing west toward them and controlled the territory east of the river. As the Twenty-Ninth Division settled in along the river, they began to take custody of thousands of German soldiers who swam, rafted, or boated over, anxious to surrender to the Americans rather than submit to the brutality of the Russians.

The end of April brought beautiful spring weather and, with the war in Europe clearly over, thoughts of going home. The news of Adolph Hitler's death strengthened those hopes as the men shifted their focus from front-line infantrymen to one of an occupation force. Arnald and the others collected a few souvenirs. The soldiers were permitted to ship these items home, and Arnald garnered a nickel-plated Luger pistol, a Mauser rifle, and a German helmet that his little brother Rick had requested.

By the third of May, the 175th tallied more than ten thousand captured German prisoners. The act of military surrender was signed on May 7 both in Reims, France, and the following day in Berlin. The war drew to a close and ended Arnald's days of combat. He had survived eleven months at war, including 201 days of front-line fighting.

Copenhagen, Denmark, November 1945

Bremen, Germany (first row, right end)

CHAPTER SEVEN

Army of the Occupation

In May 1945 the Twenty-Ninth Infantry became part of the Army of the Occupation. Almost overnight, their mission changed from an active front-line fighting unit to what essentially became a temporary military government. They were sent to what was designated the Bremen Enclave, fifteen hundred square miles of northern Germany nestled against the North Sea formerly occupied by the British and Canadian forces. Bremerhaven, the largest city, became the port of entry and departure for all American forces in Germany. The 175th set up its headquarters about twenty-five miles south in the town of Osterholz-Scharmbeck and Arnald with Item Company just east of there in Worpswede.

The men were housed in a former German army barracks whose accommodations far exceeded the muddy or frozen foxholes and crumbling buildings of the previous year. Meals still consisted of army chow, but now the men had other options available on the black market. In the flourishing underground economy, there was no more powerful currency than the soldiers' regular GI issue cigarettes, chocolate, and coffee.

In 1945 smoking was a deeply ingrained part of American and Western culture. The army issued cigarettes weekly to the men, and nearly everyone smoked. Arnald never did. "I guess in the heat of battle when I was shaking with fright, I thought it might be nice to light up, but of course then, none were to be had." Afterward, it just didn't seem like a good idea. He used his issue of cigarettes to barter for items in town.

The army instituted a nonfraternization policy to preclude excess involvement with the local populous that was, at best, lightly regarded. Despite the threat of a sixty-five-dollar fine for violating the policy (a staggering amount of money to the young soldiers), the increasingly common sight of a GI's clothing hanging on the clothesline at a young *fräulein*'s home doomed the initiative, and it was soon rescinded. Cigarettes and chocolate could buy almost anything.

Part of Arnald's duties in the Bremen Enclave was to take the legions of displaced persons (DP) home. During the war, the Germans had pressed thousands of captured foreigners into service to fill the depleted ranks of its army. They were dressed in German uniforms and threatened with being shot if they didn't comply. The DP were composed of citizens from all over Europe—Czech, French, Polish, etc.—and boxcars and flatcars were used to send them home. The cars were hitched to a train traveling in the general direction of the DP home country, deadheading the former soldiers. Arnald was in charge of the train, and with a corporal in each car to keep order, they had very little trouble because generally, "They were happy to be going home."

Arnald made two DP train trips during his stay in the Bremen Enclave. The first was to Prague, Czechoslovakia, with a stop in Pilsen, home of the massive Skoda arms factory used by the Nazis to produce countless Panzer tanks, machine guns, and other tools of the *Wehrmacht*, the German war machine. The second was to France where they were stopped at the French border. The French border guards prevented the trains from entering the country and left Arnald wondering, "Maybe they considered the DP collaborators. We never knew what happened to them."

Days off were spent at the makeshift Noncommissioned Officers (NCO) Club in the converted train station a short walk into town from his barracks. After just a few days in his new town, Arnald spotted a small boy sitting on a curb, alone. He approached the disheveled little waif and asked, *"Wo ist dein mutter und vater?"* The answer to, "Where

The Force of Destiny

are your mother and father?" was *tot*, "dead." It broke the combat veteran's heart. "I knew I had to do something for this little *kind*."

He found some scrapped olive drab (OD) uniforms in supply and, with the barter of chocolate, had one of the local *fräuleins* sew a little uniform that matched Arnald's. He set up a cot next to his in the barracks, and Günter (the young boy knew his own name) became Arnald's constant companion. Trips around town and even to the army mess hall to eat brought no complaints from superior officers. He and the other men in the company taught the little boy some English words, and he was quick to learn. When Arnald shipped out the following January, he left the boy with the British soldiers who remained in the enclave. Günter left him with a heartbreaking *danke schön*, "Thank you very much," and to this day Arnald thinks, "I have often wondered what happened to little Günter."

In early July Arnald joined the 175th Regimental Drill Team at the request of Lieutenant Butler. Nearly a year of firing a .30 caliber machine gun hadn't affected his rifle skills; the team consisted of the thirty-six best riflemen out of the three thousand in the regiment. The competition against other regiments' drill teams took place at the newly christened Ike Stadium in Bremen. At the completion of the drill championship at the end of July, they placed an impressive third place in the entire division.

Life in the Bremen Enclave continued uneventfully throughout the autumn with the only highlights of his week being visits to the NCO Club for an evening of playing cards and hanging out at the bar or into the village to trade for a home-distilled potato whiskey and companionship. An R&R to Copenhagen, Denmark, in November resulted in a great deal more of the same. The citizens of the small island country treated the soldiers as liberators and feted them accordingly. He visited the famous Tivoli Garden, and though shows of more sophistication were available at the many performance stages there, Arnald and his companions frequented the ones featuring popular songs and dancing girls.

In December 1945 the rumors began to fly concerning a return to the United States—to home. As rumor turned to fact, the men were faced with calculating a formula that would determine who would be eligible. A point system was established that considered length of service, marital status, and battle credits. Those who had accrued the requisite number would ship out, and the others would redeploy to yet another unit in the Army of the Occupation. The Twenty-Ninth Infantry Division was being disbanded.

With more than twenty-one months in-country with the Twenty-Ninth Division, the horrific D-day landing at Omaha Beach in Normandy that resulted in the award of a Distinguished Unit Citation, 201 days of front-line combat, five campaign stars,[17] two Bronze Star Medals, and a battlefield promotion of a three-step rank increase, Arnald was stunned to learn that he was shy of the magic number that would allow him to go home. Other soldiers had garnered more points due to their early participation with the Twenty-Ninth Infantry in England prior to his arrival in the spring of 1944. The fortunate men were outfitted with new uniforms, weapons, and flags for their triumphant return to the States.

Lieutenant Butler's Advice

Lieutenant Butler summoned Arnald into his office in early January 1946 to inform the shocked staff sergeant of his new assignment. Arnald was angry and depressed and felt he'd been deceived by the army. Rear echelon personnel who'd never fired a shot, who'd not lived through the horrors or felt the losses that he had were packing their bags to go home. The simple fact of their longevity and marital status trumped his experiences. In desperation, Arnald had even approached the leader of the Twenty-Ninth Infantry Band and had requested an audition as a flute player. The fact that he hadn't played the instrument in more than three years was less important than the fact that the unit was readying for their return to the United States, and he'd hoped to join them for the trip home. The bandleader, though sympathetic, saw through Arnald's ruse and informed him that it was

---

[17] Campaign stars indicate participation in major battles, or campaigns, during the war.

all about the points. He still didn't have enough. His frustration was all consuming and close to the surface as he reported to his CO.

Arnald was reassigned to the Twenty-Ninth Regiment (not to be confused with the Twenty-Ninth Division, which had ceased to exist) stationed in Frankfurt, Germany. He was to leave within the week. Lieutenant Butler also took the opportunity to present Arnald with the 175th Regiment, I Company flag, or guidon. Lieutenant Butler said, "Sergeant, you've been with us the longest. You've gone all the way with us. This belongs to you." As he spoke, he handed over the battle-torn symbol of his and his men's efforts over the past year and a half. It was an honor beyond description. It represented hundreds of men who were never going home. Ever. He was the only member of his original squad to survive the war. More than the high honor that Arnald's receipt of the guidon represented, the lieutenant's recognition of his contribution to the unit was far more astonishing to the frustrated young man. Arnald was flooded with emotion as he shakily accepted the flag and, with a lump in his throat, managed to say, "Thank you." He then saluted sharply and left the room. To this day, the 175th Regiment, I Company guidon is Arnald's most treasured possession. "It represents to me more than can be put into words," he says.

The trip south from the Bremen Enclave brought him to the Supreme Headquarters Allied Forces Europe (SHAFE), the center of all Allied military activity in occupied Europe. As the sergeant of the guard, his primary duty was to transport sentries to posts scattered around Frankfurt. Every four hours he drove his armed men to SHAFE headquarters, the Palm Garden (then, a Red Cross recreation center), the *Bahnhof* (railway station), and other strategic locations around the city.

Arnald's roommate was S.Sgt. Ross Pascalis from Mt. Vernon, New York. He was able to continue his partying lifestyle with Ross, and they spent much of their off time at the Palm Garden. It had been a high-end nightclub during the war and now drew bored GIs from around Frankfurt to its plush halls. Celebrities of the day not only entertained the troops, but spent time mixing with them as well. Arnald remembers two particularly well. Mickey Rooney used to sit in with the GI band and, as he recalls, "displayed much emotion and energy." That same drive was on tap during a game of Ping-Pong with Arnald, and because of Mickey's hyperkinetic intensity, "I thought it best that he win the game."

Arnald also danced with Maria Riva. She was the beautiful daughter of Marlene Dietrich and an actress and entertainer in her own right. He was infatuated with the young actress, who was nearly his age, and had her sign a five-dollar bill as a souvenir.[18]

The long evenings of revelry with Ross would inevitably end with a visit to the mess hall. Because Ross was the sergeant in charge of the kitchen, the closed building presented no problem to the men. Their evening on the town would end with cooking a dozen eggs, a toasted *loaf* of bread, and a gallon of coffee. It didn't take long for the lifestyle to manifest itself. Since leaving the front lines at the end of fighting nearly seven months earlier at a trim 175 pounds, Arnald ballooned to well over 200.

Still, his commanding officer, Lieutenant Butler, also noticed the dramatic change in his veteran charge. Lt. Newton D. Butler was a big Texan from Corsicana and a powerful presence in Arnald's life. He was a hands-on leader and an officer who led by example. Arnald remembers a harrowing battle where his front-line unit had been pinned by the relentless onslaught of the advancing German troops lead by a half-track mounted with a machine gun. The tide began to turn as the tracked vehicle burst into flames, a direct hit from a mortar, reversing the enemy foot soldiers. Seizing the opportunity, a wounded Lieutenant Butler leapt atop the burning hulk, manned the machine gun, and spun it toward the retreating Germans, firing on them to clinch the battle. "If you saw that in a movie, you'd say, 'Naw, that couldn't happen,'" Arnald remembers admiringly. "He was fearless." By the end of the war, Lieutenant Butler had been awarded five Purple Heart Medals for wounds he sustained on the battlefield.

In mid-January, summoned by his commanding officer, Arnald entered Lieutenant Butler's office with not a little trepidation. He was obviously aware of his debased lifestyle but was having a tough time dealing with its causes. It was an affliction not unfamiliar to most

---

18 She signed it "Maria Manton," her stage name.

The Force of Destiny

combat veterans, to anyone having faced a life-threatening trauma. The terms *battle fatigue, shell-shocked*, or, during the Civil War, *a soldier's heart* all acknowledge the malady, and yet one prevailing thought held it in the realm of a personal weakness or, more harshly, cowardice. He carried his shattered psyche grimly, not wanting to face the terrible events that abruptly ended his adolescence and forced him into the horrors of sanctioned killing. He hid behind the haze of alcohol and the comfort of food. The camaraderie he sought was false, whether with his cohorts at the NCO Club or one of the local *fräuleins*. The future didn't exist except in making plans for tomorrow; he didn't dare think about his life as a civilian back home.

Lieutenant Butler was deeply concerned about the fellow veteran who stood in front of him. Typically, the big Texan was direct. "Gabe, what the hell's wrong with you? You eat too much, you drink too much. What's go'n on?"

"Well, Lieutenant," Arnald began, and as he did, the explanation spilled forth in a torrent of words. "D-day ... combat ... Harry and Johnny ..."

The sympathetic officer stopped him. "Now hold it right there," he said as he held up his hand. The lieutenant paused, stared directly into Arnald's troubled eyes, and said easily, "Gabe, it's all right to look back, but just don't stare."

The simple, homegrown piece of advice resonated with the troubled young man. In that moment, Arnald found a way out. He was given a way to acknowledge the awful events of the past eighteen months and the permission to move forward. In that moment, he saw a small light in the darkness that might lead him out from under his overwhelming feelings of guilt at the loss of his two buddies; he found tremendous strength in the power of a simple idea that came from the heart of a man he held in the highest regard. "I really admired that guy," Arnald says simply.

His anger and frustration continued, however, and he still felt deceived by the army. Ross and he continued their lifestyle as he plodded through the days and mindless work schedule. He still resented the rear echelon guys who were shipping out and, "In my opinion, didn't deserve to go home." The bitterness gnawed at him, and he continued to bury it in food and alcohol.

Just a couple of weeks later, in early February, Arnald finally received orders home. The news came suddenly. He had never been sure how long he needed to serve to complete his commitment, and in the army's arcane system, orders just arrived one day. All he knew was that he had accrued the requisite number of points and was told to pack. He was transferred to the Port of Antwerp, a five-hour truck ride northwest, back into Belgium. He and the other soldiers who were awaiting arrival of their ship home were confined to the base with very little to do. They attended the makeshift theater on Camp Lucky Strike,[19] and with nothing else to pass the time, they watched the same movie every night for over a week. By the end of their stay in Antwerp, the men were able to recite dialogue from the musical *On the Town* before Gene Kelly or Frank Sinatra spoke it on screen.

Passage back to the United States was provided by a Liberty Ship. Hundreds of the freighters were built for the war effort primarily to ship cargo, and thus, accommodations for the soldiers in the hold of the vessel were bleak. FDR's description of the ship as "the ugly duckling" was apt. The homesick veterans had little else to pass the time but wander the ship and play cards.

After nearly ten days on the ponderous freighter, they passed into New York Harbor. The sight of the Statue of Liberty, as it has for countless others before and since, deeply moved the hardened vets. The symbol for which these men had fought, been wounded, and witnessed death, unabashedly brought tears to their eyes. Leaving the ship, each one ceremoniously dropped to his knees and kissed the ground. They were home.

---

19 The camps were named for cigarettes: Lucky Strike, Chesterfield, Pall Mall, etc.

The Hallstead Canning Factory Cooker Gang

CHAPTER EIGHT

Home

After disembarking, the soldiers were bused to Camp Kilmer in New Jersey. Arnald spent three days and two nights at the fifteen hundred-acre camp out-processing and completing the steps for separation from the army and his return to civilian life. On March 1, 1946, Arnald was presented with the United States Military Service Honorable Discharge Lapel Pin[20] and requisite paperwork and was bused to New York City. At Grand Central Station he boarded the New York Central Train heading upstate through Albany to Syracuse. The last leg of his three-year-long journey home to Cortland, he hitchhiked. In 1946 a guy in uniform had no trouble getting a ride.

He was dropped on Main Street in Cortland and immediately ran into one of his old buddies, Louie "Cheróke" Giamichael. Cheróke walked Arnald the short distance down Elm Street to the small home and grocery store where he saw his father sweeping the walk. Arnald dropped his duffel bag in the middle of the street at the same time Ferdinand dropped his broom, and father and son embraced, the emotion spilling forth in a flood of tears. His words peppered with his typical mix of Italian and English, Ferdinand then proceeded to thoroughly inspect his son's body, limb by limb, "just to make sure everything was there." The street celebration continued as Ma ran out to welcome her son home.

---

20 The gold embossed eagle pin was referred to as the "ruptured duck" by the former soldiers. It allowed them to travel home in uniform as new civilians.

Arnald dropped his duffel bag in his small bedroom in the living quarters above the grocery store at 122 Elm Street and walked across the street to Pomeroy School where his little brother Ricardo was attending sixth grade. Walking into the classroom, he searched for Rick and overlooked him until Rick stood and turned to greet his older brother. It took a moment to recognize him; his little brother was now a tall, lanky, and spectacled young man. They embraced and, with the teacher's blessing, left and spent the rest of the afternoon catching up on their respective lives during the past three years.

After Arnald's older brother Min joined the Army Specialized Training Program (ASTP) in September 1943, he was trained as an MP and stationed at the Brooklyn Navy Yard. As the war ended, he applied for overseas duty in an effort to speed his accrual of points needed for separation from the army. He was transferred to Greenland, and as such, it would be a few more months before the family was reunited. When Min out-processed through Ft. Dix, Arnald drove to New Jersey to bring his older brother home.

Throughout the past three years of army service, Arnald and his high school sweetheart had maintained contact through letters. Wartime correspondence, when available at the front lines, provided little intimacy and, due to censorship, no details as to the soldier's duty or whereabouts. It was, however, a vital link to home that Arnald and many other soldiers cherished during combat. After a couple of days settling in at home, Arnald borrowed Pa's 1937 Plymouth and drove to Potsdam, New York, on a beautiful and unseasonably warm March day to visit his girlfriend.

The surprise visit shocked the young college coed, and after Arnald heard her make a surreptitious phone call, she broke down and confessed that she'd been dating a Navy V-12 Program[21] student at nearby St. Lawrence University. Arnald learned what thousands of returning GIs also knew: maintaining a relationship over many miles of separation and vastly different lifestyles and experiences is extremely difficult. Upset, he got back in the car and drove home.

---

21 It was a navy college training program similar to the army's ASTP.

The Force of Destiny

Though he was truly home, Arnald's sense of detachment persisted. His difficulty in transitioning to civilian life was due in part to the style of speaking he had become accustomed to. "The movies do not accurately depict the language used by GIs at the front," Arnald explains. Living and fighting alongside other soldiers for more than thirty-six months had coarsened his speech, and as a means to help his reacclimation into society, he attended English classes at his alma mater, Cortland High School.

The first day he arrived in the classroom, the teacher introduced him to the class and suggested he relate some of his war experiences to the young high school students. Arnald quickly expressed his gratitude at being home, said, "I don't think you want to hear about that," and quietly sat down in the last row of chairs, anxious to begin putting the memories behind him. He attended English and social studies classes at CHS for about two and a half months.

Much of the rest of his time was spent at the Varsity Pool Hall in downtown Cortland reconnecting with the Rinkydinks and other childhood friends, many of whom were combat veterans as well. There, he learned the sad fate of some of his old buddies: Louie Perfetti and Sam Speciale were killed at Tarawa Island in the Pacific. John Locke was killed in combat in Europe. John Patriarco lost his right arm at the Salerno beachhead. Ed "Pookie" Mazzoli lost his right leg at Guadalcanal. Others suffered similar fates, and Arnald remembers, "I felt very lucky."

Arnald also enrolled in a federal program he and the other vets referred to as the 52/20 club. It was one of the provisions of the Servicemen's Readjustment Act of 1944[22] and was a kind of unemployment compensation for returning servicemen, giving them twenty dollars a week for up to fifty-two weeks. In 1946 it was enough money to bridge the span into the civilian world.

By June, although certainly entitled to it, Arnald felt uncomfortable taking the federal assistance money and decided to get a job. Because of his many years as a teenager picking beans during the summer, he went back to work at the Halstead Canning Factory. Bill Halstead

---

22 It's more commonly referred to as the GI Bill.

promoted Arnald to the factory and placed him in the warehouse; it allowed him a degree of isolation that suited the returning vet, still struggling with his feelings.

After a short stint in the warehouse, he was asked to take over as boss of the cooker gang. He and his crew were responsible for cooking the fresh-picked beans, peas, and other vegetables in huge vats about five feet in diameter and nearly as deep. The seasonal work forced them to work sixteen to eighteen hours a day for which he was very reasonably compensated at the rate of eighty-seven cents an hour.

The hot summer, long hours, and hard work helped to repair his psyche, satisfied his work ethic, and toned his body. As late August neared and the seasonal work slacked, Bill Halstead stopped by the factory one day and rewarded the hardworking young man with an offer of a full-time, year-round position in the warehouse. Arnald enjoyed the plain, honest toil and was gratified with the generous job offer as he settled into what he suspected was his life's work. August also brought another visitor to the Halstead Canning Factory.

Burton Stanley

Prof. Burton E. Stanley had been Arnald's high school band director, had given him flute lessons, and now searched out his former student to ask about his plans for a future in music. Professor Stanley was clearly not happy with Arnald's career choice at the factory and challenged him with a blunt, "What do you think you're doing here?"

Arnald responded honestly. "Trying to earn a living."

"Forget it!" the professor said. "You should go to college."

Arnald tried to explain that he hadn't played an instrument in more than three years and would be competing with top high school musicians of great skill in addition to former military band members who had played all during the war and who now played at a professional level. Additionally, he had very little money, and although the GI Bill would pay for tuition, he couldn't afford the entrance fees. Frustrated, Professor Stanley left, and Arnald returned to work at Halstead.

A week later, Professor Stanley returned to the factory and informed the chief of the cooker gang that the audition and other entrance requirements to Ithaca College and the School of Music in neighboring Ithaca, New York, had been waived, the fees paid, and, "I expect you to be there at the beginning of the fall semester." With all the hurdles cleared, Arnald faced his changed future. He was motivated by the extraordinary generosity of his former band director and was inspired by the confidence the professor had in him. Arnald's desire not to disappoint the man pushed him to practice his flute for between four and six hours each day. The old skills returned quickly, and Arnald worked hard to hone his craft, recognizing that fear of failure was a strong motivator as well.

In addition to his practicing, Arnald had much work to do before school started. He made arrangements to have the GI bill cover his tuition, but he needed a place to stay in Ithaca. He recalled that a former member of 175th Regiment, I Company mortar squad, named Les Wheaton came from the small college town on Lake Cayuga. Arnald looked him up in the phone book, jumped in the 1940 Hudson Terreplane he and Min had picked up for the three hundred dollars mustering-out pay each had received from the army, and drove to 412 South Aurora Street in Ithaca.

Arnald was met at the door by Les's wife and mother-in-law, and after introducing himself and explaining his need for a place to live, they offered him their spare room for six dollars a week, including breakfast. The house was quite a hike uphill from campus, but he felt he'd been lucky to secure affordable housing close to school.

CHAPTER NINE

Ithaca College

The fall of 1946 was a special time in the country. More than a year had passed since the victory over Japan and Germany, and a new sense of energy and excitement coursed through the nation. America turned her eyes inward and began a period of building and expansion previously unknown in history. A confidence borne of her new world standing drove the impetus and fueled the growth. College campuses reflected the expansion, and enrollment exploded due largely to free tuition provided by the GI Bill.

The incoming freshman class was as unique as any in the history of Ithaca College. Like Arnald, many were in their twenties, some busy with raising a family while carrying a full class schedule. Adding to the ranks of the students fresh out of high school were former GIs who swelled the population to record levels. The administration was forced to hold classes in makeshift locations around Ithaca, including the second floor of Home Dairy and vacant rooms over Woolworth's five-and-dime store.

Most of the older students were focused on studies and schoolwork but none more than Arnald. His desire not to disappoint Professor Stanley drove him to study and practice his instrument. Auditions for the various performing groups were held, and Arnald was up against a rich pool of talented students for the available positions. The faculty was filled with professional musicians, including the band director, Walter Beeler. He, Craig McHenry, and others had played in the Patrick Conway Band[23] and in the Army Air Corps Band at Stuart Field near West Point, New York. The director expected the same level of professionalism from his students, and the auditions were a particular challenge.

Emerging from his audition, Arnald learned that he'd not only passed, but had been selected as first-chair flute for both the band and orchestra. Now, Arnald remembers, "The pressure was really on." The first student recital was the following month in October, and he was selected as soloist for the Concertino for Flute by Cécile Chaminade. Solo performers were required to memorize their parts, and Arnald stayed in the practice rooms till midnight some nights working on his solo.

The return to school and a more sedentary lifestyle after a summer of work in the cannery had Arnald looking for an outlet to satisfy his desire to stay in shape. The Ithaca College football team had reformed after a three-year hiatus (because of the war), and he decided to try out for the team. When word filtered back to the music department about his application to play, he was summoned to a meeting with the dean. Dr. Victor Rebmann informed the hopeful athlete that music students were *not* allowed to play sports at the college. A few days later, during a visit home to Cortland, Arnald ran into an old friend, Phyllis Nagle, who was serving as supervisor of parks. The Gowanda, New York, native told Arnald about the Western New York Semi-Professional Football League and their need for players, especially in her hometown.

Arnald tried out for the Gowanda Tigers and was added to the squad, resuming his old position of left tackle. He was given the plays each weekend for the following week's game. He then returned to Ithaca during the week for school and worked out on his own throughout the week. On Fridays, he'd make the four-hour drive to the small town a few miles south of Buffalo and practice with the rest of the team. After Saturday's game, the team ended up at Skufca's Bar (their sponsor) in Gowanda for the celebration (they won most of their games). Sunday,

---

[23] Patrick Conway, along with John Philip Sousa and others, is a major contributor to the rise in popularity of bands in the late nineteenth and early twentieth centuries.

it was back in the car for the drive back to Ithaca. Another benefit of the chance meeting with Phyllis was their dating for about a year until she took a job out of the area as an English teacher.

With the football, schoolwork, band, and orchestra rehearsals and concerts, Arnald still found time for social activities. He pledged and was invited to join the Delta Chapter of Phi Mu Alpha, a fraternity of music students. By his junior year, he was elected its president, a position normally reserved for a member of the senior class.

In spite of his not having been in a classroom for more than three years and by virtue of his hard work, by the end of the first semester, Arnald's grade point average was the highest in his freshman class. He was not only elected to Adelphi, the freshman honor society, but he was chosen its president.

At the beginning of the second semester, Arnald moved into the Phi Mu Alpha fraternity house at 118 DeWitt Place. Although a few miles farther from the Ithaca College campus, the free housing provided some financial relief. His new roommate was Jack Reichard who was also a former infantryman during the war. The two were able to share their common struggles due to similar combat experiences; the healing and support each provided the other was a theme repeated often throughout the student body at Ithaca College. The faculty was equally as supportive, and Arnald thrived in the environment by immersing himself in his work. Many of his friends were former servicemen who were able to help each other through the tough transition to college and civilian life. Their shared experiences during the war provided a bond and lent understanding to the struggles they all had. Among the many who would become lifelong friends were Hank Carr, Bill Bush, Caesar Struglia, Joe Canale, Joe Chalker, Ben Hoke, Chris Izzo, and Hank Orlowski.

Musical Growth

By his sophomore year, Arnald made the decision to become a conductor. His music classes and band and orchestra practice and concerts provided him with much knowledge and a good basis for learning, but he felt he needed more practical experience. He interviewed for the vacant choir director's job at the Memorial Baptist Church in his hometown of Cortland and landed the position despite his rather thin résumé. During the interview, Arnald was asked if he had experience as a choir director, and he answered in the affirmative. "Well, I took a vocal class, after all," he reasons.

Typically, he jumped into the job with the enthusiasm of youth. In the first year, he decided to perform Handel's *Messiah* with the group. The piece requires a large choir and is quite an undertaking for a small community church, so Arnald found a few students from Ithaca College and pressed his two brothers into service to fill out the choir.

That same year Arnald assumed directorship of the Cortland Drum and Bugle Corps. The group was sponsored by the local Moose Club, and they had only been able to field about eighteen players. Through his leadership and enthusiasm, he was able to build the band to sixty musicians by the end of the first year.

Patrick Conway had begun his legendary music career in neighboring Homer, New York, playing in the local band and becoming its director within a few years. After his death in 1929, many of the players drifted away, and the group finally disbanded. During his sophomore year of college, Arnald walked into the mayor's office and inquired about the instruments and library of the old band. They still belonged to the town and were stored in the basement of city hall. With the mayor's blessing, Arnald reformed the band. He recruited local musicians and, once again, turned to his two brothers for help. In an interesting reversal of roles, he assigned Prof. Burton Stanley to play first-chair clarinet.

Spiegel Wilcox played trombone in the band. Spiegel was a professional Dixieland and big-band musician who had played with Tommy Dorsey and also with Paul Whiteman and Gene Goldket in the first RCA recording band. He had an eighteen-piece dance band that Arnald joined playing tenor sax at weekend gigs around the southern tier and Finger Lakes region. The depth and breadth of Arnald's knowledge grew in the relentless pursuit of his passion. He conducted the three groups and continued with Spiegel's dance band on weekends for the next three years while attending college full-time.

The Force of Destiny

The downside to the impressive schedule was that it left no time for football; Arnald played only one season with Gowanda in the Western New York Semi-Professional Football League, but he was fulfilled. His gratitude for Burton Stanley's persistence and remarkable act of kindness in the summer of 1946 continued to motivate the formerly confused GI and boss of the cooker gang.

In April 1948, toward the end of his sophomore year, the Ithaca College Symphony Orchestra held a concert at Arnald's alma mater, Cortland High School. Under the baton of its assistant conductor, Craig McHenry, Arnald performed the Quantz, Concertino for Flute. Burton Stanley was in attendance, and the standing ovation and thunderous applause Arnald received from the assembled patrons served as a large measure of gratitude he had for his former bandleader.

One break in the routine took place in Arnald's junior year of college. The high school director in Hornell, New York, called the Ithaca College band director, Walter Beeler, and asked if he had an outstanding senior student who could run his program in Hornell for a semester because he was to have surgery. Beeler instead chose Arnald, and the second semester of his junior year was spent in Hornell running the band program. He also carried a full college load for the semester by visiting all his instructors at Ithaca College on Friday to get the assignments for the following week. He turned in the finished work each week as he picked up the new. Arnald also continued to commute on weekends to play with the Spiegel Wilcox dance band.

Arnald's excellence in academics continued, and in his senior year he was elected to Oracle, the senior honor society. He graduated in June 1950 with a bachelor of science in Music, *cum laude*, and Ma and Pa rewarded his impressive efforts with a 1950 Pontiac. The new car was a welcome replacement for the 1940 Hudson Terreplane that Arnald and brother Min had purchased following the war. He enrolled in the graduate music program at Ithaca College and beginning in the fall of 1950. Now living in Cortland, he began his commute back and forth while maintaining his schedule with the four music groups.

The fledgling graduate program required Arnald to attend a class with sophomores due to the lack of grad school classes. Leaving class one day early in the fall semester, he was asked by a beautiful nineteen-year-old classmate for a ride up the hill to her dorm. It wasn't long before he and the bright, artistic pianist/singer, Joan Noël Graham of East Aurora, New York, began to date.

SECTION II
The Air Force

Joan and Arnald's Wedding
with Joan's sister Barbara and Min

CHAPTER TEN

Air Force Bandsman

In the spring of 1951, Arnald's parents began to think about retirement. They had been running the grocery store in the east end of Cortland, New York, for more than twenty-seven years, and Pa was now sixty-one years old. Although it's not clear where the idea came from, Ferdinand and Filomena decided to move to California. They asked Arnald to take time off from graduate school and run the store while they drove west to plan their future. Arnald dutifully assumed the operation of the store while maintaining his schedule with the drum and bugle corps, church choir, Homer Band, and the dance band on weekends.

The trip to California was cut short, and with little explanation, a plan was made to visit Florida. "They hated California," Arnald remembers. "They never really elaborated." Apparently, Florida suited them better. They returned to Cortland in April 1951 and began to make plans for their long-anticipated retirement.

By now, the United States' nine-month involvement in Korea and her demand for increased troop levels forced a decision. Having no desire to be recalled into the infantry, Arnald heard from his college bandleader Walter Beeler that there was also a need to expand the number of air force bands. The newest branch of the military had been formed about two and a half years prior, and leading an air force band seemed an exciting, and safer, alternative to combat.

Arnald had been pondering career choices throughout his college years. He thought about conducting Broadway musicals, a symphony orchestra, or a military band. "Even now, the term *band director* refers primarily to a school teacher; I wanted more than that," Arnald explains. The rather simplistic expression he remembers is: band directors have band practice, conductors have rehearsals. Arnald wanted to be a conductor.

Arnald made arrangements to take the air force bandleaders' exam in Washington, DC, and Burton Stanley, his old high school bandleader and mentor, assembled a band consisting of his Cortland High School students and adult musicians from the community to allow Arnald to practice the required selections that he was to conduct as part of the exam. Professor Stanley had an assistant, who was a classmate of Arnald's at Ithaca, named Frank Lockwood who also inquired about the exam. Frank decided to take it as well, and Arnald and he drove to Washington, DC, together in Lockwood's VW Beetle.

The exam was held at Bolling Air Force Base in May. Both Arnald and Frank passed the test, but Arnald was informed he had passed with the highest score ever achieved. As such, he was invited to sit in on the adjudication of some of the other applicants. "I did and learned a very valuable lesson," Arnald remembers. One high school director mounted the podium and was to conduct Victor Herbert's Favorites, a piece the band had performed many times. The inexperienced conductor launched into a ten-minute lecture about every nuance of the music to the group of professional musicians. As he finished, finally ready to begin the piece, the group, feigning confusion, began to shuffle their sheet music, asking, "What? What are we playing?" Arnald took the lesson to heart. "When you're working with professionals, just state the name of the selection and give the downbeat. They will follow your gestures, facial expressions, etc. In this case, less is more."

Arnald returned briefly to Cortland to settle a few personal affairs, then it was back to Washington, DC, where he enlisted in the US Air Force on May 23, 1951. The other seven enlistees who'd also passed the bandleader's exam were promoted to E-5, staff sergeant; Arnald, due to his having achieved the highest score in history, was promoted to E-6, technical sergeant. As he first walked the halls of the band building with his new stripes, he was approached by M.Sgt. Ed Grace, the band's first sergeant at the time. Grace insisted that Arnald had

The Force of Destiny

applied the wrong stripes and escorted him into the office of the commanding officer of the band. Col. George Howard mollified M.Sgt. Grace by explaining the reason for Arnald's higher rank.

Arnald stayed in the transit airman's quarters at Bolling Air Force Base in DC for a couple of weeks, and in early June 1951, he drove to East Aurora, New York, to marry Joan Graham. They had continued dating from the day he drove her up the hill to her dorm at Ithaca College more than a year and a half earlier. In Joan he'd developed a kinship that had blossomed into a deep and abiding love. Although she'd been born and raised in a small town in western New York, she had a sense of adventure and was excited about Arnald's career choice, which would certainly involve a great deal of travel.

The wedding was held at the Orchard Park Country Club, just south of Buffalo, New York, and a few miles from Joan's hometown of East Aurora. Arnald's family from Cortland and a large contingent of relatives from Brooklyn made the trip to western New York. Joan's mother, Mercedes, was not happy about her daughter marrying a musician, and the presence of the boisterous Italians from the city didn't enhance her feelings about the air force tech sergeant. Mercedes was largely a product of her upbringing and of the times. The acceptance of these first-generation sons and daughters of immigrants was slow in coming, and professional musicians were not held in particularly high regard. With few exceptions, musicians were still thought of as itinerant dreamers unwilling to engage in "real" work. The irony about her feelings toward Arnald was that she was an accomplished vocalist and piano teacher.

After the ceremony, Sgt. and Mrs. Arnald Gabriel drove to New York City where they honeymooned for a few days at the Dixie Hotel. Arnald was only able to obtain a week's leave so they reluctantly left the city and drove to Washington, DC, to begin his new career. Arnald had arranged to stay at the apartment of a couple of Air Force Band members, Oscar Ghebelian and Carl "Costy" Costenbader. The band embarked on a tour to Europe that summer, and the two new acquaintances generously offered their vacant apartment on Orange Street in southeast Washington to the newlyweds. Even when they returned from the tour, the two men graciously allowed the couple to stay in the apartment while Arnald waited for his first assignment. "I frankly don't know where they stayed. Probably with their girlfriends."

The summer of 1951 found Arnald and the seven other newly minted air force bandleaders with little to do. Because the band was on tour for the summer and their first assignments wouldn't come until the end of August, they were tasked with what can only be described as busywork. The musicians were taken each morning on a ferry from Bolling Air Force Base across the Potomac River to the Pentagon where they poured over reams of data relating to the bandleaders' exam they'd all taken weeks earlier. In the days well before computers, it made for tedious and, ultimately, pointless work. The statistics were forced into an arcane formula that yielded an incomprehensible answer: the coefficient of 9.5, to which the head statistician, upon being presented the result, nodded sagely and said, "Very significant." It was now August, and their new assignments could not come soon enough.

Arnald and the other new bandleaders received their promotions to warrant officer and were given a list of bases to choose from to which they would be posted for their first assignments. Arnald requested Sampson Air Force Base in the Finger Lakes region of upstate New York; it was close to home and Ithaca College where both Joan and he planned to continue with school. He was granted his choice, and they drove to Sampson in September 1951 to begin his career as an Air Force Band Officer.

CHAPTER ELEVEN

Sampson Air Force Base

The move to assume his new position as conductor of the 545th Air Force Band Squadron was made easier due to its proximity to Cortland. Warrant Officer Junior Grade (WOJG) and Mrs. Arnald D. Gabriel moved in with Ma and Pa for a few days in order to find a place to live. Arnald made the fifty-mile commute to Sampson with Guy Passeri, a local barber, and Joan began her semester at Ithaca College. They purchased a forty-foot mobile home with money borrowed from Arnald's brother Min, who was working as an accountant for Ames Chevrolet in Cortland, and moved to Varna, New York, a suburb of Ithaca. It shortened the Sampson commute to about thirty miles and allowed Joan to continue with her studies.

Sampson had begun as a naval training facility during World War II and only six months prior had been converted to an air force induction center. It was used to process and train all new air force recruits east of the Mississippi River, with Lackland Air Force Base in Texas training those to the west. It was a time of growth for the newly designated air force base, as the personnel permanently stationed there approached fifty thousand. It's estimated that nearly three hundred thousand recruits were processed through and trained at Sampson, which allowed Arnald time to identify musicians who were college graduates or had played with major dance bands or symphonies and recruit them into his band. He managed to hire band members from the newly formed Eastman Wind Ensemble,[24] Northwest University, Ithaca College, and other notable schools. He also convinced his younger brother Rick to join the band. Although a superb trumpet player, he had dropped out of high school and was appreciative of the direction his older brother provided.

When Arnald arrived in the fall of 1951, there were two forty-five-piece bands at the sprawling facility, the 544th and his 545th. Within a few months, the director of the 544th, Vernon Proctor, was reassigned, and Arnald took over as commander and conductor of both units. He named the combined group the Empire Band of the Air Force, prompting Col. George S. Howard, the commander of the band in Washington, DC, to wonder, "What the hell kind of an empire are you building up there?" Warrant Officer Junior Grade Gabriel explained that the name was simply a nod to New York as the Empire State. The two Sampson bands played separately for the most part but were combined for large parades and concerts. They performed not only on base, but at many of the colleges, universities, and civic functions in the Finger Lakes region, gaining a strong following among the local residents and providing additional challenges for the fine musicians.

In addition to his many duties in the air force, Arnald also taught the Ovid Drum and Bugle Corps. Ovid is a small town very near Sampson, and after about a year of living at the Tag and Wagon Trailer Park in Varna, Joan and he moved the trailer there. His relationship with the drum and bugle corps allowed their instant acceptance. "We knew practically everyone in the village." They moved to a vacant lot next to a wealthy member of the drum and bugle corps, where a septic tank and electrical hookups were installed. The move to Ovid and Joan's pregnancy ended her studies at Ithaca College; sadly, Joan miscarried shortly after the move.

---

24 Frederick Fennell formed the group in Rochester, New York, and it was widely known as one of the premier bands at the university level. He named it a wind ensemble because the Eastman School of Music didn't want a "band." Other permutations of the term are wind orchestra, wind symphony, etc., but it only serves to disguise what they are: bands. "There is nothing wrong with the noble term *band*," Arnald insists.

The Force of Destiny

As the burgeoning training facility at Sampson grew, so did the different musical units of the 545th Empire Band. The Skytones, led by Don Trube, was a dance band similar in structure to the big bands of the era à la Tommy and Jimmy Dorsey, Glenn Miller, Charlie Spivak, Woody Herman, and Benny Goodman. Arnald also formed an eighty-voice male choir from members of the band and others from around the base. The chorus was conducted by Chuck Valenza, a French horn player in the band. The evolution of the Empire Band continued from its largely ceremonial function as a typical military brass band to concert band and choir whose repertoire could be expanded to include a string section on temporary tour of duty (TDY) from Colonel Howard's USAF Symphony Orchestra in Washington, DC.

The Skytones were busy taping a series of fifteen-minute shows to be broadcast over the Mutual Radio Network. Directed by Airman Stuart Ostrow, the fourteen-week run titled *From Out of the Blue* featured popular music of the day and vocalists from the vast pool of talent present at Sampson. After Stu Ostrow left the US Air Force, he went on to become a top Broadway theatrical producer and director, collecting four Tony Awards over his career. The musical arrangements for *From Out of the Blue* were accomplished by three members of the band: Wayne Andre, Nick DeAngelo, and Dick Polumbi. After their enlistments, each achieved tremendous success in different areas of music. Wayne Andre joined Jack Franklin and Barney Mallon to form the Kai Winding Septet, a popular group in the sixties and seventies. Dick Polumbi was an arranger and conductor for Neil Sedaka, and Nick DeAngelo has been the chairman of the Music Department at Hobart and William Smith College in Geneva, New York, for nearly fifty years.

The level of talent possessed by the musicians with whom Arnald had the privilege to work is evident in the success each achieved after leaving the air force. The following, although not a complete list, are a few examples of the outstanding talent and where they went after Sampson Air Force Base: Lowell Shaw and Richard Myers, the Buffalo Philharmonic; Alan Abel, the Philadelphia Orchestra; Keith Kummer, the Baltimore Symphony; Robert Klump and Joe Kleeman, the St. Louis Symphony; Dan Dowdakin, the Atlanta Symphony; Jerry Neff, the Oakland Symphony; Joe Kloess, arranger and conductor for

Dionne Warwick; Don George, director of bands for the University of Wisconsin-Eau Claire; Sid Woloshin, jingle writer (most notable for McDonald's "You deserve a break today"); and Ricardo Gabriel, the US Air Force Band, Washington, DC.

Each of these fine musicians, Arnald stresses, came to Sampson as professionals. "I didn't train them," he says. For example, Greg Phillips had played with Tommy Dorsey, and Wayne Andre had played with Woody Herman. As Arnald saw it, his daunting task was to challenge them. As a new college graduate in his first job, his desire was nothing less than building the best band he was able to, and it was a unique opportunity to work with some of the world's most accomplished musicians.

World-class talent at Sampson wasn't limited to the performing musicians. Airman Serge de Gastyne composed a symphony commemorating the fiftieth anniversary of powered flight titled *Conquest of the Air*. Originally written as a full symphony, the rearranged for concert band piece featured female voices supplementing the choir with the addition of women from Rochester, New York, and New York City choral groups. The performances were met with packed houses and rave reviews in the local press.

At Sampson the growing reputation of the fine musicianship on base wasn't the only source of excitement. In the fall of 1952, Joan announced that she was pregnant again. There was renewed hope for this pregnancy because she was not commuting to school in Ithaca and because of her close proximity, in Ovid, to the base hospital. Around the same time, Arnald's brother Min met young Agnes Hogan and proudly predicted to his buddies, "I'm gonna marry that girl some day!" after their first encounter. Agnes's father owned a farm around the corner from Ma and Pa's place in Cortland on Pomeroy Street. Following several months of dating, and despite the warnings from Aggie's uncle to "be careful of those Italian boys," they set their wedding date for June 7, 1953, very close to Joan's due date.

Following the success of *Conquest of the Air*, the band embarked on a series of weekly radio broadcasts over the 503 stations of the Mutual Radio Network. *The Big Serenade* were live performances broadcast from Arnold Hall on Sampson in front of two thousand cheering recruits.

The live radio format required exactly twenty-nine minutes and thirty seconds of narrations and music from beginning to end. An airman sat in front of Arnald during the concert with a clock and a written script and monitored the delicate timing. The last few minutes of the show, due to a varied tempo, applause, and announcements, became an adventure in time management that Arnald artfully juggled each week. One of the broadcasts was heard by jazz clarinetist and bandleader Woody Herman. He was particularly interested in a very talented trumpet player in the Sampson Band named Gerry Esposito and called about his joining Woody's Third Herd Band at the end of Gerry's enlistment. Sadly, Gerry Esposito was killed in an auto accident several months later.

In addition to his duties with the two bands on base, the Skytones (the choral group), the drum and bugle corps, and the dance band, Arnald continued his studies at Ithaca College, and on June 4, 1953, he received his master of science degree and a mention in that year's *Who's Who in American Colleges*. In his spare time, he renewed the interest in flying he had ever since his time with the Army Air Corps. Arnald earned his Private Pilot's Certificate, taking lessons in a Piper J-3 Cub at the local airport. It was the same kind of airplane he'd flown for the army as part of the CTD in Buffalo ten years prior.

As Min and Agnes's June 7 wedding date approached, arrangements were made for the big day. Shortly after Arnald and Joan moved to Sampson, Ma and Pa had sold the store in Cortland, retired, and moved to North Miami Beach, Florida. For reasons now lost to memory, Pa had a falling out with Min and instead of attending the wedding said simply that he needed to stay in Miami to "water his flowers." Ma boarded a bus for the twenty-six-hour ride to Min's house in Binghamton, New York, and arrived a few days early.

Arnald attended the wedding with Sav Amatulli and Gerry Esposito, two good friends and band members, because Joan was late in her pregnancy, uncomfortable on the warm June day, and thus opted to stay home. Arnald's wedding gift to the newlyweds was the use of his new Cadillac convertible for their honeymoon to Canada. Arnald drove Min's beat-up Chevy and had the faulty transmission repaired by the time they returned.

On the morning of June 9, Joan's increasing discomfort gave way to labor pains, and Arnald drove her to the base hospital. They were met there by Sav Amatulli. Because these were the days when fathers were relegated to the waiting room, Arnald then drove back to Binghamton to pick up Ma who had remained in town for a few days after Min and Aggie's wedding. At 10:40 that night, my mother gave birth to me. Three days later, Arnald drove his new family home to the trailer in Ovid.

Throughout the balance of 1953, the band continued its busy schedule, supplemented with many gigs at local and regional events as varied as the National Soaring Contest in Elmira, New York, and the Pennsylvania State Laurel Festival in Wellsboro, Pennsylvania. In October the Pakistani ambassador visited Cortland, and the city declared the day Pakistan-Cortland Day. Warrant Officer Gabriel returned to his hometown with the Sampson Band to participate in the parade, and he was fortunate to have the opportunity to meet Ambassador Syed Amjad Ali. The wide range of music, from Broadway-style shows to jazz and orchestral arrangements, performed in a variety of venues around the Finger Lakes region and into Pennsylvania, was Arnald's attempt to continue to raise the bar for his talented musicians.

As the band's schedule stretched through 1954 with concerts played throughout central New York, and while they continued to support the marching mission on base, Arnald endeavored to involve young people. Working in conjunction with the New York State School Music Association, he adjudicated the spring competitions for ensembles, bands, and solos. He was also selected as guest conductor for the All New York State Sectional High School Band in 1954 and 1955, beginning a lifelong effort to encourage music education and inspire the next generation of musicians. Arnald says, "Our legacy can be measured by how we pass along our love and knowledge of music. These children are, after all, our future."

In addition to a full slate of band concerts, Arnald organized and mounted several stage shows at Sampson and drew from the base personnel, as well as local civilian talent, to fill the casts. Normally, Joan participated in these productions, displaying her talented singing voice and acting abilities, but her busy home life with a newborn became busier with the announcement of another pregnancy. She gave birth to my brother Steven Edward on September 7, 1954.

All Arnald's hard work, innovation, and leadership skills did not go unnoticed. On January 8, 1955, he was promoted to first lieutenant. Col. Russell Brock, Sampson Air Base Group Commander, pinned the silver bars on that day, making Arnald the first bandsman in US Air Force history to receive a direct commission[25] to the officer corps. His was the first direct commission of ten that would be awarded to US Air Force bandsmen that week. The normal progression would have been to second lieutenant, but because of his age, he leapfrogged to first lieutenant.

As Arnald continued his schedule with the Sampson Band, he also maintained his position as music director and drum major for three drum and bugle corps in the area: the Ovid Drum and Bugle Corps, the corps from Newark, New York, and the Syracuse Brigadiers. In September 1955 Arnald led the Brigadiers to a second-place ranking in the nation at the American Legion National Convention in Miami, Florida. They were bested by the top seed in the competition, the Hawthorne Caballeros, and it was generally agreed by those who attended that the Brigadiers should have placed at number one.

Along with Arnald's professional success, the Gabriel household continued to grow as Joan completed her third pregnancy in three years with the birth of my brother Robert Douglas on September 27, 1955. They were now straining the resources of the small trailer and had been searching for a larger place to live. They abruptly put those plans on hold when the young family received news of a change with which all military personnel are familiar.

---

[25] A direct commission allows the elevation of an enlisted man to officer without the normal prerequisite of a service academy degree, ROTC, or officer candidate school (OCS).

CHAPTER TWELVE

Langley Air Force Base

After serving more than five years with distinction at Sampson Air Force Base, the personnel office at the Pentagon issued new orders for Lieutenant Gabriel. Arnald's reassignment orders came in the late fall of 1955, and he packed up his young family and transferred to Langley Air Force Base, Virginia.

Langley is one of the oldest continuously active military bases in the country. It was established as a joint-use facility for research and development of aircraft by the National Advisory Council for Aeronautics, NACA (a forerunner of NASA), and the army and navy just a dozen years after the Wright brothers' flight at Kitty Hawk. The location near Hampton, Virginia, was chosen because of its relatively flat terrain and the need to be near water for overwater flight testing. The facility led an early research effort into hydrogen-filled dirigibles, and to this day, that section of the base is still referred to as the Lighter-Than-Air (LTA) area. The band at Langley was quartered in a converted World War II service club in the LTA.

After the war, the Tactical Air Command (TAC) was formed to train and deploy airmen around the world in rapid fashion, and Langley was selected as their headquarters. TAC's mission was defined largely through the development of jet transport aircraft, and as such, Langley Field became Langley Air Force Base in January 1948. The base personified the newest and most modern branch of the military, and the tidewater region of Virginia was a welcome and exciting change for the Gabriel family.

Arnald moved the family to temporary base housing as Joan and he looked for a place to live. With a growing family, they decided to move off base and buy their first house. They bought a home at 221 Avon Road, Hampton, Virginia, for $11,500 (the extra $500 was for a carport) in a new subdivision that was under construction and a short drive to the base. In December 1955 Arnald reported for duty to Col. Eugene "Ben" LeBailly for his new assignment as commander and conductor of the 564th Air Force Band at Langley Air Force Base.

General LeBailly was the director of public information for the Tactical Air Command and came to Langley with a distinguished record as a pilot with the Eighth Air Force during World War II. He was a no-nonsense career military man with a take-no-prisoners attitude and would prove to be a very influential force in shaping Arnald's career and life.

After having just settled in the new house on Avon Road and after a few short months at Langley, Lieutenant Gabriel came to a decision. With the Korean War over and the threat of combat long past, Arnald decided to resign his commission and return to civilian life. Ma and Pa had settled in North Miami Beach, and in an effort to be closer to them, he decided to look for a job teaching high school music in the Miami area. Colonel LeBailly did not take the news well. After entering his office and relaying the decision to his commanding officer, the colonel kept Arnald at attention as he demanded, "Why?"

Arnald expressed doubt as to his ability to compete with pilots, technicians, missile men, and other high-profile air force officers for promotions and advancement in the upcoming years. "Damnit, Gabe, we need the best truck drivers, cooks, administrative men, doctors, and, yes, bandleaders in the Air Force!" Colonel LeBailly began. He thought it foolish to squander his talents by leaving the air force, and he expressed his complete confidence in Arnald's ability to excel in his future career in the air force. He then dismissed him to ponder his future. Arnald saluted smartly, spun on his heel, and left the office. Buoyed by the colonel's persuasive talk and anxious to move forward, Arnald decided to stay in the air force. Colonel LeBailly's confidence and admiration for the young lieutenant is reflected in the comments he wrote on Arnald's Application for Indefinite Active Duty Status

The Force of Destiny

form: "I feel that every opportunity should be taken to encourage officers of this caliber to remain in the Air Force. Lt. Gabriel is one of the best qualified and most mature young officers I have known in the Air Force."

Arnald's moment of doubt was quickly cast aside as he dove headlong into his new job with renewed vigor. His sense of community has always been a motivating force, and the family's move to the Tidewater area of Virginia engendered new feelings of untapped opportunity. He began, naturally, with a drum and bugle corps. He was familiar with the Braxton-Perkins American Legion Post 25 Drum and Bugle Corps due to his involvement with the three corps he led in upstate New York, and the group was familiar with him as well. He applied for and became musical director and drum major of the Virginia Gentlemen and within a year won the Virginia State Drum and Bugle Corps Championship. The following year the resurgent group placed eleventh in the country in the National American Legion Convention in Atlantic City, New Jersey.

Arnald also renewed his efforts at involving children by beginning a series of concerts sponsored by the Hampton Roads Civic League via invites to all the grammar school kids surrounding Langley. These were concerts geared specifically to the often fidgety grade-schoolers and included a game to identify musical instruments, an opportunity for several to conduct the band, and a processional around the concert hall to the strains of a stirring march.

In the local newspaper, Arnald read about a Catholic nuns' choir that performed concerts in the Newport News area and visited them to ask if they needed a conductor. "I guess I wasn't shy," he admits. In addition to conducting their concerts, he combined them with the men's chorus of the Langley Band to form a mixed choir. The addition naturally expanded the repertoire of the group and provided a unique sound that was met with rave reviews and packed houses. Colonel LeBailly attended one of these concerts when they played Respighi's *Pines of the Appian Way*, one of his favorite pieces of music.

As time went on, Arnald and Colonel LeBailly's professional relationship evolved into a close, personal friendship. As veterans of the war, they traded war stories and discovered that while serving

Michael A. Gabriel

in England for the Eighth Air Force, Ben LeBailly had flown air cover for Arnald and the Twenty-Ninth Infantry many times: Normandy, Saint-Lô, Holland, and Germany were just a few of the locations he'd provided the fortunate protection Arnald and his infantry buddies needed. They also spent hours fishing on the Chesapeake Bay, joined sometimes by Joan and Ben's son, Steve, who was fifteen at the time. They were building a solid friendship that would continue beyond what either suspected.

The year 1957 was the 350th anniversary of the nearby Jamestown Settlement, the first permanent English settlement on the continent. That summer, the Langley Band played at the settlement three times a week, the highlight being a visit by Queen Elizabeth II. She toured the grounds to the strains of a few British and American marches following both national anthems. The band continued with their regular base concerts and ceremonies and also played at several of the local universities such as Hampton University, Old Dominion University, and William and Mary.

Arnald's desire to perform music extended beyond conducting the bands, choirs, and drum and bugle corps. He joined the Peninsula Symphony and the Norfolk Symphony (now called the Virginia Symphony), playing first-chair flute for both. He also formed an eight-piece dance band with several members of the Langley Band, augmented with vocals from Connie Poncheri, a wife of one of the band members. The group consisted of Art Poncheri and "Kosy" Koyle on trombone, Don Miller on trumpet, George Millwater on drums, Gene Gartrell on piano, Jim Danielsen on upright bass, and Arnald on baritone saxophone. The talented musicians doubled playing their instruments; Arnald played trombone, and Gartrell played French horn so they had five brass. On Latin tunes, Arnald played flute, and Danielsen played oboe while all backed up on vocals for various tunes. When Connie became pregnant and decided to quit the band, she was replaced by Joan, billed as the Lovely Joanne. They became the most popular dance band in the Tidewater area and played almost every Friday and Saturday night at the NCO and Officers' Clubs at Langley, Fort Eustis, Fort Monroe, Norfolk Navy Base, and an occasional fraternity

The Force of Destiny

house. The frat houses paid overtime, and the group sometimes played until two or three in the morning.

In the spring of 1958, after two short but very busy years at Langley Air Force Base, Arnald was offered a choice of assignments: Hawaii or Germany. The obvious appeal of the tropical island territory in the Pacific (it would not become a state until the following year) made it his first choice. Arnald approached his friend and mentor Ben, and the colonel convinced Arnald that he'd go rock-happy on the island and that Germany was the best career option. Because both Japan and Alaska had their own bands, engagements for the Pacific Air Force Band (PACAFB) would have been limited to the Hawaiian Islands. The US Air Forces in Europe (USAFE) was headquartered in Wiesbaden, Germany, and would provide travel across Europe and beyond and provided a better chance to broaden his professional career and his personal musical growth.

Before leaving for Germany in April 1958, Arnald was awarded the Air Force Commendation Medal. The Secretary of the Air Force had authorized issuance of the honor less than a month prior, and Arnald was one of the first in the Air Force to receive it. The Air Force Commendation Medal is awarded to "members of the Armed Forces ... (who) have distinguished themselves by meritorious achievement and service." The citation recognized his work over the five or so years since he'd enlisted and noted his having presented a staggering 465 band performances in the past year alone. It also noted his work with the community groups in the Tidewater area by recognizing that it reflected credit on not only himself, but the Air Force as well. The award ceremony was held at the office of Gen. Otto P. Weylan, commander of the Tactical Air Command, with Colonel Lebailly in attendance and, of course, Arnald and his young family. As the citation was being read, the pomp was interrupted by a five-year-old at play. Apparently bored with the official presentation, I had wandered to the general's desk and began twirling the propellers on several military model airplanes, disrupting the proceedings. As an uncomfortable silence descended over the room, the general broke the ice by laughing at the wayward boy; the relief from my parents was palpable.

Later that month, Arnald and Joan sold the house on Avon Drive for $12,500 (a thousand more than they paid for it), sold their station wagon, and reluctantly severed their musical ties to the Tidewater, Virginia, area. Arnald packed up his growing family, and a mere twelve years after his combat experiences there, he returned to Germany.

Remembering Harry
The Netherlands American Cemetery
Margraten, Netherlands

CHAPTER THIRTEEN

Wiesbaden Air Force Base

On May 1, 1958, Arnald assumed command of the 686th United States Air Forces in Europe (USAFE) Band stationed at Wiesbaden Air Force Base, Germany. The immediate concern was housing. Base quarters weren't available when the family arrived, so the only option was housing on the economy, meaning renting a place in the town of Wiesbaden. The accommodations "weren't very desirable," Arnald remembers, but only four weeks later they moved on base to Heerstrasse 7, Apartment D. It was a three-bedroom unit on the third floor with a balcony and government-issued furniture. Bunk beds provided an efficient accommodation for the boys. The issue of transportation was solved when Arnald bought two cars—a Borgward, a German-built station wagon, and a VW bug for Joan.

Arnald wasted no time after his assumption of command as he stepped into a very full schedule of already booked concerts. When he reported to his commanding officer at Wiesbaden, Gen. Frederic H. Smith Jr., he was told that his task was to improve relations with the German populous locally and with the different cultures across the continent. The irony was not lost on him. "Just over a decade ago we were trying to kill each other!" Arnald remembers thinking. The mission was the air force's effort to parallel a civilian program championed by President Eisenhower called People to People. It was, quite simply, a means to allow contact between different cultures on a personal, nongovernmental level. Friendship Week kicked off the following week and included a full slate of events to promote the now close ties the two nations enjoyed. The highlight of the week was a benefit jazz concert featuring the Ambassadors Dance Band and smaller Dixielanders, both units of the USAFE Band.

Arnald's work with the USAFE Band began in earnest with their first rehearsal. He chose the music for each program they were to play and raised the bar by challenging them musically. He not only changed what they played, but how they played it. First rehearsals with a new conductor can be stressful for all, but Arnald left little doubt as to what he expected of the group. The undercurrent of excitement grew as he energized and motivated the men with careful and insightful work on intonation and articulation and managed to occasionally break them up with comments like the one he made to the trombone section one day: "Could I have a little less spit and a little more tone?" He used the humor to help establish an easy rapport with the men and built an environment that encouraged their natural desire to play better. Arnald recognized that he was working with professionals, and he treated them as such. On another occasion, in an effort to clarify his point, he said, "Intonation is like shit; it doesn't get any better when you stir it up." The musicians quickly learned that although the new lieutenant had high standards, he was very approachable.

Summertime in Europe also brought back the air show season, and Arnald seized upon an idea that would allow greater exposure for the band. The Skyblazers were an aerial demonstration team (similar in mission to the Thunderbirds in the United States) based at Bitburg Air Force Base, Germany, and traveled around Europe drawing huge crowds. Arnald suggested that the USAFE Band play a concert while the team of four F-100 red, white, and blue Super Sabres flew their routine, and the approval to do so allowed the band to play in front of massive crowds. Just three weeks after Arnald assumed command, they performed their first air show/concert at Torrejon Air Base, Spain, for an Armed Forces Day celebration. The band performed for forty-five minutes in the afternoon and played for a dance at the NCO Club that evening. The following day, they performed for a morning change-of-command ceremony at Zaragoza, Spain, an afternoon concert, and a concert at ten o'clock that night in front of the US ambassador and other high-ranking officers from both the American and Spanish Air Forces. They played a final concert the third day at the principal theater before returning home to Wiesbaden.

Other concerts over the next few years with the Skyblazers would prove to be hugely successful. In Turkey, the air show/concert was on the Straits of the Bosporus and attracted more than a million people. Tens of thousands remained after the air show to listen to the band. In Athens, Greece, so many people crowded into the airfield that a four-lane road was made one-way to accommodate the crush of vehicles. Once again, tens of thousands of people remained to listen the USAFE Band and the Royal Hellenic Band of Greece. Arnald was invited to guest conduct the Greek band and had the privilege of meeting King Philip of Greece who was in attendance.

The USAFE Band's next opportunity to play under the baton of Lieutenant Gabriel was at the summer fair in Haslev, Denmark, whose performance was described later in the *Wiesbaden Post* as "the highlight of the fair." The season of fairs and music festivals was in full swing as the band traveled that first summer to Finland, Norway, France, and a visit, in late August, to the World's Fair in Brussels, Belgium. While at Expo '58 they played at the US pavilion. The pavilion was built largely to compete with the pavilion of the Union of Soviet Socialist Republics (USSR) and was billed as the largest freestanding circular structure in the world. They attracted standing-room-only crowds, and during one such performance, Arnald noticed that the bandsmen's attention was directed at a point behind him; the crowd also seemed to be distracted, and when he turned, he saw a small girl mirroring his movements on the podium. He bounded from the platform, scooped up the five-year-old, and, holding her with his left arm, used her right arm to conduct the rest of the piece. At the conclusion, the now cheering throng leapt to their feet in thunderous ovation as the little girl returned to her seat while rubbing her sore arm. It became clear to the musicians of the USAFE Band that their leader was a bit of a showman as well. The band was so well received that they were invited to return to perform at the closing of the monthlong celebration.

Michael A. Gabriel

Military Band Music

The USAFE Band's growing popularity was a result of their innovative sound. To the European ear, the band music they were hearing was the manifestation of a relatively new concept. Frederic the Great of Prussia established the first military band by decree, and for nearly two centuries, military band music was played largely for the benefit of the marching troops. Throughout that period the music was virtually unchanged until early in the twentieth century when the genre began to evolve. The innovation occurred largely in bands in England and the United States and allowed the groups to expand their repertoire to include orchestral works and popular music. The new symphonic band was built through a framework of standard instrumentation established by the newly formed American Bandmasters Association (ABA) and would soon attract the compositional talents of some of the century's most talented composers. Contemporary works from Paul Hindemith, Darius Milhaud, Dmitri Shostakovich, Aaron Copland, Walter Piston, Vincent Persichetti, Morton Gould, and Leroy Anderson, to name a few, were beginning to be introduced by the USAFE Band to packed houses all across Europe. They further endeared themselves by playing the national anthem and specially arranged regional music of every country they visited. "Music brings people together—the universal language," Arnald says.

Most of the band's travel was by bus, and one long-standing practice that Arnald was determined to stop was drinking on the bus. Although initially an unpopular decision, it was eventually seen as an effort to raise the professionalism of the group and served to feed their growing sense of pride. Cpl. Shannon Jones, a young bandsman of the day, remembers, "We used to arrive at some of the gigs pretty lit, but I can defend my fellow bandsman by saying all of us were young men who were extremely bored on those long, uncomfortable bus trips." As

The Force of Destiny

to the overall effort to transform the band, he says, "Gabe[26] will always be that young officer we all loved! And, yes ... love is not too strong a word to use to describe how much we appreciated Gabe."

Another change in the travel policy came as a result of Arnald's concern for his men. Arriving at a long-forgotten city, the local military attaché directed the band to their accommodations for the evening—a filthy, seemingly abandoned structure whose toilets consisted merely of a hole in the floor. Arnald called his superior officers in Wiesbaden and insisted that he was unable to subject his troops to the squalor. He was promised a per diem for each man that would allow billeting at the local hotel. The men were ecstatic. A more remarkable result was that the change in policy became the *de facto* norm for the balance of Arnald's tenure at Wiesbaden.

The first summer at Wiesbaden Air Force Base was also spent rebuilding the staff and band personnel while maintaining the vigorous tour schedule. Several members were lost to reassignments, and their positions hadn't been filled by the outgoing commander, so Arnald corresponded with the Washington, DC, band about replacements. In July he took a TDY to Washington and hired Robert "Bob" Cray, a flute player; Lawrence Odom, an oboe player, pianist, and arranger; Merle "Gene" Gartrell, a French horn player who would lead the Ambassadors Dance Band of the USAFE; and several others from the Air Force Bandsman School who joined them later.

The most exciting news of the summer of 1958, however, was the arrival of Joan and Arnald's fourth baby and first girl. My sister, Joanne Marie, was born on August 11 in the base hospital and was, remarkably, the first girl born to Gabriel(e) men in five generations.

Just a few days after Joanne was born, the USAFE Band participated in the World Music Festival in Kerkrade, Holland. It is an event held every four years, drawing wind and brass bands from around the world in a competitive event. Although the band didn't compete, they

---

26 In an e-mail sent more than fifty years after serving under Arnald, Shannon's respect for his former commanding officer is apparent: "First I must apologize for calling you 'Gabe' in my e-mails. In 1958 we always addressed you as 'Sir' or 'Lieutenant Gabriel, Sir,' which is proper—but between bandsmen in the barracks we always referred to you as 'Gabe'; it was NOT meant as a slight."

were able to showcase their talents on a truly world stage, and as the only American band at the monthlong festival, they garnered high praise for their performance. At the conclusion of the concert, the four thousand cheering music fans remained on their feet for a ten-minute ovation.

Hearing of the inclusion of the American group, the mayor of the small town of Margraten, just a few kilometers from Kerkrade, invited them to play at ceremonies scheduled at the local military cemetery. Interestingly, the location of the mining town on the southeastern border with Germany held special meaning to Arnald. Prior to his deployment to Germany, he had written to the American Battle Monuments Commission in Washington, DC, to find out what had happened to the two buddies he'd lost in a foxhole near Bourheim, Germany, on January 9, 1945. The commission is responsible for establishing and maintaining cemeteries and monuments overseas and holds a listing of all soldiers who fell in battle. He found that both were interred at the Netherlands American Cemetery[27] in Margraten, Holland. Kerkrade is midway between Margraten, Holland, and Bourheim, Germany. The mayor, with no knowledge of Arnald's past, wanted the USAFE Band to play at the cemetery where Harry Aschoff and Johnny Arrowsmith were interred.

After the summer of 1946 and his return from the war, Arnald had thought little of his experiences in combat. He had immersed himself in his life's work and supplanted the haunting images he'd wrestled with after Victory in Europe Day. He'd taken Lieutenant Butler's advice to heart and considered the visit to Margraten a look back without staring. It also afforded Arnald the opportunity to fulfill a pledge made to his two buddies more than fourteen years earlier. While being transported on the 40-and-8 railway through France and Belgium as army infantrymen, they had vowed that if one of the three was killed, the others would return to his grave after the war. "I have never forgotten the wartime pledge," Arnald told a local reporter. Prior to

---

27 The cemetery was established in November 1944. After the war, the land was donated by a grateful Dutch people in perpetuity. Its monuments were finished only two years after Arnald's visit and is now the meticulously maintained final resting place of 8,301 of US military dead.

the official ceremonies, the only survivor of their machine gun squad was able to lay flowers on each of his friends' graves.

Travel around the Continent and Wiesbaden

In early September, Arnald and the band left to participate in the Festival of Piedigrotta in Naples, Italy. Although the USAFE Band was formed almost fifteen years prior, this was, surprisingly, their first visit to the Italian mainland. To add further distinction to the trip, they were the first foreign band ever invited to the centuries-old religious festival. More than one hundred thousand people attended the weeklong holiday known for its noise and raucous celebration.

The band performed in a rotunda along the Bay of Naples esplanade in a ninety-minute concert. During the concert, Arnald noticed the rapt attention being paid by a five-year-old boy, and as they began Bagley's "National Emblem" march, he set the boy in a chair and helped him conduct the piece. Little Goffrido Covino held a stick with festival streamers tied to the end as a baton, and as Arnald stepped back, the boy continued to lead as the cheering crowd roared their approval. Arnald and the band continued with Mitch Miller's arrangement of the "Colonel Bogey March" and concluded with Sousa's "The Stars and Stripes Forever" and the Italian and US national anthems. Later that evening, the ambassadors played at the Flamingo Club at Allied Forces Southern Europe Headquarters at nearby Bagnoli. Their performance was extended by several hours, as the house band musicians sat in with the group to jam into the night.

It was quickly becoming apparent that travel was a major part of his new job, and after only a few days back in Wiesbaden, Arnald and the band left for the Harvest and Wine Festival in Neuchatel, Switzerland. Arnald was impressed with the organizers' high regard for the bandleaders and music directors of the various performing groups; they were housed in the finest hotels in the medieval city at no charge and feted as VIPs. During the festival, he was approached by a gentleman who was so taken with the band, he wanted to hire them for a private function attended by various dignitaries. He introduced himself as the president of ESSO Oil Company, Europe, and graciously invited Arnald to stay at his private residence for the duration of the festival. Although unable to accommodate his request to play the private function due to scheduling issues, an effort was set in motion that would allow them to do so in the future.

The USAFE Band wrapped up their fall travel with the return to Brussels, Belgium, to the closing ceremonies of the World's Fair and, a week later, to Aalborg in the North Jutland region of Denmark. While there, they performed in the three thousand-seat Aalborg Hall, which was, at the time, the largest performance hall in Denmark, for a televised concert in connection with United Nations Day celebrations.

In the late fall of 1958 Arnald was promoted in rank to captain. Most officers are required to serve a minimum time-in-grade before being considered for promotion to a higher rank. Each is given a yearly Officers Effective Report (OER) based on his or her performance and record for that year. A mere 10 percent of officers in the military are considered for promotion below the zone based on exceptional OERs. Colonel LeBailly's reports and the reports he received for his few months in Wiesbaden allowed Arnald to rise to the higher rank well before his time-in-grade requirement.

Throughout the first six months in Europe and despite the full schedule, Arnald continued to work on his master's thesis. Its theme dealt with the makeup and instrumentation of the concert band, and in November, during a visit to the Selmer Instrument Company in Paris, Arnald interviewed Maurice Selmer. Arnald was there to purchase instruments for the Air Force Band, and the two discussed the changing role of the concert band. Arnald shared his ideas concerning a standardization of its composition and the broadened repertoire that might become available; in 1958, the idea was so new that little was being written for the evolving concept. After Mr. Selmer had Arnald play an E^b contrabass clarinet and listen to a recording of the Selmer Clarinet Sextet that included the instrument, Arnald incorporated two contrabass clarinets in the makeup of his theoretical construct. They also discussed the saxophone section and agreed that care must be taken by the conductor to properly balance just one bass saxophone with the other saxophones in the section. His research

The Force of Destiny

and interviews of other experts in the field would continue over the following year or more.

Arnald's charged responsibility as musical ambassador extended to the Wiesbaden area as well, and he fell back on his proven technique by organizing musicals using German civilians and military personnel from the base. In the spring of 1959, he staged Alan Jay Lerner and Frederick Loewe's musical *Brigadoon*; the pit band was formed from members of the USAFE band and the German Bundeswehr Band in Bohn.[28] He requested the group through the public affairs office and diplomatic channels. The following year, Lt. Col. Dwight Dinsmore, Arnald's immediate superior at Wiesbaden, was invited to sing the lead part of Hajj the Beggar in Robert Wright and George Forrest's musical *Kismet*. The production was held at the German-American Club in Wiesbaden and was directed by Virginia (Ginny) Dinsmore, his wife. Each year brought another production and growing local involvement in Lerner and Loewe's *Paint Your Wagon* and Handel's *Messiah*.

Joan joined the wives' club and staged an annual spring review that featured a variety show format where they performed songs from the thirties, forties, and fifties and included vocal solos by Joe Baker (the USAFE Band's drum major), Joan, and other wives of band members. The shows and other productions were held at the Von Steuben Officers' Club, and even though it was an officers' club, it was open to all ranks and civilian employees of the air force.

The premier concert venue in Wiesbaden is the Kurhaus and is also home to exhibit halls, convention space, and a magnificent opera house. When Arnald started an annual concert in the beautiful band shell at the rear of the Kurhaus with the USAFE Band, they had the distinction of being the first American band to perform at the turn-of-the-century showcase. The outdoor space held capacity crowds anxious to hear the vibrant new sounds of the USAFE Band and its dynamic young conductor.

The first Christmas in Germany was an exciting experience in the young lives of the Gabriel children. We learned German Christmas songs and customs while attending kindergarten in the town of

---

28 Bohn was the capital of West Germany at the time.

Michael A. Gabriel

Wiesbaden and received, to our minds, exotic gifts from Arnald's travels across Europe and from the local marketplaces. We awoke each Christmas in Germany and discovered a dazzling display of strange and wonderful surprises under the Christmas tree: a hand-worked four-foot brass tray from Morocco, white leather ottomans with wooden legs and brass hinges we referred to as camel saddles from Turkey, hand-carved and painted wooden toys from Poland, and one year (although more commonplace yet no less exciting) bicycles for each. Joan displayed her artistic talent by painting a Christmas scene on the large picture window that faced the common area between the apartments and began a tradition that would repeat each year we were in Germany.

In early 1959 the marching band was asked to perform their routine to be filmed for the opening and closing credits to a movie. A crew filmed early childhood scenes on Wiesbaden Air Force Base for *The Phony American*[29] using extras from the military personnel stationed there. I was one of those chosen to participate and received ten deutsche marks as payment for perhaps ten seconds of exposure on film. The band is led by drum major Joe Baker in this little-known and seldom seen movie.

The spring tour that year brought the fifty-piece concert band along with the Ambassadors Dance Band back to Italy. To begin their four days in Rome, the Glee Club, composed of band members, played for Pope John XXIII. The performance is normally held outside, but because it was raining heavily on that Wednesday in March, the band played in the chapel singing a short selection, including William Steffe's "The Battle Hymn of the Republic." It was the first time a US service band had been honored to play for the Pope. Later that day the Ambassadors played a forty-minute jazz concert broadcast over Radio Italia. On Friday Arnald led the group in a selection of American jazz on the ramp at Rome's Ciampino Airport. The concert was filmed and recorded also to be broadcast over Radio Italia-TV. In another recording opportunity, the concert band played an hour-long concert described as serious American music to be broadcast over the Vatican's

---

[29] The B movie starred William Bendix and Christine Kaufmann and was released in 1961.

own station. Because of the short duration of the trip, Joan and some of the other wives were able to join the musicians between concerts as they toured many of the iconic sights around the Eternal City, including the beautiful Baroque classic Trevi Fountain.

The group left Rome and spent a very busy two days in Naples; the Ambassadors played a dance band concert at the Flamingo Club on Bagnoli Post, headquarters of NATO's Air South Command, but the highlight of the visit was the concert band's performance at the opera house on Naples' huge exposition grounds. At the home of the 1940 World's Fair, the band had the audience on their feet by the end of the concert with a stirring performance of Aaron Copland's "Lincoln Portrait." The universality of the views held and sentiments expressed in the moving piece proved, once again, the power of music to convey an idea and enthrall people of nearly any nationality.

Arnald made a quick visit to Wiesbaden before embarking on a unique trip. At the request of the US Ambassador there, Arnald and the Ambassadors were invited to Moscow, Russia. Llewellyn Thompson wanted the group to perform for a series of embassy receptions under some very strict conditions. Only a year and a half prior, the first man-made satellite had been launched by the USSR, and the specter of Sputnik circling overhead for months deepened already frosty relations between the two countries. Adding immeasurably to the heightened tensions, the United States had successfully tested the first intercontinental ballistic missile, or ICBM, launched by the Titan I missile less than two months prior. As a result of the inherent mistrust between the two countries, band members were joined by ever-present Russian guides during visits to Red Square and other sites around the capital city.

The concerts, however, were well received by the Russian dignitaries and were no more enthusiastically cheered than by the US citizens who were stationed there. The cloistered life under constant surveillance wore heavily on the men and women posted to the embassy who, especially after hearing their national anthem, unabashedly broke down in tears. Arnald and the other musicians were proud to bring a little slice of home to the beleaguered personnel. The success of the performances prompted Ambassador Thompson to invite the group and Arnald, to include Joan this time, for a return visit the following spring. Unfortunately, a further spike in the tension between the United States and USSR scuttled the planned visit when, not a month later, Capt. Gary Francis Powers was shot down while flying a U-2 spy plane over Russia.[30]

Arnald's travel schedule with the various units of the USAFE band continued, and mid-April found him in the divided city of Berlin. Access to the city was less strictly controlled through surrounding East Germany than it would be only eighteen months later and was accessed by one of three methods: by train, by air, or by driving. The authorities allowed a precise two hours to drive the approximately 110 miles; arrive earlier and be accused of speeding, arrive late and be suspected of taking pictures of military installations along the route. The air routes were equally restrictive and were the same ones used for the Berlin Airlift a decade prior. Increasing oppression of its citizens in the eastern zone was causing a vast exodus to the west through the still-open gates connecting the two halves of the city. During an evening at the famous Ballhaus Resi[31] nightclub, Arnald noted the presence of many patrons who had slipped over the porous border, most with no intention of returning.

The Ambassadors' spring tour of 1959 was an ambitious sixteen-day tour of the Middle East, one of the first for a Western military band. Just prior to leaving on the trip, Arnald took the concert band to Oslo, Norway, for several days of evening concerts and matinees. Although good rest is a challenge on any trip, the visit in May, only a month prior to the summer solstice, made it tough to acclimate

---

30 Interestingly, the event further eroded the already tenuous relationship between the two superpowers to a degree that a planned summit meeting in Moscow between President Eisenhower and Soviet Premier Nikita Khrushchev was also canceled.
31 The bar was known for elegant dining, music, and a unique water ballet involving choreographed fountains and jets of water. The most interesting feature, however, was the more than two hundred telephones and a pneumatic tube connection with each table used to call or send messages to the dozens of women in attendance.

to the twenty-four hours of daylight.[32] Immediately after returning to Wiesbaden, the sleep-deprived captain boarded an airplane with the dance band. The flight was an all-day ordeal aboard a military transport called the Lockheed C-130. The flight was four hours to Athens to refuel and four more to Tehran; the four-engine, turboprop airplane (still in production and use today after more than fifty years) is built for efficiency, not necessarily the comfort of the troops. It was a "very, very noisy airplane" Arnald remembers.

They played two to three concerts a day in Tehran and most notable in attendance was Mohammad Reza Pahlavi, the Shah of Iran. The tour continued for sixteen straight days on that schedule to enthusiastic crowds anxious to hear the uniquely American big band sound. The relentless itinerary was not without cost, however: by the end of the trip, the twenty-piece group was down to thirteen functioning musicians, four of them described as litter cases. The exhausted men left Dhahran, Saudi Arabia, for Wiesbaden in a C-124 Globemaster II; the double-decked interior had been converted to a flying hospital complete with litters for the nonambulatory. As he wrapped up his first full and very busy year in Europe, the optimistic Captain Gabriel described the tour in a postcard home: "The band is just plain burned out, but it's been a tremendous trip." And then admitted, "I'm pooped!" They arrived home on June 9, Arnald and Joan's eighth wedding anniversary and my sixth birthday.

NATO Band

The summer of 1959 marked the anniversary of the formation of the North Atlantic Treaty Organization (NATO), and Arnald struck upon an idea to help commemorate the event. "I thought it would be a great idea to form a band comprised of musicians from the fifteen NATO nations." To that end, he was directed by his commanding officer in Wiesbaden to request permission from the Supreme Headquarters Allied Powers Europe (SHAPE) in Paris. He met with representatives

---

[32] Although the sun does dip below the horizon this time of year, it doesn't get completely dark.

of Gen. Lauris Norstad, Supreme Allied Commander, Europe and Commander in Chief, US European command, and garnered their approval. They contacted each nation and requested five musicians comprising a band of seventy-five players. It was Arnald's intent to play at the Arnhem Tattoo[33] to be held in June in the southeastern Dutch city and later to tour every NATO country with the international group. Organizers of the tattoo had a similar idea but were planning to invite bands to represent only a few of the member countries. Arnald then went to Arnhem to negotiate a compromise and convinced them of his idea. They agreed to the formation of the band but only for participation at their event; they would not sign off on a follow-up tour.

Initially frustrated at the decision, Arnald arrived in Arnhem to rehearse the unique compilation of musicians. As he began to work with the men, he realized that the couple of local concerts that had been scheduled for the marching band would prove to be quite an undertaking; this was the most disparate and least homogeneous group, both culturally and musically, with whom he'd ever worked. Because each nation possessed different dietary requirements, just feeding the men was a problem. The Frenchmen required wine at each meal, and he soon realized no single menu would satisfy each nationality. Breakfast was also different for every country. For example, the Americans wanted fried or scrambled eggs to begin the day, and to accommodate their need, the efficient Dutch prepared them the night before, refrigerated them, and served them in the morning. As a result, the Americans ate cold eggs every day.

Of greater concern was how the music was played. As Arnald began the rehearsals, he realized that, although talented musically, the instrumentalists had played only with their respective countrymen, and each brought his own cultural nuance to the piece. "The Germans played a little late, the French played early, the Italians played with a more romantic interpretation, and so on." Also, their styles were different, and nationalistic pride was probably responsible for their stubborn refusal to totally surrender to the conductor's vision.

---

33 A tattoo is an outdoor concert or pageant of military musical groups.

The Force of Destiny

The unique melding of the NATO group was ultimately a success in Arnhem, and "eventually, we played somewhat together." Arnald was left to only imagine what difficulties they would have in trying to satisfy the demands for distinctive meals in each country.

The opportunity to perform at the Arnhem Tattoo allowed Arnald to hear a wide array of military marching bands from across Europe. Coupled with his experience conducting the combined NATO band, he came away with a new appreciation of the cultural differences that existed between the different national groups. He was also fortunate to meet Maestro Domenico Fantini, conductor of the Carabinieri Band of Rome. Arnald was not only invited to conduct the band that weekend (to which he gladly accepted), but he and the maestro were able to discuss at great length Arnald's theoretical construct of the concert band. Specifically, they analyzed the woodwind section, mostly with respect to the clarinets.

Arnald inquired as to the need for the four A^b soprano clarinets that the Carabinieri Band utilized at the time in addition to the four E^b clarinets. Maestro Fantini admitted that the A^b clarinets were not absolutely necessary, but because his predecessor had used them, he had inherited the arrangement. The conclusion Arnald reached in his master's thesis as a result of this discussion was that although, while conducting the fine group, he noted the "overwhelming sonority in the reed section," it "rapidly identified itself as a thick hodgepodge of instruments not necessary to a concert band at all." There is some irony in that the section is very close to Arnald's own recommendation as to the makeup of a concert band but with a key difference: in Europe, "the tendency is to add different instruments as the size of the organization increases. The tendency should be to have fewer different kinds of instruments." The result, he posited, would "place more reliance on simple, unmixed colors from a single instrumental family at a time."

Arnald and the band continued the busy summer concert season with performances at the largest Fourth of July celebration outside the United States. Rebild Bakker is a national park in Denmark whose land was donated by Danish-Americans, and its rolling hills are the site of the annual event. Arnald and the concert band joined other bands for the daylong tribute that ended with a very American fireworks display in the evening. The flags flown that day featured the new forty-nine star field acknowledging Alaska's statehood earlier that year. While in Denmark, Arnald was approached by Capt. Jorgen (pronounced "Yon") Fogg and asked to help form and rehearse the Danish Home Guard Band. The Home Guard is a largely unpaid volunteer civilian adjunct to the military (formed ostensibly in response to the proximity and threat of the USSR) to assist in the defense of their country. Arnald began by donating surplus supplies from the Air Force Band, such as sheet music, reeds, etc., and also assisted Captain Fogg with his administrative and musical expertise. Arnald made it a point to visit Copenhagen at least once a summer to rehearse with the fledgling group for the balance of his tenure in Europe. As a result of his efforts, he was awarded the Danish Home Guard Cross of St. George in 1959.

After his return to Wiesbaden and after fifteen months of nearly continuous travel, Arnald set aside some time for his family. He bought a tent and camping supplies and returned to Denmark for two weeks of camping at the end of July. We camped near the beach on the Skagerrak, the strait that separates Denmark from Sweden, between the cities of Copenhagen and Helsingor. It was a carefree and much deserved time of exploring the beautiful country with visits to the Copenhagen Zoo, Tivoli Gardens, Frederiksborg Castle, and, of course, days at the beach. Arnald admitted in a postcard home to brother Armand, "These are the most relaxed days for a long time. No telephones, etc., and the Air Force doesn't even know where I am!" He concluded enthusiastically, "It's a great life!"

Our trip to Copenhagen was made by driving the Borgward to Lübeck, Germany, just northeast of Hamburg, and taking a ferry across the strait to Denmark. Being the only Americans in the camp presented no language problem; we organized the Scandinavian kids and taught them to play softball. We ate a breakfast of Danish rolls delivered by truck each morning and drove the Borgward to the local grocery store for lunch and dinner. Late one week, a massive thunderstorm flooded the camp and drenched everything we had. We were rescued by Jorgen Fogg of the Danish Home Guard Band of Copenhagen. Jorgen took us

The Force of Destiny

to his home where he served hot chocolate to the soaked children and hot toddies to the adults.

Unfortunately, the idyllic respite ended, and early August was filled with making plans for the fall tour of Northern Greece and an upcoming seven-day trip to Finland. A concert midmonth in nearby Koblenz was typical of the musical selections Arnald chose for the performances: the lively "Hall of Fame" march by Olivadoti was followed by the quintessentially American composer Don Gillis's "The Man Who Invented Music." The concert continued with medleys from *Porgy and Bess, The King and I, Oklahoma*, and one of several arrangements featuring the music of George Gershwin. Copland's "Lincoln Portrait" and the jazzy "Cuban Fantasy" by Air Force Chief Warrant Officer Charles Kepner separated the medleys, and as always, the concert ended with a march, "March to the Battle of Jazz" and a rousing version of "The Stars and Stripes Forever" that never failed to bring the houseful of Europeans to their feet.

The weeklong trip to Finland was split between the four days in Helsinki and three in Pori, a city in the northwest on the Gulf of Bothnia. The success of the Finnish tour was marred by a strange medical affliction Arnald discovered one morning: he had lost the vision in his left eye due to an unexplained hemorrhage of the blood vessels. The doctor he consulted told him that, "There's a good chance it will come back," and his only concern was possible scarring that may cause permanent damage. Arnald had already planned to return to the United States in November to submit for the oral exam for his master's degree and now added a visit to Walter Reed Hospital in the Washington, DC, area. A postcard to Armand telling him of the malady implored, *"Please* don't tell folks about it!" He didn't want to worry his parents with the news.

Arnald's vision problem apparently did little to slow his travel schedule. After the Finland tour and a "few days in Berlin," he returned home in early September and interviewed Franz Groffy of the Heckel Instrument Company in neighboring Biebrich on the Rhine River. This was another in a series of interviews where he garnered information that he incorporated into the master's thesis he was writing. With Herr Groffy he discussed the double reeds in the concert band; as a manufacturer of double-reed instruments, he was uniquely qualified to speak to their inclusion in the construct of the concert band. They talked in-depth about the technical aspects of, for example, the necessity for the complex finger patterns of the bassoon and how the instrument might be manufactured more simply. Arnald described the discussion as "spirited" but ultimately both benefitted from a fruitful exchange of ideas. At Arnald's urging, Herr Groffy suggested a makeup of double-reed instruments for the concert band. Arnald's final build pared the variety of instruments Herr Groffy suggested because, as with Maestro Fantini of the Carabinieri Band, Arnald felt, "the trend should be toward more homogeneity of sound rather than polyphony." Arnald's idea, once again, was to increase the number of instruments and not the number of *different* instruments.

The 1959 fall tour was by bus to northern Greece. They traversed the rugged Pindus Mountains through the cities of Kozani, Kavala, Alexandropoulos, and Salonika. They also played many smaller villages whose names are lost to memory and whose residents had likely never seen Americans, much less heard an American band. Though many of the towns' populations rarely exceeded a few thousand, the band would fill to capacity the local soccer stadium, drawing from the surrounding area and playing to a crowd that often exceeded the population of the town. Arnald worked with the local American Consulate to play local songs arranged by Lawrence Odom, the band's oboist and arranger. The inclusion of the familiar tunes always brought the crowd to their feet, clapping in unison to "their" music. Accommodations in the tiny villages were, at best, meager. In one town, Arnald was given the finest room in the hotel. For the equivalent of eighty-seven cents per night, he had the only room with running water; the sink drained into a pail that, when full, was tossed out the window into the street.

By contrast, however, in Salonika[34] Arnald was honored with a unique distinction: a march was written for him by a Greek music professor. Spyros Haikians, professor of music at the Aristotelis Institute of Music, presented him with "The Captain Arnald Gabriel

---

34 Also called Thessaloniki.

Greek-American March" just before their concert in the port city on the Aegean Sea. In the second-largest city in Greece and home to the prestigious university, the acclamation was humbling to the thirty-five-year-old air force captain.

In postwar Europe, the Marshall Plan provided many millions of dollars of aid and support to rebuild the war-torn countries. In Greece, one program taught farmers to more efficiently cultivate the rocky soil that, paired with the abundant sunshine, increased agricultural yields dramatically. Band members were heaped with the bounty. Nearly all went home with sacks full of fruits, vegetables, and "especially the great, sweet corn."

Early October found Arnald with a rare stretch of time at home in Wiesbaden. When home, Arnald continued his personal musical growth. There were three full-time opera companies within twenty-five kilometers of the base located in the towns of Wiesbaden, Mainz, and Frankfurt, and Joan and he attended whenever possible. They also continued each year to mount the musicals and organize and perform in the variety shows utilizing the local populous as actors and musicians.

In late October 1959 the band flew to Tehran, Iran, for the fortieth birthday celebration of Mohammad Reza Pahlavi, the Shah of Iran. The band marched into a packed stadium and passed in review in front of thousands of jubilant Iranians. As they passed the Shah's box, they halted, turned in unison, and shouted, "Happy fortieth birthday, Shah of Iran!" Later that evening, the Ambassadors played a gala ball attended by leaders and the elite from around the world. Arnald was struck by not only the opulence of the ruling class, but the disparity of living conditions compared to the common people. The stark reality was that most of the country lived in poverty.

During the weeklong birthday celebration, the band and Arnald played for the Shah, his family, and various dignitaries at the Golestan Palace, one of the oldest historic royal buildings in Tehran. The throne room in the palace had served as the location of Reza Pahlavi's coronation and on this birthday as a place to receive his guests offering their good wishes. Each segment of society (medical community, press corps, academic, government, etc.) was allocated a different hour throughout the day to convey their sentiments in a short audience with the Shah. At five o'clock, Arnald was summoned and ushered into the magnificent throne room. He entered, by tradition, in his stocking feet into a massive room stacked nearly three feet high with hundreds of Persian rugs. The Shah was perched upon a lavish throne[35] studded with countless emeralds, diamonds, rubies, and other precious stones, the titular head of a twenty-five-hundred-year-old monarchy. Arnald was presented with one of the beautifully handwoven Persian rugs, and the gift hung on our living room wall for many years.

After a total of nine days in Iran, Arnald and the band spent four days in Brussels, Belgium, performing two concerts a day and continued into northern Germany through Hannover, Hamburg, Itzehoe, and Flensburg, performing the same exhausting schedule. After a one-day visit home to Wiesbaden in mid-November, Arnald boarded an airplane for his planned trip to the United States. As he passed through Washington, DC, he visited Walter Reed Hospital where he found there was little the doctors could do; his vision had returned, and the eye problem had resolved itself as mysteriously as it had occurred. On November 21 and 22, Arnald submitted his sixty-page typewritten master's thesis and sat for the oral exam at Ithaca College. He was able to reconnect with brother Min and sister-in-law Agnes, staying at their home near Binghamton, New York. The first week of December he took seven days of leave and visited Ma and Pa in Miami before returning to Germany.

After returning to Europe, Arnald and Joan spent several romantic days in Paris.[36] They explored the city of lights as unabashed tourists visiting the artistic community of Montmartre and its Basilique du Sacré-Coeur, Les Invalides, the burial site of Napoleon, and the Louvre. They spent a perfect evening sitting at a sidewalk café sipping a cognac

---

35 The Peacock Throne is a reference to early Indian and Persian emperors' thrones and a name oftentimes mistakenly given to this one.
36 Shortly after arriving in Germany and moving into base housing, Arnald and Joan hired a maid who was able to stay with the four kids. A very affordable and common practice at the time, Barbara lived in quarters on the fourth floor of the apartment building and over the years became part of our family, even accompanying us on our vacations around the continent.

as Joan's postcard home remarked blissfully, "The weather is beautiful." The decade ended with a few holiday concerts in and around the Wiesbaden area as Arnald enjoyed his home life in southern Germany.

In addition to his duties as commander and conductor of the USAFE Band in Wiesbaden, Captain Gabriel was command band director of four other air force bands in Europe. They were the bands at Camp Griffiss in Bushy Park, England; Torrejón Air Base in central Spain; Wheelus Air Base in Tripoli, and the air base in nearby Ramstein, Germany. His position required him to periodically travel to each of the units in order to conduct inspections and supervise the overall operation. Even though a picturesque locale on the shores of the Mediterranean, Arnald always felt uncomfortable traveling to Wheelus because he thought "it was dangerous to Americans." His travels off base were always in the company of others, but he mostly confined himself to his duties within the relative safety of the base. The trip in mid-January was particularly tiring because it was sandwiched in the middle of a nearly monthlong ordeal of travel.

He had begun the trip with eight days of frigid temperatures in Oslo, Norway, with the band playing at various locales around the northern city. Although most of his travel by air was by military transport, the tight schedule required him to use Alitalia Airlines and to connect to Tripoli through Rome. Low clouds and fog grounded the new DC-8 jetliner and forced him to stay in Rome for two days before continuing on to Tripoli. He spent two days in the Libyan capital with temperatures in the high eighties; by contrast, the temperature in Oslo had been a cold (even for Oslo) -10°F. Leaving Tripoli, he returned to the chill by joining the band in the northern city of Kiel, Germany, a port city on the Baltic Sea for four days. From there it was on to damp and cold London for three days, followed by snowy Luxemburg for another two. His return to Wiesbaden at the end of January gave him just three days to ready himself for his periodic trip to Washington, DC, to report to his superiors at Bolling Air Force Base and the Pentagon.

Arnald's duties required him to visit Berlin several times a year, and after his return from the States, he found himself once again in the divided city. After the various meetings and planning sessions for upcoming concerts, Arnald loved walking the Kurfürstendamm

Strasse. The main street in West Berlin was lined with shopping, restaurants, and clubs, and his favorites were the Ballhaus Resi (or just Resi bar) and the Zigeunerkeller, a gypsy nightclub featuring a Hungarian band from Budapest. The lively music in the arch-roofed cellar was a nice diversion, and one night Arnald approached the zither player for a request: he suggested "Kalinka," "a wonderful folk song," he remembers fondly. Offended, the musician exclaimed, "*Das ist Russki!*" His initial outrage to a request for a *Russian* folk song was likely due to the Soviet crushing of the Hungarian Revolution only four years prior, but he then smiled and played the song anyway. The politics of the relatively new Cold War were creating a tricky dynamic in the world and particularly in this unique city split between East and West.

In early April Arnald and Joan seized another break in his travel schedule and flew to London for a week. Staying at the Columbia Hotel[37] on the north side of Hyde Park, they toured the capital city and visited Westminster Abbey, the Tower of London, Buckingham Palace, and many other tourist sites. Evenings, they devoured the cultural scene, attending the latest movie releases of *My Fair Lady, Ben Hur, West Side Story*, and *A Majority of One* and visited museums and live music venues. They were no less adventuresome on the culinary front, sampling the vast spectrum of available cuisines in the cosmopolitan world capital. At the end of their whirlwind week, they headed to the airport for their flight back to Germany and ran into an unexpected delay: British immigration officials informed the couple that Joan's passport had expired the previous week. They returned to the hotel and after "many hassles with the embassy" were able to fly home a couple of days later. It is likely that the passport was not checked on the flight over; generally, authorities were very lenient with uniformed military personnel and their families with regard to security and paperwork.

---

37 It was called the Columbia Club at the time and began life as five separate Victorian townhomes and during World War I an American Red Cross Hospital. It became the Palace Hotel after the war and then the Columbia Club; the hotel catered to American GIs and charged one British pound per night: about $2.80.

The Force of Destiny

The following month, in early May, Joan was able to join Arnald on one of his many trips to Berlin. The Ambassadors Dance Band was scheduled to play for six nights at the Silver Wings Officers' Club located at the Tempelhof Central Airport.[38] There was probably nowhere in the world where increasing tensions between East and West were played out as they were there, and Joan was enthralled with the dynamic city. The border was still largely an open one, and there were approximately sixty thousand people commuting from the East Sector to the West daily for jobs and nightly for entertainment. She summed up her feelings in a postcard home to Min and Aggie: "This is a lovely city (West) with sharp contrasts in the East Sector." Arnald took advantage of his increasing familiarity with the city and showed his young wife around to his favorite sites.

A Growing Recognition for Excellence

In showcasing the different units of the USAFE Band, Arnald's penchant for innovation didn't end with his work on the band's sound and makeup. The marching band participated in many festivals and stadium-type shows whose performance was judged as much by their precision marching as by the music they performed. He drew on his many years of working with the drum and bugle corps in upstate New York and the Tidewater region of Virginia and devised drills that were as groundbreaking for military marching bands as had been seen to date. The drills involved marching along complex geometric patterns that, paradoxically, appeared random and disorderly and that ultimately reformed into precision lines or shapes all while maintaining a sharp, clear, and musically top-notch performance.

Arnald chose to debut this unique marching band drill he called the Cavalcade of American Music at the Maggio di Bari (literally, Bari in May) in Bari, Italy. Because the city was a bastion of Communism in poor, southern Italy, it was profoundly anti-American. The monthlong celebration features wide-ranging cultural events, regional costumes

---

38 Formerly called Tempelhof Air Base, it was renamed only a few months prior, in November 1959.

and music, sports, road rallies, fireworks, and even a bridge tournament. With his position as command band director, Arnald was able to combine the bands from Bushy Park, England; Ramstein; and his Wiesbaden marching band for large events such as these in an effort to more closely match the size of European marching bands of the time. The combined band, numbering about eighty men, entered the International Festival of Military Bands at the spring gathering.

The Egyptian band led the show and, dressed in period costumes, played an excerpt from the opera *Aida*, complete with herald trumpets. Next, the Carabinieri Band of Rome took the field to cheers and shouts of approval from the partisan crowd. Arnald remembers that they "hated to march" and, as such, moved perfunctorily to the center of the field and played the "William Tell Overture" from memory. As Arnald led the band into the arena to perform, they were roundly booed. Their show featured military marches and jazz classics from Glenn Miller, Irving Berlin, George Gershwin, and other popular American artists all choreographed to the complex precision marching. By the conclusion of the routine, they had all fifty thousand Italians on their feet cheering wildly. He admitted that the "small step for democracy" didn't change their politics, but it was a step in the right direction owing to the power of music, and "had members of Congress been there, they wouldn't have been so adamant in cutting military band budgets." Of equal satisfaction to Arnald and the air force musicians was the effect on the other participants in the festival; comments to his brother Min stated, "Bands from England, Belgium, France, Italy, and Greece crawled out of the stadium!"

Late spring/early summer brought the annual music festival season back, and Arnald toured with the concert band through Finland, visiting Tampere, Vaasa, and Pietarsaari, located along the rugged northwestern coast. After returning, the band was invited to play at a newly formed music festival featuring military bands from NATO countries in the northwestern German city of Mönchen-Gladbach. It is certain his thoughts must have gone back over fifteen years prior to the spring of 1945 and his role as an army infantryman in helping to capture the city, then the largest city in Germany liberated by the Allies.

The Force of Destiny

They performed their show along with four other European bands at the stadium filled with thousands of enthusiastic music lovers. After the performances, they were all invited to the local *rathskeller* for dinner where Arnald was approached by the *Bürgermeister*[39] and his staff. "Captain?" he began. "This was not a contest, but we all thought that the American band was the best and so we want to present you with the city flag of Mönchen-Gladbach." The following week in the *Stars and Stripes*, the newspaper of the armed forces, the headline read: "Gabriel captures Mönchen-Gladbach in war and with music!"

The popular Fourth of July celebration at the park in Rebild Bakker, Denmark, drew thousands of Danish Americans and each year featured a keynote speaker. That summer US vice president and candidate for the 1960 presidential election, Richard M. Nixon, and Val Peterson, US ambassador to Denmark, spoke to the enthusiastic crowd. Dinah Shore, popular singer, film, and television star, sang with the USAFE Band on the brilliant, cloudless day.

During rehearsal, as the band began the intro to her popular "Sweet Violets," Ms. Shore stopped and asked, "Captain? Can you play this a little lower?"

Arnald asked if she would like it in a lower key that would allow her to sing it in her vocal range.

She responded, "Oh, I don't know, just play it lower." He directed the band to drop the written key, and the men transposed each of their parts on the fly.

The largest venue annually was, by far, Berlin's Olympic Stadium. Each fall, The Berlin Police Show was held in the one hundred thousand-seat arena and featured acrobatics, police dog shows, trick motorcycle riding, marching bands, and other music from countries across Europe. Arnald and the band performed their Cavalcade of American Music precision marching routine to high acclaim, and the Ambassadors Dance Band won first prize in their division. It marked the highlight of each year to compete against the best on the continent in front of the massive crowd.

---

39 Local official or mayor of the city.

The fall tour of 1960 was an ambitious six-day, eighteen-appearance tour of Turkey. On the first day in the southern city of Adana, the band performed in a parade, two marching demonstrations, and a concert at the Civic Sports Stadium that drew a record fifteen thousand Turks. The band traveled next to nearby Incirlik Air Base and played to an audience of American military personnel on the newly lighted baseball diamond. The Ambassadors played to fifteen hundred people for an evening dance sponsored by the Turkish-American Society of Adana that raised funds for Turkish charities. The air force musicians worked their way around the country by bus and military transport airplanes, and they traveled as far east as Diyarbakir and northwest to Eskişehir, both US military installations, where they played mostly on the bases. Crisscrossing the country, they performed in the beautiful Aegean Sea port of Izmir and ended the tour in the capital city of Ankara.

The concerts were mostly a mix of Western music and Turkish songs arranged by Sergeant Odom. The complicated asymmetrical meters were familiar with the audiences and hugely popular. Each performance also began with the US and Turkish national anthems. The final concert at the university in Ankara exceeded all expectations and left an indelible impression on the men. In a concert slated to begin at nine o'clock at night, the one thousand-seat auditorium was crammed with two thousand restless students by seven thirty. The concert began with a medley of international tunes, and by the time they played the British "The Bridge over the River Kwai," the students were on their feet whistling and singing along with the band. The second half of the show featured Dixieland band music from the Dixielanders (a smaller segment of the Ambassadors), which caused pandemonium. Spontaneous applause and standing ovations roiled the night, and Captain Gabriel remembers, "They were hanging from the window sills and dangling from the balconies. It was the most frantic, unrestrained audience that we have ever played for—and we've seen plenty of enthusiasm." Arnald had scheduled a one-hour show, but to calm the jubilant throng, he once again played the Turkish national anthem. The students leapt to their feet during the playing of the anthem and drowned out the band in full voice. "I have rarely

The Force of Destiny

heard that kind of response," Arnald says. The one-hour show ended at eleven o'clock that night.

At the conclusion of the evening, Arnald and the exhausted band members retired to the bar at the club on base to celebrate the successful end of the tour. The club admitted both officers and enlisted men, and as the night slipped away in revelry, one of the musicians, noting the late hour, said to the man next to him, "It's 3 a.m. I need to go to bed. I have a flight at seven." The disconcerting answer he received was, "I know. I'm your pilot."

The year ended with a tour of Morocco, including the cities of Rabat, Marrakesh, Ben Guerir, Nouasseur Air Base near Casablanca, Sidi Slimane, and Fes. The country had achieved independence about four years prior, and the new government had insisted that the United States withdraw its forces and close its bases. The decision to close the high-security Strategic Air Command Base Nouasseur had come only a year earlier, and although tensions were running high, the band drew enthusiastic capacity crowds to each concert. Throughout the tour, theft was rampant, and concerns about personal safety increased the stress of the bandsmen; each was grateful to board the air force transport for the return flight to Wiesbaden eight days later.

Changing Times

By any measure, the world at the end of 1960 was in a state of flux. Emerging nations, mostly in Africa and the Mediterranean, unfurled eighteen new national flags and engendered an attendant unrest that helped to ratchet up global tensions. The member nations of NATO were grappling with the weighty issue of nuclear proliferation and testing, finding little common ground. Most of the Central and South American countries were in the throes of revolution or at least some sort of political upheaval, and there was a fear that a majority of the hemisphere would follow Fidel Castro's brutal Marxist regime as an ally with Communist USSR. The 1961 New Year's parade in the Cuban capital featured, for the first time, a display of Soviet weapons and tanks.

President John F. Kennedy took the oath of office on January 20, 1961, after one of the closest elections in US history. After the highest voter turnout of the twentieth century and a winning margin of only 1 percent of the popular vote, the new president faced a truly divided country. His inaugural speech sought to bind the nation together with a clarion call to service coupled with the importance of maintaining our military vigilance. There was concern among military personnel abroad about President Eisenhower's order to slash by nearly 50 percent the number of dependents stationed in foreign countries. Cuts are rarely across the board and are prone to ignite turf wars in a battle to retain hard-fought-for manning positions and equipment. In the military, rumors abound, and Arnald could do little but focus on the overwhelming success of the USAFE Band's role as musical ambassadors. General Smith's mandate to reach out and improve relations with the peoples of Germany, the rest of Europe, and the Middle East continued to drive Arnald.

Back home in the United States, the country continued to grapple with the painful issues of integration and civil rights that were generally unknown in the military. Since President Truman signed an executive order ending segregation in the armed services more than a dozen years prior, each branch had worked to comply and, although not unheard of, blatant discrimination was rare. In early January 1961, Arnald rehearsed the band and attended to the myriad of details for an upcoming trip to Reykjavik, Iceland, the following month. During the preparation, he received a message that halted all the work.

An agreement between the United States and Iceland in 1951 opened the door to the establishment of a permanent US military base on the island country that was vital to US Cold War strategy and turned over control of the airport at Keflavík to the Air Force Military Air Transport Service (MATS). Subsequent to the approval, the Icelandic government instituted off-base restrictions on personnel stationed there. Due to their isolated history, the citizens of the North Atlantic country were one of the most insular and fiercely patriotic populations on the planet, and the restrictions were a misguided attempt to preserve that homogeneity. Another more disturbing provision, passed in secrecy by the government, was a prohibition against black servicemen serving on Icelandic soil.

US officials had been lobbying for a lifting of the ban for years, but even after public disclosure in late 1959, the restriction remained. Arnald was told to leave behind bassoon player James A. Johnson for the six-day tour or set in motion a logistically complicated and politically sensitive tangle (by then most of the travel details had already been set). For Arnald, the choice was simple: he refused to do the tour unless *all* his men were allowed to go. Doubtless, a flurry of meetings and phone calls transpired over the following days that resulted in an approval for the tour to proceed as planned with Captain Gabriel's full complement of musicians. His decision was less about the complicated questions surrounding the civil rights movement than it was a basic question of fairness. Not only was the man a member of the organization, and as such deserved no less consideration than any other in the group, but operationally, it was simpler: he was the only bassoon player and was crucial for the performances. The six concerts in Reykjavik were played without incident, and the ban was subsequently less strictly enforced. It was officially rescinded less than two years later.[40]

Back in Wiesbaden in mid-March, Arnald performed in a concert that typified the concept laid out by Gen. Smith almost three years earlier. The USAFE Concert Band joined with *Musikkorps 5* (literally, Band 5) for a German-American Military Band Concert at downtown Wiesbaden's premier venue, the Kurhaus. It was a three-part performance. First, under the direction of Hauptmann Schlüter, the German group played a selection of European composers beginning with Giuseppe Verdi's overture to *The Sicilian Vespers,* followed by Frenchman Charles Gounod's *Margarethe,*[41] and three movements from *Das Pensionat* by Franz von Suppé, an Austrian composer who was born in what is now Croatia. He concluded with German countryman

---

[40] It is important to view the policy in the context of the history of the Icelandic people. Their isolationism was manifested in the desire to remain neutral during World War II, and it is felt that the postwar policy was a result more of a fear of the unknown rather than of enmity.

[41] Called *Faust* outside of Germany.

Michael A. Gabriel

Eduard Küenneke's *Intermezzo from the Dance Suite*. Next, Arnald selected a popular program of American composers beginning with Gershwin's *Rhapsody in Blue* featuring the multitalented Lawrence Odom on piano. He continued with "Fanfare and Allegro" by Clifton Williams, a Lerner and Loewe's *My Fair Lady* medley, and selections from Don Gillis's *Tulsa*. The third part of the concert featured the bands seated together playing the mixed selections of "Berliner Luft" (Berlin Air), "The World Is Waiting for the Sunrise," "Alte Kameraden," (Old Comrades), and the grand finale, "The Stars and Stripes Forever." Two encores capped the evening that found the capacity crowd of Germans and Americans on their feet.

In the spring of 1961, Arnald led the musical ambassadors on their spring tour north of the Arctic Circle through the cities of Bardufoss, Bodø, Andøya, and Oslo, Norway. They returned from the tour with a gift from the commander of Bardufoss Air Base. Norwegian Col. O.J. Jonesberg built a drum crafted from a portion of the wing tank of a jet as a token of their visit. Upon their return, Colonel Gabriel and Tech. Sgt. "Gene" Gartrell posed for a picture with the uniquely styled instrument that ended up on the front page of the *Wiesbaden Post*.

The first few years flashed by as Arnald neared the end of his three-year military service in Germany. They were by far the most successful years in the existence of the band's fifteen-year history, traveling more than thirty-five thousand miles across Europe, North Africa, and the Middle East and playing to more than 2 million people. Because of the USAFE Band's resounding success, he was asked by the commanding officer of Wiesbaden Air Base, Gen. Truman H. Landon, to extend his service for an additional year, and he agreed. General Landon had replaced General Smith and chose to reiterate the importance of Arnald's role in improving international relations in Europe and especially in Germany. The goal matched perfectly with Arnald's own sense of responsibility to his community. In his mind, community meant not only the local civilian populous but the US Air Force, music education, and the international community.

The extension imbued him with a new sense of purpose, and as temperatures warmed, so did Arnald's travel schedule. After his return from Norway, "a few exciting days in the exciting city of Madrid" led to an exhausting twelve-day itinerary in Helsinki, Finland, for the International Trade Fair. They packed thirty engagements into their schedule, including parades and two daily concerts and also provided dance music for official functions each evening. In keeping with the international nature of the event, the music selections were chosen accordingly. A few of the pieces played were Morton Gould's "Jericho Rhapsody" and also "Finlandia" and "Aurora March" by native Finnish composers Jean Sibelius and Josef Kaartinen. The latter was written and dedicated to former President Eisenhower in 1960. Arnald summed up the upcoming season in a postcard to brother Min: "We're in for one hell of a hectic summer!"

EUROPE

Arnald's hectic summer began with a trip to Geneva in early June. He attempted to make arrangements for an upcoming Fourth of July concert but found it impossible to secure the approximately fifty hotel reservations required for the group. Disarmament talks between the United States and USSR being held in the Swiss city, in addition to peace talks for the growing conflict in southeast Asia, made rooms scarce. He was finally able to arrange boarding for the musicians in private homes through the American Women's Club of Geneva, and Arnald and Joan were invited to stay in the home of the president of ESSO, Europe, whom Arnald had met during the September 1958 Harvest Festival in Neuchâtel, Switzerland.

A short visit with the band in mid-June to Naples, Italy, was followed quickly by another planning trip to Bree, Belgium. Arnald was accompanied by my brother Steve for the two-night stay in the small northeast town where final arrangements were made for the band to play at the upcoming International Music Festival. It was then back to Geneva for the Fourth of July concert (actually held on the fifth) and the Festival in Bree a few days later.

The concert in Geneva was part of the Independence Day festivities and was attended by US Ambassador to the United Nations, Adlai E. Stevenson. The Ambassador was not the only one to express high praise

Michael A. Gabriel

for the group; Arnald was quoted after the performance as saying, "Tonight this band reached its peak musically." The program included Gould's "Jericho Rhapsody," the *Overture to La Forza del Destino* by Verdi, Tchaikovsky's rousing *1812 Overture*, Clifton Williams's "Fanfare and Allegro," and the highlight of the evening, *Escalles* by Jacques Ibert. The symphonic work was masterfully transcribed by Lawrence Odom, and the Geneva patrons were treated to its first ever performance by a military band. The overwhelming acceptance of the piece prompted Arnald to send the arrangement to Col. George Howard, Chief of Bands and Music in Washington, DC, as a gift from his 686th Air Force Band.

The International Music Contest in Bree featured a similar program that included Odom's now-popular concert band arrangement of *Escalles*. The addition of Johann Strauss' *Die Fledermaus*, Sousa's "Hands across the Sea," Morrissey's "Caribbean Fantasy," and Percy Grainger's "Irish Tune from County Derry" rounded out one of the more talked about concerts at the contest. The wildly successful performance brought the grateful and exhausted musicians to their semiannual leave; during the previous six months they'd played to more than 275,000 fans in seven countries.

Just one day after the concert in Bree, Arnald loaded his family of six (seven with Barbara, our maid) and camping gear into the Borgward and drove to a campsite just outside of Copenhagen, Denmark. We spent a week returning to our favorite places in Tivoli Gardens and other sites around the capital city, including the iconic statue of the Little Mermaid in the harbor. Most of the time we spent at the beach while Joan and Arnald were able to get away and spend evenings alone, thanks to Barbara.

After a relaxing week in Denmark, we were up early, drove all day to Garmisch, Germany, and camped overnight. The beautiful setting in the southern Bavarian Mountains was home to the 1936 Olympics and was a beautiful contrast to the previous week's stay at the beach. Up the next day, we drove through Innsbruck, Austria, over the Swiss Alps, and spent the night in Verona, Italy. From there it was a morning's drive to pitch our two-room tent at a campsite on Tirrenia Beach near Pisa, Italy. We spent two weeks exploring the city and beach enjoying the relaxed Mediterranean climate and people. The days were filled with sand and surf and the occasional sightseeing trip followed by evenings at the campsite's central kitchen eating pasta.

One day Arnald wandered into a small bodega to buy a bottle of the local wine for dinner and when he placed it on the counter, the shopkeeper said, "*Settecento lire.*"

Arnald responded in Italian, "*Settecento lire, per questo?*" asking "Seven hundred lire, for *this?*"

The surprised shopkeeper said, "*Oh, Italiano? Trecento lire,*" immediately dropping the price by over half for a fellow *paisano*.

During the first week of August we headed back to Wiesbaden and, for Arnald, to rehearsals.

Berlin, Germany

After several days of rehearsals in preparation for the upcoming tour of Turkey, Arnald was visited by Capt. John Yesulitis, conductor of the Air Force Symphony Orchestra in Washington, DC, and one of his superiors. It was, ostensibly, an inspection visit that is required periodically, but because Captain Yesulitis had never been to Berlin, the two men hopped military transport and flew to the city. They arrived the morning of August 14 and drove first to the Brandenburg Gate. Constructed more than two hundred years ago, the Gate is a prominent example of some of the classical architecture of the city and served as one of the entrances to East Berlin. Access to the West by East residents had been virtually unrestricted, but in order to stem the alarming exodus of its citizens, as of midnight the previous night, Communist officials started to shut down travel across the border. They began by placing massive concrete planters across the entrance of the columned structure, strung barbed wire along the entire length of the border, and started construction of a block and concrete wall.

Arnald and John arrived to find a crowd of demonstrators (including West Berlin Mayor Willy Brandt) facing heavily armed soldiers nervously restricting access to East Berlin. In response to the growing demonstrations, the soldiers then totally sealed off access and announced by loudspeaker, "*Das tor ist nun geschlossen.*"

Michael A. Gabriel

The broadcast announcing, "The gate is now closed," ratcheted up tensions throughout the restless mob. Arnald, seeking to preserve his unexpected brush with history, stepped off the curb to snap a couple of pictures of the East German soldiers and was immediately fired upon by a water cannon in an attempt to force everyone to stay on his side of the street. He spun quickly back to the sidewalk, avoiding the jet of water and immediately attracted a bevy of reporters covering the historic event. He and John were, thankfully, in civilian clothes, and a curt, "No comment," avoided what could have been an uncomfortable situation for the two air force officers, off duty or not.

They remained in the high-voltage city for another couple of days as Arnald escorted John around town exploring the Gedächtniskirche[42] on the Kurfürstendamm and of course the Resi Bar and basement gypsy bar, the Zigeunerkeller. A hastily scribbled postcard home captured the mood of the city: "The refugees are panicky and desperate—this city is dynamite." One of the photographic slides he had developed when he returned home shows heavily armed East German soldiers partially obscured by a jet of water, frozen in midflight.

In late August the USAFE Band began their tour through Turkey by playing for America Days as part of the International Fair in Izmir. Leaving the beautiful port city on the Aegean Sea, they traversed the country much as they had during their tour only a year earlier, visiting the air bases at Diyarbakir, Eskişehir, and Incirlik, near Adana in south-central Turkey. The tour ended with performances before the enthusiastic students in the capital city of Ankara and finally to Istanbul. Travel around the country was mostly by bus, and after ten long days, the musicians returned to Wiesbaden.

Arnald was excited about the upcoming Berlin Police Show at Olympic Stadium. It was their third year of attendance, and he'd fine-tuned the precision marching routine the band had now come to be known for. He once again combined bands to expand the fifty-piece marching band to eighty musicians and billed this year's program as, A Musical Tour of the United States. The September 11 festivities were

---

42 Also called Remembrance Church, it is a nineteenth-century church heavily damaged by bombing during World War II and left in disrepair as a stark reminder of war.

The Force of Destiny

slated to run nearly eight hours in front of the massive crowd, and as the air force musicians marched off the field at the conclusion of their performance, they were clearly the outstanding event. The program began with "Fanfare" followed by "California, Here I Come" and "Oklahoma!" They moved musically around the country by following with "St. Louis Blues March," "The Sidewalks of New York," "Miami Beach Rhumba-Cha-Cha," and the "Basin Street Blues." They finished with "The Stars and Stripes Forever," *Allied Nations in West Berlin* Medley (*Ich Hab' Noch Einen Koffer in Berlin*), and naturally, "*Auf Wiedersehen*." Not to be outdone, the Ambassadors Dance Band, once again, took first place in the dance band competition. We four kids were able to watch the spectacle and were totally swept up in the revelry. We'd joined Arnald and Joan traveling to Berlin by train and spent a couple of days exploring the fascinating city.

Despite our young ages, we recognized the unmistakable tension the day we went to see the newly constructed wall around West Berlin. Those on the West were allowed to walk right up to the structure but under the constant watch of the armed guards in the towers that lined it. At one point, Joan bent down to pick up a small piece of cinderblock as a souvenir, and several East German soldiers abruptly swiveled their weapons in our direction. The four of us stood nervously for a photograph in front of the wall flanked by a mound of flowers placed there in tribute by West German citizens. The sobering fact was that someone had been shot and killed trying to scale the wall and escape to freedom in the West. The picture shows a benign-looking, hastily built concrete and cinderblock wall barely cresting five feet and topped with barbed wire, it's true danger evident in the collection of flowers behind us.

Throughout the fall months and the balance of the year, the band stayed close to home playing at gigs in the Wiesbaden area and in northern Germany. The USAFE Band joined with the Second Musik Korps of the German Air Force and raised several hundred dollars in support of school programs and to provide equipment for local schools and orphanages. Approximately one thousand German and American citizens jammed the Kurhaus to watch Captain Gabriel and Hauptmann B. Meyer conduct the combined group.

In November, the band ended a bus tour of northern Germany in Hamburg where they played a series of concerts for the US Food Fair. It was attended by Secretary of Agriculture Herr W. Schwarz, Mayor Dr. P. Nevermann, and other dignitaries from northern Germany. The highlight of the week was a performance in front of sixteen hundred workers at the local Volkswagen factory who packed the largest hall in the area and whose thunderous ovation at the end of the concert prompted the band into four encores. The Ambassadors, conducted by Merle Gartrell, played two dances at the festival hall in Hamburg's Platen un Blomen Park sponsored by a local German American group. They also appeared on a regional TV program.

The Taunusaires were a Wiesbaden-area choral group composed of Americans and formed by Col. Dwight Dinsmore, one of Arnald's immediate superiors. They also appeared on a regional TV show; some footage of the show was used in a newsreel in theaters around Germany, Western Europe, and the United States. In addition to the six thousand attendees in Hamburg, it is estimated that some 8 million saw the Taunusaires in the newsreel and another 3 million saw and heard both groups on television. Local newspapers labeled them, "truly, the musical ambassadors of the US Air Force." During their just completed tour, the band played for an estimated ten thousand people who heard selections from *Porgy and Bess*, *My Fair Lady*, and *Oklahoma*. At the conclusion of the weeklong fair, Mayor Nevermann of Hamburg presented Arnald and Sergeant Gartrell citations for their "continuing efforts in furthering German-American relations in Northern Germany." Another notable performer at the Food Fair was a young puppeteer who caused quite a sensation at his Hamburg Town Hall performances. Jim Henson and Jerry Juhl entertained the crowds with their Muppet routines, including characters from their popular Washington, DC, show, *Sam and Friends*.

In December Arnald staged two shows that went to the heart of his tasked mission to improve relations with the local populous. The first was a seven-night run of the Broadway musical *Kismet*. It was performed at the American Community Center and involved the efforts of the Wiesbaden Little Theater, the Taunusaires (a twelve-piece string section composed of members of two German armed forces bands), and an eighteen-man component of the USAFE Band. Colonel Dinsmore played Haj the beggar in a cast that included Dee Tallman, Susan Hopkins, and Betty Christiansen, wives of band members and other personnel from the base, as well as local community.

Another truly international effort was their performance of Handel's *Messiah*. The sixty-voice chorus was made up of the Wiesbaden Officers' Wives' Club Vocalettes, the Taunusaires, the Hainerberg Chapel Choirs, and members of the community. The symphony orchestra, conducted by Captain Gabriel, was composed of members of the USAFE Band, the Bundeswehr Band from Siegburg, and the Hessian Police Band. The choral directors were Charles Neal and Virginia Dinsmore, Colonel Dinsmore's wife.

The spring of 1962 found Arnald wrapping up another successful year at Wiesbaden Air Force Base and at the same time anxious to pack up his family and return to the United States. His unprecedented service (he'd served longer than any previous commander and conductor at the base) was by any measure an overwhelming success. General Landon summoned him to his office and surprised him by asking Arnald to extend his tour by yet another year. Although he was anxious to satisfy the needs of the general and of the US Air Force, Arnald explained his concern about his family: we'd not left Europe since our arrival four years earlier, had little memory of home, and hadn't seen any of our extended family in as long. In fact Joanne, who'd been born in Wiesbaden, had never been to the United States. Because both Arnald's and Joan's parents now lived in South Florida (North Miami Beach and Boca Raton, respectively), the general offered to pay for round-trip tickets on Pan American World Airways (as opposed to military transport) to Miami to allow a visit and two-week vacation in return for the additional year. Arnald agreed and embarked on his final year in Europe with the same successful plan as the previous four.

Final Year in Germany

After returning from the States, the spring tour took the band across North Africa, ending at Wheelus Air Force Base in Tripoli. Although the men were housed in the relative safety within the confines of the high-security SAC Base, late one evening one of Arnald's trumpet players knocked on his door. Standing in his underwear, he informed Arnald that everything he owned—his instrument, clothes, personal items, *everything*—had been stolen. He was literally wearing the only items that remained. The final leg of the tour the following day took them to the Azores, and wearing Arnald's borrowed clothes, he continued with the band. The commanding officer of Lajes Air Force Base was Arnald's old friend Gen. Ben Lebailly, and when he heard what happened to the young airman, he took him to the BX (base exchange) and bought him new clothes, including a new uniform. The band played at several venues around the Azores in conjunction with their Armed Forces Day celebrations. May 13, 1962, was also not only Mother's Day, it was the day my brother Steve received his first communion; Arnald lamented in a postcard to Min: "I wish I were with him!"

Shortly after arriving home from the Azores, the band embarked on yet another trip to Turkey, performing four days of concerts in Istanbul before flying directly to the Maggio di Bari Festival to compete in the International Festival of Military Bands. The USAFE Band was to compete against bands from four other nations: Italy, West Germany, the Netherlands, and Egypt. Once again, Arnald planned to perform their A Musical Tour of the United States, but a medical emergency threatened their ability to stage the precision march. One of his trombone players had contracted sinusitis and had been left in Istanbul, unable to fly. Although only one of eight trombones in the section, due to the intricate maneuvers executed for the routine, every man was vital, and because the trombones occupied the front row, all the other musicians gauged his movement on them. That day, more than forty thousand spectators saw Captain Gabriel pick up a trombone and lead the group from the front row, marching alongside sixty-four of his fellow musicians as Bari's Victory Stadium erupted in unrestrained adoration.

As was the case each year, the summer leave in July provided a much-needed respite from the nearly constant travel and local concerts. Our summer adventure that year found us in Madrid, Spain, where we stayed at an American-owned hotel on the Av del

Generalissimo, one of the main boulevards. Sightseeing under clear-blue skies around the beautiful city was followed by a daily swim in the hotel pool and nightly by Spanish food at nearby restaurants and listening to live flamenco music. On Sunday we attended the bullfights. The centuries-old spectacle fascinated us, its brutality softened somewhat by the news that the beef was donated to a local orphanage. A week in the capital city was followed by a short drive to the ancient city of Toledo. It was a fascinating tour of medieval castles and cathedrals, and we were able to watch craftsmen hand-fashion knives and swords with a workmanship developed over the centuries. We ended what Arnald describes as "absolutely the best vacation we've ever had!" by spending several days in Barcelona. For the children, the Gothic architecture and museums were no match for the Mediterranean beach where we spent most of our time.

Back home in September, Arnald's schedule found him playing gigs close to Wiesbaden and late in the month to southern Germany through the Black Forest and the towns of Lahr, Freiberg, Badenweiler, and others. In November the Wiesbaden Little Theater joined once again with the Taunusaires and members of the USAFE Band and Wives' Club to stage Lerner and Loewe's *Paint Your Wagon*. The *Wiesbaden Post* raved about the show and gave high praise to female lead Lynn Strange as Jennifer Rumson; Dwight Dinsmore as Ben Rumsen, her father; and a group called the Fandangos, "seven eye-filling gals who present a wonderful can-can."

The first tour of 1963 would be Arnald's last major tour as commander and conductor of the USAFE Band. At the invitation of General Lebailly, they returned to the Azores to play thirteen performances in seven days with concerts all across the archipelago. The newspaper *Diario Insular* was enthusiastic in its praise of the group: "Under the vibrant and sure direction of maestro Captain Arnald Gabriel, this famous band ... captured the audience." From there, they played for three days in Lisbon (Arnald's first visit to the Portuguese capital), including a broadcast on a national television show before returning to Wiesbaden for an emotional farewell.

In March 1963 Arnald received a letter from his old boss and friend General Lebailly. Ben told him of efforts by the Personnel Office in

Michael A. Gabriel

Washington to assign Arnald to Chanute Air Force Base in Illinois. Chanute was a training base, and after his assignment in Germany, he felt that would have been a demotion of sorts. The general stepped in, changed the orders, and informed Arnald that he would assume command of the one hundred-man Air Force Academy Band in Colorado Springs, Colorado. It was an exciting opportunity to serve at the nation's newest service academy, having graduated their first class only four years prior.

The final concert on April 17 at Wiesbaden's premier venue, the Kurhaus, served as a farewell to the community Arnald had grown to love and an opportunity for the city to express her thanks as well. It was billed as the culmination of "a five year study of community relations expressed in the beautiful international language of music" and brought the capacity crowd to their feet many times at the conclusion of the concert. Arnald accepted a floral wreath on behalf of the entire band, and in an unprecedented gesture, he was given the city flag of Wiesbaden by the mayor.

In addition to the many local concerts and tours around Europe and the Middle East, the band was responsible for the frequent ceremonies held at USAFE headquarters at Wiesbaden Air Force Base. In late April 1963, Arnald assembled the band and reported for one, not knowing the purpose or honoree of the ceremony. Because he was soon to rotate to the States, he suspected that he was to be the recipient of some kind of award. The presiding officer at the ceremony was Commander of US Air Forces, Europe, Gen. Truman H. Landon, and after being summoned by the words: "Captain Gabriel, front and center," the adjutant began to read the citation for the Legion of Merit. It is the sixth-highest (second-highest peacetime) military decoration this nation may bestow and is primarily awarded to general officers and colonels. Additionally, medals, promotions, and other recognition in the military are usually given by one's immediate superior (in Arnald's case, a colonel). Captain Gabriel's citation read in part: "for exceptionally meritorious conduct in the performance of outstanding services and achievements ... and for improving international relations, through music, in twenty-four countries in Europe, North Africa, and the Middle East."

The Force of Destiny

In a way, this ceremony was a reunion of distinguished World War II vets; while Arnald and Lebailly were fighting in Europe, General Landon fought in the Pacific. In late 1941 Colonel Landon was commander of the Thirty-Eighth Reconnaissance Squadron in California and was leading the group to the Philippine Islands. They arrived at Hickam Field in the territory of Hawaii for a fuel stop on the morning of December 7 during the Japanese attack. Although unarmed and low on fuel, he safely landed his aircraft "through his skill, coolness, and daring under fire." For his bravery that day, he was awarded the Silver Star Citation.

The next couple of months had the family in full preparation for the move back to the United States. They sold Joan's VW, shipped the Borgward ahead, and finished the packing. As was the custom, a party was held by the USAFE Band for the departing leader and was capped by the traditional farewell playing a tearful rendition of "*Auf Wiedersehn*, Until We Meet Again."

Doc Severinsen and Arnald Gabriel

CHAPTER FOURTEEN

The Air Force Academy

The Gabriel family disembarked the military transport at Charleston Air Force Base, South Carolina, in early June 1963, picked up the Borgward from the ship, and drove to south Florida to visit with Joan's and Arnald's parents. After a short stay, the car was traded in for a new Rambler Classic 660 station wagon and the light-green family car was driven across the humid Deep South states of Alabama, Mississippi, and Texas without the benefit of air conditioning, arriving at the Air Force Academy in mid-June.

As is the case common to the arrival of any new leader, there is always some skepticism with regard to how the new guy will run things. More than just a little of that skepticism met the new captain as he reported for duty. The fact that he was as young as he was, claimed to have been in combat, and had been awarded two Bronze Star Medals and the Legion of Merit drew considerable attention. The information officer at the Academy, to satisfy his own questions, felt it necessary to write to the Records Section in St. Louis (the vast repository of all military personnel records) and verify Captain Gabriel's claims.

Since the cadets (students) were slated to arrive at the Academy in July, Arnald set to work with the staff and band members as soon as he arrived. One of the band's missions was to play for the noon formations where the cadets were marched from their dorm, Fairfield Hall, to the dining hall and back. It was a popular event, especially in the summer vacation season, and attracted as many as three thousand spectators who gathered above the formation level to watch the cadets' striking precision and to listen to the highly regarded band. Earlier that year, as a cost-saving measure, Washington, DC's, Air Force Drum and Bugle Corps was cut, and all their assets were transferred to the Academy. As part of the transfer, members of the DC Drum and Bugle Corps were offered transfers to one of two existing drum and bugle corps in the Air Force, one at the Air Force Academy in Colorado and the other at Lackland AFB, Texas.

The NCO in charge of the drum and bugle corps was Ricardo, Arnald's younger brother. Rick brought a rich history of drum and bugle corps experience with him to the position due to his years of playing in the Cortland Drum and Bugle Corps and the Syracuse Brigadiers when Arnald led them. In an effort to integrate the corps more fully into the Academy's musical programs, Arnald arranged several marches for the band and drum and bugle corps that were played at the weekly parades for the twenty-five hundred cadets.

As Arnald stepped into his role as commander and conductor of the band, he was joined by another familiar face. Capt. Frank Lockwood, his old Ithaca College classmate and the friend with whom he had driven to Washington, DC, from upstate New York and taken the Air Force bandleaders' exam with in the spring of 1951, was now the assistant conductor at the Academy.

The one hundred–man Air Force Academy Band was actually broken down into smaller component parts: a fifty-six-man concert band, a fifty-five-man marching band, an eighteen-man dance band, a forty-five-member drum and bugle corps, and a twenty-five-man Glee Club.[43] There was a monthly performance featuring the concert band at Arnold Hall (essentially, the student union) and regularly scheduled broadcasts over area radio stations. The marching band and drum and bugle corps participated in the Monday through Saturday noon formations and for halftime festivities at home football games at the newly christened Falcon Stadium. They had been nationally recognized for functions as diverse as Frontier Days in Cheyenne, Wyoming, the Cotton Bowl festivities in Dallas, Texas, and the Presidential Inauguration Parade in Washington, DC.

---

43 Obviously, the men played in more than one group.

The Force of Destiny

In early July, one of Arnald's first official duties was to play for former President Eisenhower, who visited the Air Force Academy to dedicate the golf course named in his honor. Just before he began his remarks, the old soldier turned to Arnald and said, "Captain, please give your band 'at ease.' I hated standing at attention when I was a cadet at West Point." After his speech, he proceeded to the first tee, set down a ball, and promptly sliced it into the spectators lining the fairway. "Don't print that," he ordered the assembled press corps. "I'm going to take a mulligan." His second shot that was rifled down the center of the fairway was the one shown in the news reports of the event.

In addition to the Monday through Saturday mealtime formation, rehearsals for upcoming events began immediately for a very full September schedule. The first two football games beginning in mid-September were home games, and the marching band was slated to play at halftime. For the fiftieth anniversary of the US Air Force silver wings (the wings worn by air force pilots) in 1963, the drum and bugle corps joined with the marching band to kick off the celebration with a concert at Falcon Field.

On September 22, the band played for the dedication ceremonies for the new chapel. The just-completed structure featured a unique design of seventeen aluminum, glass, and steel spires that soar 150 feet into the Colorado sky. Attending the dedication was Air Force Secretary Eugene Zuckert and Chief of Staff of the Air Force, Gen. Curtis LeMay. Although neither man could know, Arnald and General LeMay would meet again within the year under very different circumstances.

The first performance of the concert band under the new commander was held the following Sunday at Arnold Hall. The back-to-school theme was echoed throughout the concert with "Academic Festival" by Brahms, "Summer Memories," "School Days," and *Autumn Collage*, which included "Autumn Leaves," "September in the Rain," and "September Song." They also played a college medley "Halls of Ivy" and "The Stein Song" and a medley of service academy songs from West Point, the US Naval Academy, and the Air Force Academy. Each was arranged by the talented arranging staff, including Tech. Sgt. John

Caughman, Senior M.Sgt. Wes Adams, M.Sgt. Dale Chamberlin, M.Sgt. Dick Hubbard, and Capt. Frank Lockwood.

The following month, on November 2, the band was able to join the entire twenty-five hundred–man Cadet Wing and play at the Air Force-Army football game held at Soldier Field in Chicago. They played not only at halftime, but as the cadets marched from the train station on Dearborn Street to the Hilton Hotel and from there to the stadium. They also performed a concert prior to the game.

Later in the month at one of the noon formations as Arnald and the band waited for the cadets to leave the mess hall, the commanding general of the Air Force Academy, Maj. Gen. Robert Warren, approached him and informed him of the tragic shooting of Pres. John F. Kennedy in Dallas, Texas, that morning.[44] After the formation, he broke the news to the stunned band members who, despite being dismissed, milled about in disbelief for several minutes, shocked that their vibrant, young commander in chief and president had been assassinated.

Doc

Because television programming in Germany was sparse, or nonexistent, the family never owned a television; Arnald bought the family's first one after arriving in Colorado. One evening, while watching *The Tonight Show*, he noticed the extraordinary tone and range of the first trumpet player in *The Tonight Show* Orchestra. Arnald knew that the bandleader, Skitch Henderson (real name: Lyle Cedric), was a major in the Air Force Reserves and decided to call him. He was told that the talented young man was known as Doc Severinsen (real name: Carl). After talking to Skitch, Doc gave his permission for Arnald to call, and he was invited to play with the concert band at the Air Force Academy. Doc's first question was, "What is a concert band?" Doc was a largely self-taught musician who'd left home at age fifteen to play in the Ted Fio Rito Orchestra, a dance band, and had little knowledge of the type of music with which Arnald was involved. Doc's second question was: "What will we play?" Arnald chose a piece

---

44 JFK was shot at 12:30 p.m. Central time, 11:30 a.m. Mountain time.

The Force of Destiny

written by John Krance called "Dialogue for Trumpet and Band" and another called "The Hummel Trumpet Concerto." The meeting of the two dynamic, young virtuosos would be the beginning of a lifelong personal and professional relationship.

In spite of the work schedule, there was plenty of opportunity for recreation. Many weekends the family drove up into the Rocky Mountains to Farish Memorial USAF Recreation Area. The resort was maintained by the air force for use by its personnel, and the setting, at an elevation of higher than nine thousand feet, was spectacular. The days were spent horseback riding and the evenings in front of a crackling fireplace. The cost for the idyllic weekends for the family of six was twenty-five dollars per visit.

In December Arnald wrote to the board of directors of the Midwest Clinic and secured permission for the band to perform at the Midwest National Band Clinic held in Chicago. The prestigious event has been held each year since its inception in 1946 and exists to promote music education through performances by groups across the spectrum of instrumental music. Community bands, as well as high school, college, and military organizations perform jazz, orchestra, chamber, and band concerts to many thousands of music educators from around the world. The Air Force Academy Band was the first military academy band to appear, and the professional musicians garnered high acclaim for their performance.

The band had the distinction of presenting the Grand Opening Concert in the Grand Ballroom at the Sherman House, which was described as one of the highlights of the four-day event. At the conclusion of the band clinic, the organization presented Arnald with the Midwest National Band Clinic Medal of Honor, awarded for "an inspiring contribution to music education." The award had only been established the year before, and Arnald was one of its first recipients. Showcasing the talents and promoting the opportunities available in the air force was one of the stated goals Arnald was tasked with, and the band's attendance at the Midwest Clinic was another in a growing list of innovative concepts he would employ.

Back home at the Air Force Academy in the spring of 1964, Arnald bought an eighteen-foot Shasta travel trailer. It slept the six of us comfortably, and for summer vacation that year, the family set out first heading north to Wyoming then west into California, camping at preselected sites along the route. Although the trailer was quite an improvement over the two-room tent we'd camped in all over Europe, the stop in Los Altos allowed a respite from the trailer. The family stayed with old friends from Germany, Bill and Leah Fry. The trip continued south to Anaheim and a visit to Disneyland, then back east to Las Vegas, the Painted Desert, the Grand Canyon, and home to the Academy. The arrival back home was met with the news that Arnold had been chosen to take over the Air Force Band in Washington, DC. The choice assignment to head the premier band of the US Air Force in the nation's capital at such a young age, and at that point in his career, was a surprise, but a welcome one. He had vaulted over a number of other higher-ranking and more experienced men all vying for the coveted position. The only response the children could give when faced with leaving beautiful Colorado was: "Why?"

The new assignment would not become effective for a few more months, and there was much work left at the Academy. Doc Severinsen had enjoyed playing with the band so much that he'd expressed interest in returning for cadet graduation week. He played with the concert band again, but the highlight of the week was the Cadet Senior Ball. Arnold knew that Commander of Academic Affairs for the Academy Brig. Gen. Robert McDermott had attended the Latin School in Boston and played the trombone. He asked the general if he wanted to sit in with Doc and the dance band, the Falconaires, and he agreed. "I will never forget the look on the faces of the cadets watching their general and Doc jamming with the band!"

Arnold's success in the air force continued, and he was promoted to the rank of major just prior to leaving the Academy. He had been in the air force only twelve years, and at the age of thirty-eight, he was the youngest air force musician to attain the rank. He also knew that not only a great opportunity lay ahead, but one of the biggest challenges of his young career.

Major Gabriel, Doc Severinsen, and Chief M.Sgt. Floyd Werle

CHAPTER FIFTEEN

Bolling Air Force Base

Maj. Arnald D. Gabriel arrived to assume command of the United States Air Force Band on Bolling Air Force Base, Washington, DC, in June 1964. Although the band had been the preeminent musical organization in the air force and the coveted position was the top of his career ladder, Arnald found a skeleton group fighting for survival. The once-proud unit had been gutted from a high of about five hundred musicians and support staff to 177 demoralized and fearful souls. The Airmen of Note, the dance band, had been cut to fewer than twenty men and were folded into the ceremonial unit. The drum and bugle corps had been cut with all assets transferred to the Air Force Academy's Drum and Bugle Corps. The choral group known as the Singing Sergeants had been slashed from forty voices to twelve. A once-vibrant symphony orchestra out of which the Strolling Strings operated had just a few string players left. The remaining musical groups consisted of a small fifty-piece concert band, out of which a smaller Ceremonial Band was drawn for official functions such as funerals, awards ceremonies, etc. There was also a small pipe band (bagpipes and drums) that had been retained because, it was thought, they were a favorite of President Kennedy. Morale throughout the organization was at rock-bottom and determined to stave off further cuts, Arnald began to formulate a plan.

He reported to work to his old friend and former boss Eugene "Ben" LeBailly who had been promoted to the rank of major general and was now Director of Information for the Air Force and stationed

Michael A. Gabriel

at the Pentagon. In typical fashion, Ben got right to the point and asked Arnold what plans he had to restore the band to its former position as the premier military service band in Washington. The general prefaced the discussion with an analogy he knew the war veteran would understand: "Gabe, being in Washington is not unlike being in combat. The only difference is in combat, you always knew where the enemy was!"

Arnold was familiar with the reason for the devastating cuts in the budget and subsequent slashing of personnel. The former leader of the Air Force Band, Col. George S. Howard, had retired the previous August under mounting pressure due to alleged improprieties with regard to funds allocated during the band's national and international tours. Thirty-three charges and specifications were originally brought against him with six remaining during his court martial, and although found "not guilty, as charged," the sordid mess damaged the reputation of the proud professionals who remained in the organization—and so began their systematic dismantling. The man at the forefront of the movement to shrink the band was Chief of Staff of the Air Force, the legendary Gen. Curtis E. Lemay.

General Lemay was as tough, innovative, and polarizing a military man as any in history. During World War II he revolutionized the bombing missions of the new B-17s that were pressed into service with largely inexperienced crews, and leading by example, commanded many missions by flying the lead airplane. When he took over the Bomber Command in the Pacific later in the war, he eliminated a largely ineffectual campaign and instituted one that, arguably, won the war against Japan. He was the commanding officer on the island of Tinian when Lt. Col. Paul Tibbits took off in the *Enola Gay* carrying the world's first atomic bomb. After the war, it was under his command that humanitarian supplies were flown into Berlin, Germany, after the Soviet Union blockaded the city. The Berlin Airlift continued for eleven months as an average of five thousand pounds of supplies a day were delivered to sustain the grateful citizens of the isolated city. More recently, General LeMay had commanded the Strategic Air Command. He oversaw the modernization of the group, and owing to the development of long-range bombers and aerial refueling, he instituted the concept of aircraft that remained aloft around the clock. It was another revolutionary development wrought largely as a result of his tough, hard-nosed personality.

In the summer of 1964, Lemay was under pressure to cut budgets throughout the air force, and because of the fallout from the investigation of Colonel Howard, the band became an easy target. Lemay's intent was to shrink the group to a ceremonial band performing at funerals, award ceremonies, and other official functions in the Washington, DC, area, stripping the band of a much larger mission. Gone would be the band concerts locally and the national and international tours that brought music to enthusiastic patrons around the world.

Arnald was told to prepare a report that he would present directly to General Lemay. He spent weeks of intense research and study, pouring over reams of data from past operations and policies that governed the day-to-day running of the band, including past tours. The result was a flip-chart presentation that outlined his vision for the organization. It was, by any measure, a bold initiative that would not only reverse the reduction in staff, but also offer a number of innovative concepts designed to avoid the mistakes of the past while spurring unprecedented growth. Arnald previewed the proposal to Gen. LeBailly and Gen. John P. McConnell, Vice Chief of Staff, who both offered a few suggestions and subsequently granted their approval for the presentation.

Barely a month after assuming command of the US Air Force Band, Major Gabriel stood next to his paper flip-chart proposal facing Gen. Curt Lemay, Gen. Ben LeBailly, Gen. John McConnell, and the generals in charge of personnel, budget, and several other departments. "It was the most difficult and stressful twenty minutes of my life," Arnald says without hyperbole. It was clear that the work represented within those pages would either launch his career in the air force or end it.

Since Arnald's induction into the Air Force more than a decade earlier, he had always proudly donned the medals he'd won during the war. They were medals the army had awarded him: the Bronze Star Medal with oak leaf cluster, and atop those and his Air Force ribbons sat the Combat Infantryman's Badge that represented his sacrifices on the battlefield. As he snapped to attention in front of the roomful of US Air Force generals, General Lemay barked his first question: "Major, do you know that the Air Force discourages the wearing of army insignia?" Standing his ground, Arnald stiffened and boldly responded, "Yes, sir, I know that." An uncomfortable, momentary silence settled over the room before someone nodded for him to begin his presentation to a scowling Lemay.

Arnald outlined the sweeping changes he wanted for the band, beginning with a request to increase personnel from the current 177 to 225, an increase of almost a third. He could almost hear the officer in charge of personnel gulp. Arnald pushed on; he wanted the entry grade increased from E-5 staff sergeant to E-6 technical sergeant. It would result in raises for nearly every man currently on staff and increase starting pay for everyone they hired. The string orchestra was to be reinstated, and the choral group, the Singing Sergeants, numbers increased along with the Airmen of Note, the big band-style dance band. Arnald paused as each page was turned and asked for questions, and each time, General Lemay unceremoniously shook his head and continued to chomp on his ever-present cigar.

The most innovative concept Arnald proposed was the funding of the Air Force Band's domestic tours. To date, an admission was charged at each concert, and in each city, a sponsor was found to make up the shortfall between the gate receipts and actual costs. A civilian tour manager booked the band and coordinated the payments; it was a system rife with dubious accounting and open to abuse. It was under this system that charges were brought against his predecessor, Colonel Howard, that resulted in his forced retirement. Arnald suggested that all concerts be free to the public and travel be accomplished on government funds, paying government per diem, thereby establishing a clean and accountable system. To that end, the band would need four touring buses, two trucks, and a staff car. Obviously, a new department and additional staff would be required to operate and maintain the vehicles.

Arnald concluded his report and as General Lemay mulled over the request for a budget increase of several million (1964) dollars, he paused momentarily before brusquely asking, "Whose ass do I have if this doesn't work?"

Arnald's old friend, mentor, and boss, Ben LeBailly stepped forward and cut the palpable tension in the room by saying, "You can have mine, sir!"

All were dismissed, and as they filed out of the room, General Lemay called out, "Ben, I need to talk to you."

Arnald's wait outside the closed door seemed much longer than the few minutes it took. When General Lebailly exited the room, he told Arnald what Lemay had said: "Ben, I don't know what makes a good leader, but getting shot at can't hurt." The proposal was approved.

Arnald immediately got to work setting up meetings with the officers and support staff remaining at the band. He discovered not only a demoralized group of musicians, but a fractured command structure as well. Lt. Col. Sale "Bud" Tulin had been appointed commander of the band, because after the debacle resulting from Colonel Howard's investigation, it was thought that General Lemay lacked confidence in a musician to command the organization. Because Arnald was hired as commander *and* conductor, the Stamford, Connecticut, native returned to his former job in the information officer career field.

In 1964 the band's command and support staff consisted of the following: Maj. Arnald D. Gabriel, commander and conductor; Capt. Franklin J. Lockwood, associate conductor; Capt. Harry H. Meuser; Capt. Robert L. Landers, special assistant to the commander who was told to remain outside of the squadron until after the Howard investigation was complete; 1st Lt. John J. Osiecki, director of dance units; 1st Lt. David E. Elliott, OIC, support services; 2nd Lt. Theodore E. Wiltsie, director, Singing Sergeants; Chief Warrant Officer 4 Charles F. Kepner, director, Ceremonial Unit; Chief Warrant Officer 3 Robert J. Dunn, operations officer; Chief Warrant Officer 3 Edward G. Grace, administrative services officer; Senior M.Sgt. Robert A. Turner, NCOIC, Ceremonial Unit; M.Sgt. Stuart B. Seavey, first sergeant; and M.Sgt. Francis E. Cox, supply sergeant. Arnald would soon fire Ted Wiltsie and put Frank Lockwood as director of the Singing Sergeants. Capt. Harry Meuser, who had been assistant conductor under Colonel Howard, had been appointed conductor when Howard retired. Arnald reassigned

Captain Meuser and Lt. Col. Paul Weckesser, who was deputy director of the bands and music office, to the Bands Branch at the Pentagon and removed any guilt by association with Colonel Howard (they were innocent of any wrongdoing) and thus preserved their air force careers.[45]

Of Lt. Dave Elliot, Arnald would say, "He was a guy Bud Tulin brought in, and I didn't know what he did." A flurry of reassignments and restructuring occurred that not only streamlined the organization, but served tacit notice to those who remained that a dynamic, new era was at hand. Arnald began a series of staff meetings soliciting ideas from his sometimes skeptical administrators. He employed the simple technique of agreeing with those whose ideas fit his plan, while at the same time backing dissention that didn't. Through a deft hand, he drove the agenda, utilizing their suggestions, to build the vision he had.

Rebuilding the Air Force Band

One of the first changes Arnald made on the performance side was to increase the size of the Ceremonial Band. Their most important function was to ensure that US Air Force war veterans would receive full military honors during their burial services at Arlington National Cemetery. The cutbacks had reduced the number of musicians to a small unit, and Arnald immediately restored them to a full Ceremonial Band. The action was compelled by his own wartime experiences and long-ago memories of loss.

In the midst of all the necessary and exhausting administrative work, Arnald found solace in the music. The gentlemen[46] he had the privilege to conduct were, although a bit fearful of their future and not just a little worried about the new guy, consummate professionals.

---

45 It is interesting to note that Arnald was able to effect the transfers although one of the men outranked him and his command was not yet official; he merely assumed de facto head of the organization from the moment he arrived.
46 The musicians were all men at the time.

The Force of Destiny

However, the first rehearsal with their new conductor was as thorough as they'd experienced in their tenure with the band. In the past, in preparation for a performance, the previous conductors would do a read-through once or twice and felt the music was ready to perform. Arnald worked through each number, challenging every one of the musicians, but the bulk of the first session was devoted to Slavonic Rhapsody Number 1 by Carl Friedemann. He had chosen the popular piece for band because of its challenges in tempo, style, dynamics, and articulation. As he ended the first half of the rehearsal, the band broke out in applause. Arnald was humbled and surprised; up to that point, he wasn't sure how the men were taking his direction. As the applause tapered, he said honestly, "I hope you feel that way a year from now!"

Senior M.Sgt. Al Bader played first-chair alto saxophone in the band and had also been an instructor at the Bandsmen School at the base. The school trained air force musicians in performance, arranging, conducting, and other areas, and Senior M.Sgt. Bader had taught music theory and harmony. (The school was closed as a result of the downsizing the prior year.) Bader says, "I'll never forget that first rehearsal ... [he] really whipped us into shape." Sergeant Bader's feelings, surprisingly, weren't universal. During their first break, the men mustered back to a storage room where Oscar Ghebelian had set up a coffee shop. As Sergeant Bader entered the room, he expected joy at the results of their first actual rehearsal. Instead, he found dead silence as the men glumly stood around listening to a lone voice bemoaning what was sure to be their fate. Principal horn player Joe Freni had always been the mother hen of the group and took it upon himself to look out for the group's welfare. Because of his Italian heritage, he claimed he was familiar with the way "they" work: "He'll fire all of us and bring in his own people!" Joe ranted. Sergeant Bader finally interrupted and attempted to impose a little reason on the group. "Look," he began, "this is the first time anyone has ever rehearsed this US Air Force Band and made it sound decent within one hour. I say let's give him a chance." The men largely agreed, and it wasn't long before they had further reason to believe their luck had changed for the better.

Although the wheels of a massive bureaucracy like the Pentagon turn slowly, with the backing of Secretary of the Air Force General Lemay, Arnold was able to institute some of his proposals with surprising quickness. The entry grade of the bandsmen was one of the first to take effect. In one afternoon, Arnold promoted seventy-seven musicians from an E-5 and E-6 to an E-6 and E-7 rank.[47] The result was a significant pay raise, and the day it was announced, the jubilant men streamed across the street to the NCO Club where the afternoon celebration stretched into the evening. Arnold spent a large part of that evening fielding calls from concerned wives as to the whereabouts of their husbands.

Normally, the air force requires NCOs[48] to attend training academies as a prerequisite for promotion. Arnold resisted the mandate for those under his command by successfully arguing that he could teach them to be leaders. The effort not only allowed him to mold the men as he saw fit, but it strengthened morale and served to foster loyalty throughout his organization. Over the next few years, each of the other service bands in Washington, DC, raised their entry-level pay to match Arnold's initiative.

The staff promotions weren't limited to the enlisted personnel either. Arnold had unprecedented authority to commission those from the NCO ranks for leadership roles—that is, to promote enlisted to the officer corps. It removed the need for the men to meet a promotion board and have their fate decided by committee.

Senior M.Sgt. Al Bader was called into the new commander's office one day, and because he hadn't been offered a raise yet and was told to close the door behind him, he was sure his days with the Air Force Band were over. Arnold began with, "I suppose you were wondering why you did not get promoted." As Sergeant Bader nodded yes, Arnold shocked the principal saxophone player by offering him not only a commission as a captain, but the position as assistant conductor of the band. Sergeant Bader was as qualified and accomplished as any under his command. He had seen combat in the Pacific Theater during World

---

47 That is, from staff sergeant to technical sergeant and technical sergeant to master sergeant.

48 "Noncommissioned Officers" are enlisted personnel in leadership roles.

War II as an infantryman with the Fortieth Infantry at Guadalcanal, New Britain, and the assault landing at Luzon in the Philippines. After returning home to St. Louis and earning his bachelor degree in music, he was recalled to the army and served in Korea until his discharge in 1951. He was a knowledgeable and well-liked teacher at the Bandsman School, and Arnald's choice to place him in the leadership position was obvious to all except the modest man standing before him. The band's information director, Chief M.Sgt. Harry Gleeson remembers, "Al is a far better musician than he will ever let on ... and was one of the main forces behind the US Air Force Band reaching such astounding musical heights under Arnald Gabriel." Al Bader would retire from the Air Force as a major in 1976.

Over the next decade, Arnald would recommend incoming officers, currently tech sergeants at OTS, be commissioned to first lieutenant, including Bruce Gilkes, whom he placed in charge of the Singing Sergeants, and Lowell Graham, who took over leadership of the Strolling Strings. Lieutenant Gilkes enlisted in the Air Force Band as a euphonium player, but Arnald knew of his vocal background and training at the prestigious Eastman School of Music. In addition to doubling the size of the Singing Sergeants choral group from twelve to twenty-four, Arnald also mandated that each would be full-time singers. Arnald was mining the talents of his high-caliber musicians in his quest to build the organization into world-class status.

Arnald also had the unprecedented authority to recruit musicians from other military bands around the country. This is a practice long since abandoned; now, auditions are held in person, veiled behind a curtain and before a panel of judges to preclude any charge of discrimination or bias. While stationed at the Air Force Academy, Arnald had an opportunity to guest conduct the NORAD Band under the direction of Lt. Col. Mark Azzolina.[49] The big band–style group was composed of military musicians from Canada and the United

---

49 Lieutenant Colonel Azzolina was not only a renowned jazz percussionist and vocalist and founder of the NORAD Band, but he came from a talented musical family. His brother Nick was the conductor of the band at nearby Ramstein Air Force Base when Arnald was in Wiesbaden, and their father was also an Air Force Band conductor.

States and featured a saxophone soloist named Jimmy Scott. When Arnald learned of his own transfer to Washington, DC, he offered "Scotty" a position with the premier Air Force Band, and he accepted. The otherwise unremarkable inclusion of the virtuoso musician might go unnoticed except that Scotty would become the first black instrumentalist in any of the Washington-area service bands. It is interesting to note that in an era of rising racial tensions, forced integration (the Civil Rights Act of 1964 was signed in July, the month after Arnald arrived in Washington), and a strengthening call to end segregation, his acceptance in the band was based solely on his ability to play music. Scotty's roommate on tours, Jim Murphy, became a close, lifelong friend and was at his bedside when he passed away.

The first Air Force Band concert conducted by Major Gabriel was part of a summer concert series held on Tuesdays at the US Capitol building in Washington. The patrons sat outside on the east-side steps of the building and listened to the program of music chosen and constructed by a formula employed by Arnald for nearly all his concerts. He would typically start with a march or overture (at this concert, they started with "Washington Greys March" and "Procession of the Nobles") followed by a soloist from the band ("Blue Bells of Scotland" featuring virtuoso trombonist Larry Wiehe). He would then move to a lighter or more contemporary piece, and on that day he followed with "Moon River," "Amparito Roca," "Irish Tune from County Derry," and "El Relicario." The first half ended with a barn burner—in this case, the focus of most of that first rehearsal: Slavonic Rhapsody Number 1. The second half of the concert featured the Singing Sergeants in a George M. Cohan medley. Arnald would end with a patriotic piece or a march; the first concert showcased both "Armed Forces Medley" and "Americans We March" as encores.

In addition to the Tuesday night performances at the Capitol steps, the band performed Fridays on a stage built on a barge moored at the Watergate on the Potomac River. The name for this venue was linked to the Water Steps or Water Gate, a set of ceremonial stairs west of the Lincoln Memorial that lead down to the Potomac. The steps had been originally planned as a ceremonial gateway to the city and an official reception area for dignitaries arriving in Washington, DC, via water taxi from Virginia, though they never served this function. Instead, beginning in 1935, the steps faced a floating performance stage on the Potomac River on which open-air concerts were held. Up to twelve thousand people would sit on the steps, on surrounding grassy areas, and on boats anchored nearby to listen to military bands and other performing groups. Both venues offered free concerts and were held largely for the benefit of the throngs of tourists that flock to the nation's capital each year.

These were long, stressful days dealing with a myriad of administrative details and rehearsals, and in the midst of it all, Arnald and Joan needed to find a place to live. For the first time since leaving Langley Air Force Base in 1958, they decided to find housing off-base. Bolling Air Force Base is located on the east shore of the Potomac River in southeast Washington, DC, and most who were stationed there lived in Maryland. Until recently, travel to Virginia required crossing two bridges (across the Anacostia and Potomac rivers) and making a trip through downtown Washington. No bridges existed between Maryland and Virginia. A couple of years prior to the family's arrival, construction of a new Circumferential Highway (as it was first called) had begun, which ringed the District and built the Woodrow Wilson Bridge as its southern crossing of the Potomac. Now, travel from Bolling to the Old Dominion was a short ten minutes.

We had driven from Colorado to the Washington area hauling our nineteen-foot Shasta travel trailer, and with a nod to expediency, it would now serve as our cramped home for that first summer. Arnald had located a small trailer park on Route 1 just south of the new Washington Beltway in Alexandria through a colleague with whom he had served at the Air Force Academy and who had preceded us to Washington. With all the trailer's louvered windows open in an attempt to provide some ventilation during the hot, muggy Virginia summer (once again, no air conditioning) and near the noisy highway, it is a wonder how any restful sleep was possible with a family of six in much less than two hundred square feet of living space.

Arnald and Joan quickly found a new subdivision about a mile from George Washington's Mt. Vernon Estate, worked with the builder to choose a model, and began construction. We would fill the five-bedroom home very quickly; Joan was pregnant again, and the new arrival was due in December. At the end of August, we moved to a duplex in a quiet, working-class neighborhood on Edgewater Drive in the Franconia area of Fairfax County, Virginia, which we rented on a month-to-month basis. Joan drove us to our new elementary school each morning until October when we moved to our new home. Five months after arriving in the area, we were finally settled.

Washington, DC, Concerts

Historically, the Air Force Band embarked on a tour in the fall and spring, but Arnald's successful efforts to restore the devastating budget cuts came too late to plan one for the fall of 1964. Instead, he scheduled a series of concerts at Departmental Auditorium (now called Andrew W. Mellon Auditorium) on Constitution Avenue that ran from mid-October to the week before Christmas. Attendance at the Friday night performances gradually increased at the relatively small (750-seat) venue as local patrons rediscovered the resurgent group.

In addition to several concerts in the Washington area through the holiday season, late December also saw the arrival of the newest member of the Gabriel family. My brother Christopher Arnald was born on Christmas Day, the perfect gift to Joan, who celebrated her thirty-third birthday that day. It would be the first of many memorable Christmases we would have in our home on Battersea Lane.

Arnald's analysis of the band's performing schedule indicated a gap of several months when they were idle. In addition to the planned spring and fall tours (the money and logistical support had not yet arrived but was promised by the fall of 1965) and the summer concerts at Watergate and the Capitol, he added a series of Sunday afternoon pops concerts at the Departmental Auditorium in February and March. The concerts featured soloists from the band and notable musicians from the Washington area.

The featured soloist on the March 22d performance is yet another example of the top-flight caliber of musician Arnald found in the band when he arrived. M.Sgt. Lawrence Wiehe Jr. spent twelve years as a trombonist with the Navy Band before joining the Air Force Band the year before Arnald's arrival. He was recognized as not only the finest trombone player in the military, but probably in the world. Arnald first noticed the extraordinary talent in those early rehearsals, but after that first concert performance at the Capitol steps, he knew he wanted to continue to feature Sergeant Wiehe as a soloist. Arnald asked the band's chief composer and arranger, Senior M.Sgt. Floyd Werle to write a piece of music that would cover every genre of trombone music and that would challenge Larry and showcase his talents. The result that he debuted that Sunday was a medley titled *Trombone Chronology*. It begins with a Bach fugue (although Bach never wrote for the trombone) and covers Dixieland, big band jazz (Tommy Dorsey's "I'm Gettin' Sentimental over You"), variations on a theme à la Arthur Prior, and a Beatles' tune and includes narration to describe each section. The selection is about twenty minutes long, technically demanding, and a perfect vehicle for the amazing virtuoso.

Despite his crushing work schedule reorganizing, growing the organization, and performing the busy concert schedule, Arnald managed to find time for outside work. He was invited to guest conduct the Pennsylvania Music Educators Association (PMEA) Band Festival in Waterford, Pennsylvania, in the spring of 1965. Bob MacCubbin was Director of Bands for the Fort LeBoeuf School System in the small western Pennsylvania town and had seen Arnald conduct the Air Force Academy Band at the Midwestern Band Clinic. The band consisted of the best high school musicians in the state, and the music festival allowed the young instrumentalists the opportunity to perform under the country's best conductors. This would be the first of more than one thousand guest conducting jobs with high school and college bands, other military groups, community organizations, symphony orchestras, and international bands from around the world that Arnald would lead in the coming years. The jobs not only satisfied his desire to teach but expanded his own musical growth by allowing him to work with a wide variety of music and musicians.

Seventeen-year-old Judith Baker, a senior from Lockhaven, Pennsylvania, remembers the young air force major nearly fifty years after the festival. "He was personable and inspired us to do our best.

On the podium he never looked at a score and had *everything* in his head for the rehearsals and the performance." In stark contrast, the guest conductor the prior year was from another Washington-area service band and "had bodyguards that kept the students away from him ... no one could talk to him." Judy remembers the speech Arnald gave at the festival banquet where he emphasized the value of music and exhorted the students to "'be the best you can in everything you do.' He pushed us to a higher level of musicianship than any of us had ever been." He also invited them to visit Washington, DC, that summer to hear the Air Force Band, and after relentless begging, Judy's parents acquiesced. Judy and her parents attended one of the Friday night concerts at the Watergate, and despite the demands on his attention after the performance, Arnald took a moment to say hello to the young horn player from Lockhaven. "I have never forgotten that kindness," Judy says simply. "He is the reason I became a band director." Judy (Baker) Shellenberger spent more than thirty years as a music teacher and is the manager of the Repasz Band in Williamsport, Pennsylvania; it is the oldest nonmilitary band in continuous existence in the United States.

In January 1965 in Pres. Lyndon Johnson's State of the Union address to a joint session of Congress, he announced that he would form a White House Conference on Natural Beauty whose goal would be to improve and protect the environment of the United States. The massive initiative proposed to establish more parks, seashores, and open spaces "as a green legacy for tomorrow." In conjunction with the huge undertaking, the Air Force Band was chosen over the other service bands to begin a series called America the Beautiful concerts.

The first concert was slated to be played on May 24 at a venue the band used for their summer concert series, the Watergate barge on the Potomac River. To kick off the summer concert season, the White House was able to secure the help of one of Hollywood's most popular and distinguished actors. Edward G. Robinson was booked to read a narration of Aaron Copland's "Lincoln Portrait," the stirring tribute to our sixteenth president. Because of the high-profile nature of the concert (Lady Bird Johnson was going to be there), the US Secret Service decided to inspect the barge to ensure the safety of the musicians and their celebrity guest. It was discovered that the barge was not only unseaworthy, but it had actually settled into the mud in the shallow east shore of the Potomac River. A hasty rescheduling had the concert relocate to the Carter Baron Amphitheater about six miles away in Rock Creek Park. There was no time to reprint to accommodate the last-minute change, so programs from the concert show the Watergate as its venue.

As a nod to the concert's theme, it was, unabashedly, an all-American selection of music. They played *American Overture for Band* by Joseph Jenkins, Carmen Dragon's "America the Beautiful," Morton Gould's *American Salute*, and "Americans We," a march by Henry Fillmore. The Singing Sergeants sang the Floyd Werle medley titled *A Musical Tour of the United States*, and the concert ended with a rousing rendition of Sousa's "The Stars and Stripes Forever." Edward G. Robinson's narration of "Lincoln Portrait" was received with wild enthusiasm by the overflow crowd, and through it all, the veteran actor fell in love with the Air Force Band and its artistry.

He was not only a highly regarded actor with forty Broadway plays and more than eighty motion pictures to his credit, Eddie (as he insisted Arnald call him) was one of the best-known art collectors in America. He was a true patron of the arts and a warm and humble man. At one of the rehearsals prior to the concert, he learned that the band was scheduled to play at five venues in the Los Angeles area for their upcoming fall tour (he lived in Beverly Hills) and asked to be included. The concertmaster of the band, Russ Mitchell, told him that the Air Force is only allowed to pay sixteen dollars per diem, and leaping at the chance, Mr. Robinson said, "I'll take it!" He participated in each of the concerts, and after the tour, they sent him a check for eighty dollars in compensation for his six appearances. The check was never cashed. Over the years, Arnald and Eddie became close friends, and during one of the many dinners at his home in Los Angeles, Eddie showed Arnald the check. He'd had it framed and proudly hung it on his wall. Of his appearances with the Air Force Band, he said, "In my long and extensive career, nothing I have ever done or been associated with has given me such great pleasure, pride, and joy."

National Tours

The resumption of the twice-a-week summer concert series marked the end of Arnald's first year in the nation's capital. He'd successfully reversed the shrinking of the Air Force Band and, more importantly, increased morale. Their growth, however, was slower than Arnald had hoped. Although he'd been able to restore the Airmen of Note, he was still fighting for the funds that would allow the dance band to tour. He was certain that the legacy of Maj. Glenn Miller's music would be a big draw around the country, and hoping to prove the concept and the value of touring, the concert band and the Singing Sergeants set off on their first national tour in several years.

The fall tour of 1965 offered Arnald yet another opportunity to innovate. Previously, the band had taken just one program of music on the road with them to be played at each matinee and evening performance. Arnald changed that programing philosophy by creating two matinee programs that alternated each day and two evening programs that alternated. The change freed the musicians from the monotony of playing the same music twice a day for three weeks and kept the performances fresh. The one exception was Sgt. Floyd Werle's *Trombone Chronology* performed by Sgt. Larry Wiehe. Sergeant Wiehe played the challenging and popular piece at every evening concert to standing ovations. It is truly a tribute to his professionalism, talent, and stamina that he performed the difficult piece each night on tour through the fall tour of 1967.

The tour began on October 15 in Salt Lake City, Utah, and continued through Idaho, Washington, Oregon, Northern California, and finally, Southern California. They crammed thirty-five performances into twenty-three days and played to more than seventy-seven thousand people in venues whose capacity rarely exceeded three thousand. As promised, Edward G. Robinson joined the tour for the six concerts in the Los Angeles area, and with one exception (a matinee), attendance *exceeded* the seating capacity of the concert halls. Another matinee in downtown LA's MacArthur Park, with a stated capacity of fourteen hundred, was attended by twenty-five hundred music lovers.

The Force of Destiny

The final concert on November 7 in San Diego's Community Concourse Civic Theater was typical of the successful trip. An SRO crowd of thirty-eight hundred packed into the thirty-five hundred-seat hall and were treated to the overture from *Nabucco* by Verdi, *Robinson's Grand Entry March* by Karl L. King, virtuoso Larry Wiehe performing his now signature *Trombone Chronology*, *Swan Lake* by Tchaikovsky, *Incantation and Dance* by James Barnes Chance, and Respighi's *Pines of the Appian Way*. After the intermission, *March of the Steel Men* by Charles Belsterling, "Intermezzo" from *Vanessa* by Samuel Barber, and "Song of the Golden Calf" from *Faust* by Charles Gounod all led to Sergeant Werle's *West Side Story* medley performed by the band and the Singing Sergeants. "America the Beautiful" brought the crowd to their feet and "The Stars and Stripes Forever" and "Armed Forces Medley" served as encores.

The exhausted men returned to Bolling Air Force Base to resume their duties and played at various concerts and ceremonies over the holiday season in the Washington, DC, area. Toward the end of the month, the Ceremonial Band garnered special recognition from Gen. J. P. McConnell, who was by then Chief of Staff of the Air Force. The Ceremonial Band is a stripped-down version of the concert band whose function it is to play at award ceremonies, for visiting dignitaries, and on this particular day, a special military funeral for a general officer. The letter read, in part, "the Air Force Band merit special commendation for their flawless performance." Not surprisingly, the renewed unit pride and high morale was naturally manifest in the high-quality music they were performing.

STUDENT ARTIST SERIES

As the winter/spring concert series at Departmental Auditorium neared, Arnald decided to enhance the pops concerts with yet another innovative concept. In an effort to directly contribute to music education in the Washington metropolitan area, he decided to feature an outstanding student musician as a soloist at each concert. Arnald was inspired by the popularity of past celebrity guests like Edward G.

Robinson and Doc Severinsen and others with whom he'd performed in Europe. The inclusion of the students, he felt, would spur interest in music education and perhaps help to span the widening generation gap that was very much a part of the turbulent decade of the 1960s.

He called it the Student Artist Series and launched the series within a series on February 20 with a talented French horn player named Errol Floyd from the University of Maryland. The mature twenty-six-year-old junior had originally spent three years at the school as an electrical engineer major before his interest in music had him join the Army Band. Following his discharge three years later, he reenrolled in the U of M as a music major. His impressive performance of Second Horn Concerto, First Movement by Mozart had the near capacity crowd on their feet at its conclusion.

The following week, a seventeen-year-old clarinet soloist named Richard Harman, who was a senior from Thomas Jefferson High School in Fairfax County, Virginia, played *Rigoletto* by Giuseppe Verdi. Week three was an ambitious effort that was rewarded with the first overflow audience of the season. A trio of musicians from Oxon Hill High School in Maryland shared the billing with the popular radio morning duo of Frank Harden and Jackson Weaver. Lynn Rimmer and Robin Cottfried, both on flute, and Mark Bader, clarinet, performed Concerto Grosso for Two Flutes and Clarinet by Handel. If the clarinet player's name sounds familiar, it's because his father, Capt. Al Bader, was principle saxophone and assistant conductor of the Air Force Band.

The Harden and Weaver Show was at the top of the ratings for morning drive-time radio on Washington's WMAL for nearly thirty years and was number one in the Washington Metro market when asked to join the Air Force Band on Sunday March 6, 1966. Their six-day-a-week show featured several offbeat characters brought to life by Weaver and an inventive brand of comedy that had most of the DC listening public glued to their radios. Also, their considerable influence was a force that supported many charitable and humanitarian causes in the area. That day they narrated *The Man Who Invented Music* by the American composer Don Gillis and provided exposure for the band previously unheard of. The clever piece is a story about grandpa telling Wendy a bedtime story about how he invented music. Throughout the rehearsals and even during the performance, Frank Harden and Jackson Weaver strayed from the printed script in a hilarious rendition that had both the audience and the band in stitches.

The following week featured Concerto for Clarinet performed by Melissa Carr, a senior from Bethesda-Chevy Chase High School in Maryland, and the final two concerts of the series saw Katy Klietz, from Wakefield High School in Virginia, perform Concerto for Flute and Carl Metz, from Hammond High in Virginia, play Concerto for Saxophone in E Flat. By any measure, the Sunday pops concerts featuring the outstanding high school students was a resounding success. They were filling the small performance hall and generating an exciting buzz not only in the Washington, DC, area, but around the country.

Only a few short weeks separated the last concert from the beginning of the Air Force Band's spring tour but sandwiched between the two was the Mid-East Instrumental Music Conference in Pittsburgh on April 2. Arnald was aware that world-renowned tuba virtuoso Harvey Philips[50] would also be there and asked Chief Arranger Floyd Werle to compose "a short encore piece" that would feature Harvey on tuba, Larry Wiehe on trombone, and a trumpet part that would eventually be played by Doc Severinsen. The result from the prolific composer was a three-movement masterpiece titled Concertino for Three Brass that he completed only twelve days prior to the concert. It was debuted at the Saturday night performance with M.Sgt. John Maiocco on trumpet, and its acceptance in front of hundreds of musicians would help to establish it as a signature piece of music for the Air Force Band.

Ten days later, the band boarded their newly acquired buses for a twenty-four-day tour that included forty-six concerts throughout Pennsylvania, New York, Massachusetts, New Hampshire, Rhode Island, Connecticut, and New Jersey. One of their first stops was in Binghamton, New York, and Arnald's hometown of Cortland. The matinee and evening performances were sold-out affairs as the

---

[50] Among his many accomplishments, Harvey Philips was inducted into the American Classical Music Hall of Fame, the only wind instrument player to have received the high honor.

citizens turned out to celebrate the return of its native son. Further, the week was declared Air Force Band Week by Mayor Morris Noss and the day of the concerts Major Arnald Gabriel Day as they reveled in unabashed pride proclaiming, "that April 25 ... be set aside and designated as Major Gabriel Day so that we may all be reminded of his wonderful accomplishment in the field of music and our pride in him as a member of this community."

Arnald's selection of music for the evening concert was typical for the tour: each concert began with the national anthem and followed with "Festive Overture" by Shostakovich, "Washington Greys March," *Trombone Chronology*, and Concertino for Band. Just prior to intermission they played "Swan Lake Waltz" and "Pines of the Appian Way" by Respighi. The second half featured the Singing Sergeants performing "Sin Tu Amor" and a medley of songs from the popular *West Side Story*.

The concerts on this tour were remarkable for their unmistakably patriotic flavor. In a time of increasing social turbulence driven by the drumbeats of a strengthening antiwar movement and attendant enmity for the military, the performances' most enthusiastically received numbers were the ones that celebrated America. The final selection for the evening was a stirring Singing Sergeants rendition of "This Is My Country" by Don Raye and Al Jacobs as arranged for chorus by Sgt. Robert Walters of the Air Force Band. It began, in dramatic fashion, without introduction. From the snare drum intro to the powerful bass voice of Sgt. Chuck Kuliga ending with: "this is my country, to have and to hold," the audience would leap to their feet as one and erupt in full voice with cheers and shouts of *"Encore!"* while simultaneously wiping tear-streaked faces. Encores of "Armed Forces Medley" and "The Stars and Stripes Forever" did nothing to calm the enthusiastic patrons.

Soaring Popularity

The exhausting days of travel and concert performance on tour had little letup once Arnald returned to Bolling Air Force Base. The increased popularity of all the units (the Airmen of Note embarked on their first tour in several years that spring too) caused an equal increase in Arnald's workload. Their schedule was far from routine. The Ceremonial Band might get as little as forty-eight hours' notice of an early-morning funeral or award ceremony that strained logistics for an already scheduled afternoon or evening concert and made for some very long workdays. Twice-a-year tours and weekend and evening performances strained family life because, as Major Gabriel describes it, "We work when other people play." When asked by the Air Force publication *The Airman* how he managed the demands placed on him he answered with a broad smile, "I've never worked so hard in my life."

Arnald's days began early and ended late, often working through lunch. He attended to the endless details relating to upcoming concert series and tours for the concert band, string orchestra, pipe band, Singing Sergeants, and Airmen of Note. He conducted interviews and attended auditions intent on hiring the best musicians in the country. In the midst of the staggering workload, in June Arnald found time to redesign the uniforms the men donned.

Arnald felt the Air Force "blues" was too informal a uniform when playing ceremonial functions such as funerals, presidential parades, and other patriotic events. Working with his staff and the Uniform Board at the Pentagon, Arnald chose the deep-blue aquamarine from the Air Force flag for the uniform jacket and sky-blue pants with a silver-trimmed stripe down the seam. He also proposed a leatherneck rather than a tie because the stiff high collar presented a cleaner look. The board held a discussion about whether or not to wear stripes depicting rank. Because Arnald had raised the entry grade to E-6 technical sergeant, one board member worried that other Air Force enlisted men might be envious of the five chevrons each bandsman wore. Gen. J. P. McConnell, the presiding officer on the board, put to rest concern about those who might be jealous with a dismissive, "Then let 'em learn to toot a goddamn horn!" They ultimately decided to leave the sergeants' stripes off the uniform sleeve, and the end result was a sharp, professional image that further bolstered the unit's pride.

Applications to join the elite organization had skyrocketed in the past year, and only one out of seventy-five candidates who applied was accepted. It is an organization unique in the military. Recruits to most other career fields required Air Force training in their specialties; bandsmen came highly trained, and most had college degrees. Additionally, about 35 percent of the men continued their musical education at their own expense. Many of the men wore two hats by taking on a second job within the organization. One of the vocalists ran the Protocol and Public Information Office, and musicians drove the two new trucks that transported the instruments and equipment to appearances.

Over the past year, accolade-filled letters poured into headquarters at Bolling Air Force Base, and their numbers surged following the spring tour. One Air Force Reservist wrote, "Such concerts do much to strengthen popular support for the military in general and the Air Force in particular." That one comment encapsulated the mission of the band and validated their work. Arnald's OER (report card), written by his immediate superior, Colonel Lemon, in June further validated the effort:

> Major Gabriel has continued to perform, during the past year, in an outstanding manner. As Director of the US Air Force Band, he has no peer. The band's performances have been played to Standing Room Only audiences in all their local performances, and drew over 200,000 enthusiastic listeners on two extensive United States tours. As commander, he has exhibited outstanding leadership qualities. Morale, retention rates, and administration have phenomenally improved to the point where the band is now the best unit in the command. I recommend that Major Gabriel be promoted to lieutenant colonel at the earliest opportunity.

The Force of Destiny

An addendum on the same OER stated: "I strongly recommend he be promoted to lieutenant colonel *now*" (author's emphasis). It was signed by Maj. Gen. Rollen H. Anthis of Headquarters Command, USAF.

Arnald pioneered the use of recordings by military bands, and after success in Europe, he decided to continue to expand the idea in Washington, DC. During his leadership with the USAFE Band in Wiesbaden, Arnald wanted to recognize the great support he was receiving from his commanding officer, Gen. Truman H. Landon. Arnald learned that although Department of Defense funds were in short supply, he could request funding from the General Services Administration (GSA). President Truman had combined a half dozen agencies into one federal agency "tasked with administering supplies and providing workplaces for federal employees."

The discovery of the newfound funding source allowed Arnald to visit the Philips Recording Company in Amsterdam, Holland, where he brokered a deal to record an album called *American Salute*. The band recorded works by Morton Gould and other patriotic tunes, including "The Stars and Stripes Forever." The back of the album cover featured a picture of General Landon standing at salute above a caption reading: "Saluting our European Friends." It was a relatively inexpensive and highly effective piece of PR. The gift, given to a visiting dignitary or other VIP, allowed a piece of America and her music to be enjoyed and spread across the continent. By distributing the album to radio stations, the music was made available to millions who might never have had an opportunity to hear the US Air Forces Europe Band.

The first recording with the concert band in Washington, DC, was titled *The United States Air Force Band: A Symphony in the Sky*. The albums were sent to recruiters, university and high school groups, and radio stations and were tremendous recruiting and PR tools. Arnald expanded the concept and made recordings with the other groups; the Airmen of Note chose recordings from *Serenade in Blue* and *Music in the Air*, two radio programs produced by the Air Force, and included them in an album called *The Surprising Sounds of the Airmen of Note*. Just as an *American Salute* did in Europe, the albums were well received and immeasurably helped to increase the band's popularity.

Each year, Arnald and his staff compiled a worksheet that attempted to lay out a plan for each of the band's units for the following year. The twentieth anniversary of the Air Force and the twenty-fifth of the Air Force Band would occur in 1967, and a schedule was formulated that would celebrate the events, the highlight being a world tour by the concert band and Singing Sergeants. It would be the first by any major musical organization and would travel to twenty-five countries in twenty-nine days. Other plans included several separate domestic tours that, combined, would blanket the country and included national network broadcasts featuring celebrity guests. These worksheets were, however, little more than a wish list and were subject to the scrutiny of and modification by the Pentagon. Although much of their plan would be approved, the world tour was deemed overly ambitious and lengthy and was pared down considerably.

The summer concert series of 1966 resumed at the Watergate concert site and the Capitol steps but with increased attendance. In August the concert band was invited to play for the American School Band Directors Association (ASBDA) Convention in Milwaukee. The organization's stated goal is "to promote the concert band as the focus of an educational curriculum which teaches music as artistic expression." It was a unique opportunity to meet music educators from across the country, and the trip allowed Arnald to strengthen his commitment to music education by showcasing his approach to concert band music. The discerning audience was treated to a sparkling performance by the Air Force Band led by their enthusiastic, young conductor. The highlight of the concert was Chief M.Sgt. Floyd Werle's Concertino for Three Brass featuring Larry Wiehe on trombone, Senior M.Sgt. Glenn Orton on tuba, and the trumpet player for whom the piece was written, the incomparable Doc Severinsen.

The convention was also memorable to Arnald for having the opportunity to meet fellow attendee Don Gillis. The prolific American composer, teacher, author, and producer was particularly impressed with the air force major, saying some years later, "We as composers are fortunate and also we, as listeners, are lucky to have this man to bring us music."

The Force of Destiny

The return to DC offered little respite from work as final details of the upcoming fall tour were attended to. At the beginning of October, the band flew to Omaha, Nebraska, and boarded their prestaged buses for a monthlong trip through the Midwest. Their second stop on the tour in Fort Dodge, Iowa, allowed the opportunity to meet another renowned American composer.

At the conclusion of the matinee at the St. Edmond High School gymnasium, Arnald was approached by a tall, stately figure sporting a shock of white hair. Karl L. King is widely known as the Circus Bandleader and March King. His composition of more than two hundred marches place him alongside John Philip Sousa, Henry Fillmore, and Patrick Conway as one of the true masters of the genre. Mr. King invited Arnald and a few others in the band, including Captain Bader and Chief M.Sgt. Harry Gleeson, the band's announcer, back to his home for the afternoon. What followed was described as a "master level" symposium on band music composition and performance. Over the course of the freewheeling discussion, Arnald inquired of the maestro what tempo his *Robinson's Grand Entrée* should be played. Arnald had chosen the technically difficult and popular piece as his encore for the evening performance and wanted to get it right according to the composer's intent. Mr. King explained that the tempo varied according to which circus act was performing: slower for the entry of the elephants and perhaps more quickly for the tumbling acts.

At the end of the evening performance, Arnald introduced the piece to the packed gymnasium and ended with, "You'll probably never hear it played as quickly as this!" From the circus whistle that opens the thrilling piece, Arnald set a blistering pace as his highly accomplished musicians struggled to keep up with the impossible runs and lightning trills that pepper the iconic march. Less than a minute and a half later, the piece ended and was replaced with the cheers of Karl King's hometown crowd, all on their feet. As the applause tapered, Mr. King left his front-row seat, walked across the gym floor to the podium, and whispered something to the young major. Arnald broke up in barely controlled hysterics as he exited the stage and told Harry Gleeson, the first person he saw, what Mr. King had said: "Keep it up, Sonny. Someday you'll get it up to tempo!"

The tour continued through Wisconsin (with a return to Milwaukee), Illinois, Indiana, Michigan, Ohio, and concluded in Clarksburg, West Virginia. In twenty-six days they'd played thirty-seven performances in twenty-six cities in front of tens of thousands of people.

Upon their return to Bolling, Arnald gave the band and support staff a week off while he continued to work on the details of the upcoming Christmas album. He enlisted the help of two of Hollywood's most popular entertainers via the Command Services Unit: singer Jack Jones and Arnald's old friend, Edward G. Robinson.

Jack Jones had just released an album titled *Jack Jones Sings* featuring "The Impossible Dream—The Quest" (the song would reach number one on the Adult Contemporary Chart), and he was in the midst of a promotional tour but somehow found time to record several numbers with the Airmen of Note to comprise one side of their Christmas album. He arrived at Bolling Air Force Base in a large RV with a motorcycle attached to the rear, and when Joan arrived one day to meet the young singer, he surprised her with a motorcycle ride around the base. Mr. Jones was also an airman in the Air Force Reserve, and Arnald suspects that his willingness to make room in his very busy schedule was due to the obligation he felt to his service and country.

Edward G. Robinson arrived a week later, just ten days following a serious automobile accident. His doctor advised against making the cross-country trip, but Mr. Robinson told him, "The Air Force Band is calling for me!" and he wouldn't let them down. Arnald remembers, "He was a little lame, but he did a great job." He narrated *Christmas in Washington* for side two of the album titled *Sing a Song for Christmas*. The album was distributed to every AM and FM station in the country and internationally to Armed Forces Radio and the Voice of America, reaching millions of listeners.

After the holidays, the announcement of the upcoming winter concert series at the Departmental Auditorium revealed a truly ambitious undertaking. In addition to the continuation of the Student Artist Series featuring outstanding local high school student musicians, many of the pops concerts would showcase a celebrity performer. Also, because this was the twentieth anniversary of the formation of the Air Force as a separate service, each concert would contain a selection celebrating the event. Finally, fifteen minutes prior to the beginning of all but two of the concerts, the Air Force Pipe Band would perform.

The pipe band's opening of the pops concerts was a stirring and powerful start to the afternoon. The group entered the auditorium at the rear, split, and marched down the twin isles to the front where they formed at the foot of the stage facing the patrons just a few feet from the front row. The impressive military precision and obvious musical talent held the transfixed audience in thrall and set the tone for the concert band's performance to follow. The inclusion of the bagpipers and drummers also allowed many of the younger patrons the opportunity to hear a type of music they might never have before.

The first concert of the season on February 5, 1967, once again featured the popular radio duo of Harden and Weaver performing a narration of George Kleinsinger's *Tubby the Tuba*. The talented pair were staunch supporters of the military and of the service bands in Washington, DC. Every morning at 7:20 sharp they played a march performed by one of the area service bands, and in the weeks leading up to the concert, they enthusiastically plugged their upcoming appearance at Departmental Auditorium. The result was another standing-room-only crowd. To play the lead tuba part in *Tubby the Tuba*, Dan Brown of Thomas Edison High School in Alexandria, Virginia, was selected.

Described as "a serious student of the tuba," Mr. Brown faced not only an overflow crowd that Sunday afternoon, but the antics of the radio personalities. Their loose adherence to the script once again broke up not only the audience but band members as well. Young Dan Brown gave a stirring performance in a concert that featured a wide variety of music, including *Roman Carnival* by Hector Berlioz, *Wings of Victory* in observance of the Air Force anniversary, *Folk Song Suite, Incantation, and Dance* and even former Airmen of Note member Sammy Nestico's "Toboggan." The Singing Sergeants then performed selections from *Kismet* featuring S.Sgts. Joe Ilardo, Manuel Melendez, and Al Wilber as soloists.

Michael A. Gabriel

The following three concerts were without celebrity performers with their emphasis on the student artists and the observance of the twentieth anniversary of the US Air Force. On February 12, Maj. James C. Sparks was the guest narrator performing Aaron Copland's "Lincoln Portrait." He would retire as an air force pilot, ending a celebrated career that spanned World War II, the Berlin Airlift, and the Korean War. He also had degrees in radio arts and journalism and worked with the Department of Defense attached to NASA where he was involved with the early space program. Other selections included in the Air Force tribute included the march "Chimes of Liberty" by Edwin Goldman and the Singing Sergeants selections, "A Salute to Loring" and "A Salute to the Armed Forces."

The outstanding student artist that day was Leroy Fleming from Coolidge High in Washington, DC. He was a talented musician who played saxophone, bassoon, bass clarinet, clarinet, and drums and performed the Concertino for Clarinet by Carl Maria von Weber. In an interesting parallel to Arnald's life, the Coolidge High Band had to perform without Mr. Fleming during the fall months because he played tackle on the school's football team.

Mr. Henry Gore from Bladensburg High School Band in Maryland was one of the busiest student musicians yet to play with the band. The cornet soloist on the February 19 concert played with the Prince Georges County Youth Symphony, the Metropolitan Boys Club Band, the Police Boys Club Band, and his high school band, and he even found time to play with the Washington Redskins Band. He performed Joseph Haydn's Concerto for Trumpet First Movement. The concert was beautifully balanced with Mendelssohn's *Fingal's Cave*, *Summer Day Suite* by Prokofieff, *Dance of the Seven Veils*, and to celebrate the Air Force anniversary, *Shield of Freedom March* by Mark Azzolina and the Singing Sergeants with Selections from World War II.

The following day, on February 20, 1967, the office of the Department of the Air Force issued Special Order AB_316. Arnald D. Gabriel's name was included in the document that listed the current majors who were, effective immediately, promoted to lieutenant colonel. He was now the youngest air force musician to achieve the rank. Arnald had been in the US Air Force less than sixteen years, and at the age of forty-one, the promotion to lieutenant colonel was, although not unprecedented, exceedingly rare. The elevation was not without merit: Arnald had rescued the foundering organization and increased its size to 223 enlisted and seven officers and was authorized to hire even more. The popularity of all the performing units was soaring and standing-room-only concerts were now the norm. Morale among the musicians and support staff was at an all-time high, and they were described by Arnald's commanding officer, Colonel Lemon, as "the best unit in the command." The solid support from his bosses and the rise in rank only served to drive Arnald to continue to motivate, innovate, and expand the band's mission.

At the final February concert, Douglas Forbes represented a departure in showcasing the outstanding high school instrumentalists in the Washington area. Mr. Forbes was the first student conductor to ever appear with the Air Force Band. He'd begun studying trumpet at the age of four, and by age nine, he'd joined the National Cathedral Choir of Men and Boys. As a sophomore at Wilson High School in Washington, DC, he became student conductor of the orchestra and concert choir, and as a junior, he was appointed to the band. He led the Air Force Band in Dmitri Shostakovich's Scherzo from Symphony Number 5.

Skitch Henderson's appearance with the band at the March 5 concert marked the resumption of celebrity guests, but it was not the first time he'd performed with the Air Force Band. Although best known for his leadership of the NBC Orchestra and *The Tonight Show* Band, Arnald knew of his membership with the Air Force Association, a civilian organization composed largely of former air force personnel, and as a major in the Air Force Reserve.

The prior year Arnald had contacted him through NBC and asked him to guest conduct a concert the band was slated to play at the band shell in Central Park, New York, on June 15. Skitch agreed, and Arnald sent him a long list of selections to choose from that the band had recently played. He chose the "Finale" to the Shostakovich Fifth Symphony, and when Arnald asked him if he'd like to attend their rehearsal of the lengthy and intricate piece, Skitch said, "No, your band knows it, and so do I. Just drop off the score at my office early in the day and tell me about your tempos."

"It wasn't the tempos that were a problem, but in one place there is a tricky meter change," Arnald remembers. During the concert that evening, it was "touch and go for a while, but the band got him through it!" It was yet another tribute to the professionalism of the fine musicians.

The area student artist that first concert in March continued the trend of Outstanding Student Musicians with a talented and involved young player. Eighteen-year-old Neal Neuman from Springbrook High School in Silver Spring, Maryland, was first-chair clarinet with the Montgomery County Youth Orchestra, the George Washington University Orchestra, the Montgomery Light Opera Association, and with the school's band and orchestra. Additionally, he was first chair in the Maryland All-State Orchestra, the School Orchestra of America, and the All-Eastern Orchestra held in Boston that year. The audience that Sunday was treated to Mozart's Clarinet Concerto in A Major, K. 622.

The final two concerts of the season served to display the innovation and forward thinking of the leader of the Air Force Band. The Skylarks were a choral group of the Air Force Officers' Wives' Club of Washington, directed by Robert Kuzminski, the director of the Singing Sergeants. The top-notch group joined the Singing Sergeants on a special Palm Sunday program performing a medley of songs from *The Sound of Music* and, in observance of the Air Force's twentieth anniversary, "Air Force Hymn" and "America, the Beautiful." The inclusion of women's voices obviously serves to expand tremendously the repertoire of any choral group, but it would be several more years before Lieutenant Colonel Gabriel would have the opportunity to hire a woman vocalist to join the Singing Sergeants.

The last concert of the season on March 26 was a clear departure from the standard Sunday afternoon fare and would prove to be unmatched in its festive spirit and pure fun. Merle Evans, the legendary bandleader of the Ringling Bros. and Barnum & Bailey Circus, The Greatest Show on Earth, was slated to perform in Washington, DC, that week. Arnald noticed that they had no matinee scheduled for

Sunday. Having met him through their membership in the American Bandmasters Association (ABA), Arnald invited the iconic bandleader to guest conduct the Air Force Band. Mr. Evans eagerly accepted and asked if he could bring along a few of the circus performers.

That afternoon (the concert had to be moved to one o'clock from four o'clock that afternoon to accommodate the evening circus show), the arriving concertgoers were met by Mike and Frank, two clowns passing out balloons and popcorn. A beautiful girl in sequined top and circus tights on stage to the left of the band changed a placard mounted on an easel that announced the next piece. The concert was all Merle's, and the professionals in the Air Force Band worked desperately to keep up with the seventy-five-year-old dynamo. He set a blistering pace as each of the thirteen selected numbers ran into the next and was separated only by the whistle he blew as a segue. Additionally, the band had to sight-read the music because there was no time for a rehearsal. The result was controlled pandemonium that had the patrons in the packed auditorium on their feet and cheering wildly.

Merle Evans would retire from the Ringling Bros. and Barnum & Bailey Circus Band in two years after an astounding fifty-year career where he reportedly never missed a performance. It is a record made even more remarkable considering each performance was three hours of nearly nonstop playing and two or sometimes three shows per day. The self-taught cornet player was an accomplished musician who was in demand as a guest conductor around the world and was as gracious and unassuming as he was musically talented. The Toscanini of the Big Top was actively conducting until the year prior to his passing at the age of ninety-six.

Since long before Arnald's arrival at Bolling Air Force Base, the band's facilities had consisted of five separate buildings that had been built during World War II as temporary structures. Each had been repurposed in an attempt to accommodate the unique organization; the rehearsal hall and recording studio had been a theater, the instrument storage and music library building a morgue. As the unit grew (they were now almost 250 musicians and support personnel), they not only strained the capacity of the old buildings, but they had the challenge of scheduling six performing groups for daily rehearsals in one hall. Arnald wanted to consolidate the unit under one roof, and in April, a proposal was drafted to begin construction of a ninety-nine thousand-square-foot facility that would become their new home. The inexplicable cancellation of the project can only be attributed to the vagaries of military budgets. It would be several more decades before the band would move into its new home in Historic Hangar II.

Although there was a break of about two weeks until the start of the spring tour, there were very few days off. There were recording sessions, funerals at Arlington Cemetery, daily rehearsals, dinner dances, award ceremonies, diplomatic functions involving foreign and domestic dignitaries, public parades and concerts, wreath-laying ceremonies, and even little league baseball games and a boxing tournament at Bolling Air Force Base. Some involved the full concert band and others the smaller ceremonial band or the Singing Sergeants, Strolling Strings, or pipe band; yet all scheduling and coordination was overseen by the commander. Arnald relied heavily on his competent staff, but the final decision was always his. It was a delicate balancing act whose consideration was an equal measure of planning for future events, dealing with the day's logistics, and assessing past performances with an eye toward improvement. One of the single biggest challenges was the planning for the annual spring and fall tours that involved the transportation, feeding, and housing of more than a hundred musicians and support personnel. The upcoming tour beginning in Denver, Colorado, would prove to be record-setting despite events that would upset some of the careful planning.

The matinee at the Denver Municipal Auditorium that began the tour was largely for the area high school students and was enthusiastically received. The medley the Singing Sergeants performed were songs from *The Music Man* and had the students on their feet shouting and cheering their approval. The packed house at the evening concert buoyed Arnald's spirits with hopes of a great tour and had him looking forward to the next stop, a return to Colorado Springs and the Air Force Academy and to many old friends among the faculty and band.

The Force of Destiny

At the conclusion of any concert, the loading crew immediately began to pack up the equipment, music stands, podiums, large instruments, and electronics and hit the road. On this occasion, because of the backstage meet-and-greet and the reception that followed, the three buses of musicians and one of the two equipment trucks were as much as several hours behind the lead equipment truck. The light snow that had begun during the concert started getting heavier as the occupants of the lead truck took a break to snack on some Fig Newtons and wait for the morning sunrise in Colorado. When John Hickox and Red Brower woke up, they found themselves among more than five hundred other vehicles stranded on I-25 southbound. Fortunately, they were able to put on the snow chains and waited for the state's bulldozer to clear the way for them to make it to the Academy.

The buses carrying the bandsmen and the second equipment truck had been turned back to Denver by the state police, and once the storm passed and plows cleared the roads, it would be nearly forty-eight hours before the band reunited in Pueblo. Four concerts were canceled, all three in Colorado Springs and the matinee in Pueblo, and it was, remarkably, the first cancellation of an indoor concert in the twenty-five-year history of the Air Force Band. Owing to his ties at the Academy, Arnald's disappointment was especially acute, but the balance of the tour would help assuage those feelings.

A unique honor was bestowed upon Arnald at Dodge City, Kansas, the following night: he was made deputy marshal of Dodge City by the actual Marshal Ramon K. House. He joined the company of, among others, newsman Chet Huntley, President Kennedy, and James Arness (who played Marshal Matt Dillon of Dodge City in the television show *Gunsmoke*).

The tour continued across Kansas through Hutchison, Wichita, Emporia, Lawrence, Topeka, and Kansas City, garnering effusive praise at each stop as they played to packed houses. In Emporia, as only one example of many rave reviews, the paper said: "It took four encores to get the job done, but the U.S. Air Force Band sent a crowd of over 3,000 home happy from Civic Auditorium."

In Kansas City, dangerous weather once again threatened as both the matinee and evening performance were played under the threat of tornados in the area. Despite the danger, more than thirty-five hundred patrons showed up for the evening concert. Just after the downbeat for the opening march, a power failure plunged the Municipal Auditorium into darkness. Adhering to the show business mantra of "the show must go on," the musicians continued to play, and Arnald continued to conduct. A quick-thinking M.Sgt. Harry Gleeson, who was information director and served as announcer for the concerts, grabbed a flashlight and illuminated the conductor from below as the band finished the piece from memory. As the march ended, the lights returned, and the crowd leapt to their feet and roared their approval.

The tour wound through Missouri, Illinois, Indiana, Kentucky, West Virginia, and Virginia, the final concert just an hour's drive from Bolling Air Force Base. The spring weather moderated on the trip east, and the crowds continued to pack each venue, setting two attendance records for the Air Force Band. Although they held ten fewer concerts than any previous tour, they set a tour attendance and average audience record. Thirty-three concerts in twenty-four days were played in front of an astounding 117,000 music lovers.

In mid-August, toward the end of the summer concert series in Washington, Arnald was invited back to his hometown of Cortland to a banquet held in his honor. Joan accompanied Arnald to the Thursday night celebration held at the Sons of Italy San Rocco Lodge, which was attended by family and lifelong friends, including Filomena and Ferdinand (Ma and Pa visiting from their home in Miami Beach), brothers Min and Rick, Joe and John Tucci, Nick D'Adamio, Fr. Carl Denti of St. Anthony's Church, and Burton Stanley, Arnald's high school music teacher and mentor. Music played that evening was taken from a variety show Arnald was asked to stage by the priest at St. Anthony's while he was still at Ithaca College. He had arranged the music and, together with Beatrice Sardo who had written parts for the actors, mounted a production that was fronted by an all-star pit orchestra, including brother Min, Spiegel Wilcox, Burton Stanley, and students from both Cortland High School and Ithaca College.

Although the tributes that evening were honest and heartfelt, including Burton Stanley's modest, "I am proud to have had some

The Force of Destiny

small part in working with you and your brothers," many, due to their lifelong friendships, took on more the flavor of a roast. Arnald's football coach from Cortland High, Ross Shafer, related a story of the honoree's tenacity at the bottom of a scrum of players during a game and his talent for not getting caught by the referees. There was no one more proud that evening than Ferdinand. He was able to celebrate the success of his three sons in the company of friends in his adopted hometown in the club of which he was a founding member. Arnald concluded the evening by saying, "My job of spreading American goodwill through music is just beginning," and deflected praise with, "No man ever makes it alone. He is the product of his environment, his family, his friends."

In late August back in Washington, Skitch Henderson returned to perform once again with the Air Force Band, this time conducting the Air Force Symphony Orchestra at the Capitol Plaza. The Tuesday night Capitol and Friday night Watergate summer concerts were occasionally performed by the Symphony Orchestra or the Airmen of Note, especially during the two-week summer vacation the concert band took in July.

Although attendance at all concerts was surging, Arnald and his staff quickly realized that the most popular performances were the ones featuring celebrity guests (Doc Severinsen, Edward G. Robinson, etc.) and decided to recruit more. Arnald flew to Los Angeles and met with Barbara Eden on the set of her hit show, *I Dream of Jeanie*, but the demands of the show and her Las Vegas commitments precluded her from performing with the band. A meeting with Gavin MacLeod of *The Love Boat* produced the same disappointing result. Undeterred, Arnald's persistence would convince many others in the coming years.

Sgt. Ed Dawkins of the Air Force's Command Services Unit had written a moving Christmas story about an elf named Timmy and his chance encounter with the Christ Child in Bethlehem, and Sgt. Floyd Werle set it to a brilliant score for band and chorus. A narrator relates the tale of the lonely elf and the meeting that changes not only his life, but the lives of children the world over. Sergeant Dawkins told Arnald that the narrator's voice was one of "an understated British humor," and it was decided to approach the famous Boris Karloff.

Michael A. Gabriel

William Henry Pratt (his real name) performed in more than 150 films and is best known for playing Frankenstein's monster (ironically, a nonspeaking part), first appearing in 1931. In 1966, the year prior, he'd narrated Dr. Seuss' *How the Grinch Stole Christmas* for an animated television film. Arnold wrote to the actor asking to contribute his voice for the Christmas radio program they wanted to record. Mr. Karloff graciously accepted the invitation but was unable to travel due to what he described as his bronchitis.[51]

Arnold grabbed a couple of men from the air force sound studio and some recording equipment, flew to London, and drove to *Roundabout*, Mr. Karloff's home, to tape the voice-over. They spent the morning working with the rudimentary setup. Arnold listened to the music through headphones and cued Mr. Karloff when to begin each line. When they finished, Mr. Karloff was unhappy with the quality of his voice in the recording and, being a consummate professional, wanted to rerecord it that afternoon. He invited the men to stay for lunch, and after what Arnold referred to as "a delightful conversation over a relaxing meal," they recorded a new version of the narration. That final rendition is what was pressed into an LP record, distributed to every radio station in the United States, and heard around the country in the upcoming Christmas season.

As plans for the Christmas concert at Departmental Auditorium were being finalized, Arnold once again called Mr. Karloff to ask about his ability to travel to Washington to narrate the piece live. Still unable to make the long journey, he suggested his good friend John Carradine, who was performing in a play in London. Although Mr. Carradine expressed interest in the project, he wasn't able to commit due to his schedule.

After a call to his old friend Skitch Henderson with the explanation that one was "too sick to travel" and the other was "too busy," Skitch exploded in mock indignation. "Gabe! I thought you were my friend!" He, naturally, accepted and was scheduled to do the narration for the upcoming Christmas concert at the large ballroom in Washington's Sheraton Park Hotel in December.

---

51 More likely complications from emphysema that he fought for years.

The Force of Destiny

The fall tour of 1967 kicked off on Monday, October 9, in Phoenix, Arizona, with an ambitious schedule. The band would play thirty-seven concerts in twenty-five days across the southern half of the country, ending in Florida. The third day of the tour would mark the first ever performance of the United States Air Force Band in Mexico. The citizens of Ciudad Juarez packed the fifteen hundred–seat Pronaf Center Auditorium with an overflow crowd of almost twenty-three hundred boisterous fans. Arnald enlisted Sgt. Manuel "Manny" Melendez, a native of Roswell, New Mexico, to announce the concert in Spanish. The final number featured Sergeant Melendez singing the popular Spanish tune "Granada" by Mexican composer Agustín Lara, and the response was an astounding six standing ovations that led to an article in *El Continental*, the local newspaper, the next day with the headline: "The US Air Force Band conquered the hearts of the people of Juarez."

The band continued their busy schedule with ten stops in Texas, two in Oklahoma, and one each in Louisiana and Alabama before blanketing the state of Florida with eleven performances in eight cities. A consistent theme in each rave review was virtuoso Larry Wiehe's mastery of the trombone as the featured soloist on *Trombone Chronology* and the Singing Sergeants' treatment of Sgt. Floyd Werle's arrangement of *The Gershwin Years* with Sgts. Allen Wilber and Charles Kuliga as soloists. Ma and Pa were the honored guests at the Halloween night concert at the Dade County Auditorium in Miami that drew more than two thousand Miamians; the SRO crowd treated the band to three standing ovations after four encores.

One impressive measure of success is that more than ninety-four thousand people attended the thirty-seven concerts, filling more than 97 percent of the available seating capacity, and a total of eighty-nine encores were met with eighty-seven standing ovations. Their return home to Washington in early November left just a few short weeks to rest before beginning rehearsals for the Christmas concert with Skitch Henderson.

The winter concert series at the Departmental Auditorium began on January 21, 1968, with the youngest musician to date to perform in the Student Artist Series. Fifteen-year-old Edward Bierly, the first-chair clarinet player from Springfield High School in Virginia, performed the first movement of C. M. von Weber's Second Clarinet Concerto, a remarkable accomplishment considering his only three years' experience playing the instrument. There is little doubt that his teacher, Sgt. William "Bill" Hilferty, the Air Force Band's own clarinet soloist, lent a deft hand in guiding the young musician.

The final concert in January featured a student artist with vastly more experience. Ray Scheuring from J.E.B. Stuart High School in Virginia had begun playing his trumpet in the first grade under the tutelage of his father, Sgt. Francis Scheuring, a former member of the Metropolitan Police Band. The young man's impressive résumé included six medals from the Virginia Band and Orchestra Director's Association and membership with the Northern Virginia All Regional Band and the Repertory Brass Ensemble, all while playing first-chair trumpet with his high school. His lively rendition of the Latin-flavored *Chiapanecas* by Raphael Mendez brought the appreciative audience to their feet.

Nadine Asin held the distinction of being the only female student to appear with the band that season, and because they accompanied her in the performance of Kent Kennan's *Night Soliloquy*, she was also the first female to perform with the US Air Force Symphony in Blue Orchestra. Additionally, her accomplishments were no less impressive than the prior week's student. Miss Asin was first-chair flute with the Montgomery County Youth Orchestra, Springbrook High School Band, Washington Civic Symphony, the George Washington University Orchestra, and Maryland All-State Band and was able to attend the prestigious Interlochen, Michigan, National Music camp for two years on a scholarship, once again, playing first-chair flute.

The student who graced the stage at Departmental Auditorium on the February 11 concert took a decidedly tougher path than most. William Greene was born in the District of Columbia, began playing the violin in the public school system at age nine, and, within a year, switched to the clarinet. A gap in his formal instruction during his middle school years evidently had little adverse effect, because he was accepted into the DC Youth Band and was selected as the outstanding junior high school musician in the city by the DC Music Educators in succeeding years. Having to switch high schools after the tenth grade, he not only played first-chair clarinet in both bands, but he was the captain of the Ballou High School's Cadet Band. Private lessons throughout high school were funded with his work at a local drive-in, and his perseverance was rewarded with a beautiful performance of Concerto in A Major-Allegro, a tough yet melodic piece that would be one of the last Wolfgang Amadeus Mozart would write.

The weekdays between the Sunday concerts were filled with rehearsals, planning sessions, local performances, and the occasional out-and-back trips to regional locations in the northeast and mid-Atlantic states. On February 17, 1968, Arnald and the band boarded buses for a concert venue about which every musician dreams. Arnald later described Carnegie Hall as "the best hall I have ever played, including Symphony Hall in Chicago, the Dorothy Chandler Pavilion in Los Angeles, and others." The trip was coordinated through the Air Force Association, a civilian, nonprofit advocacy and educational organization, and their Iron Gate Chapter based in New York City. Skitch Henderson was a member and facilitated the booking. The sophisticated audience was treated to Larry Wiehe's now-iconic *Trombone Chronology* and a band Skitch enthusiastically described as "a well-oiled machine."

The next day, a resumption of the Departmental series featured George Nield of Annandale High School in Virginia, who played first-chair trombone with the school's symphonic band and was a feature performer with the stage band. He was also a member of the Repertory Brass Ensemble, drum major for the Annandale Marching Band, and the recipient of one ratings in the Northern Virginia Band Festival for the prior two years. For his February 18 concert appearance, he chose "Starlight," written by perhaps the most seminal composer for the instrument, Arthur Pryor.

The final concert of the 1968 season at Departmental Auditorium featured David Scaub on clarinet in C. M. von Weber's *Concertino*. He was, surprisingly, the first musician from an air force family. Due to his upbringing as an air force brat, he had the opportunity to play with a number of different groups in his travels from base to base. He began playing music in the fourth grade in Atlantic City, New Jersey, and when they moved to Illinois, he became a member of the Park Forest Junior Orchestra. After moving to the Washington, DC, area he played first chair with both the Suitland High School Band and the Maryland All-State Band. His performance at the Maryland State Music Festival earned him superior ratings for two years.

The regularly scheduled concert series throughout the year were interspersed with local gigs ranging from high schools in Damascus, Maryland, and Alexandria, Virginia, to the Arts Council in Rockville, Maryland, the Innercourt of the Pentagon, and the DC Receiving Home for Children. Arnald varied the programs of the concerts, tailoring each to the varied and wide-ranging audiences. The increasingly deep repertoire heightened the challenges to both the musicians and their conductor and, at the same time, piqued their interest. The performances became fresh and lively, matching the enthusiasm of their dynamic conductor.

Arnald's attempts to engage young people in music didn't end with programs like the Student Artist Series or his increasing involvement with summer band camps at universities across the country and guest conducting jobs with all-state bands and music festivals. Just in the past couple of months he'd received a letter of appreciation applauding his and his staff's support of President Johnson's Council on Youth Opportunity Program. The council was just one front on the president's War on Poverty that had begun several years prior. The program's aim was to target disadvantaged young people between the ages of sixteen and twenty-one, coordinating the resources of state and federal agencies. The letter had originated in the vice president's office, filtered through the chain of command to land on Arnald's desk and was little more than a pat on the back, but combined with the other accolades arriving from the tours and other concerts locally and around the country, it helped to focus attention on the extraordinary results he was reaping in an extraordinarily difficult time.

Each newspaper headline and television news broadcast seemed to explode off the page and screen. At the end of January, the North Vietnamese sent seventy thousand troops surging into the South in what became known as the Tet Offensive, resulting in the highest US death toll of the war; 543 Americans died in one week. The shocking

Pulitzer Prize–winning photograph of a South Vietnam officer with his gun to the head of a suspected North Vietcong prisoner just moments before the trigger was pulled further served to empower the antiwar movement. The number of US troops in Vietnam continued to rise and would reach more than a half million by the summer. Protests against the war manifested itself as enmity for the military and elevated the importance of what Arnald and his musicians and support staff were doing. His belief in the power of music as the universal language, especially when performed by uniformed military personnel, was a powerful counter to the images evoked by an increasingly unpopular war.

South American Tour

In the midst of the social turmoil and upheaval, Arnald convinced the State Department and Pentagon officials of the need to spread a more positive view of the United States and her military with the first international tour since 1960, before his assumption of command. Arnald and his staff organized a twenty-city, twelve-country tour of Central and South America. It was a bold initiative considering most of the region's governments cycled between populist rebellions and military coups and was laced through with a broad streak of anti-American sentiment. The band and Singing Sergeants left Andrews Air Force Base on the morning of March 10, 1968, aboard a C-118 (the military version of the McDonnell Douglas DC-6) bound for Caracas, Venezuela, a nearly eight-hour flight. The four-engine propeller-driven aircraft would transport them around the continent for the next three weeks or so into some of the world's most challenging airports tucked between mountains that soar to more than eighteen thousand feet.

The concerts in Venezuela would set the tone for the rest of the tour and featured inexplicable delays at the airports and hotels and wild bus rides along narrow and sometimes dirt roads through slum neighborhoods that bordered walled compounds of the privileged. The concerts were well attended and enthusiastically received. As he did on the tour through Mexico in the fall tour, Sgt. Manuel "Manny" Melendez announced the concert in Spanish and sang several numbers in the concertgoers' native language. The highlight was always the performance of a regional favorite titled "A Banda," a popular tune by Brazilian Chico Buarque that had the audience on their feet cheering, whistling, and singing along with the band and Singing Sergeants.

After the open-air concert at the Plaza Bolivar in downtown Caracas, the men were bused down the coast to Maracay. The evening performance on March 12 was held in the local bull ring in front of a very lively crowd who filled every seat, and afterward, the band members were feted by local dignitaries at a private club. Their stay at the Hotel Maracay initially held promise when they found out about the pools, golf course, and gym, but hope turned to disappointment when it was learned that the pools were drained for cleaning, no golf clubs were available, and most couldn't afford the cost of the gym.

The group returned to Caracas the next day to refuel the airplane for the nine-and-a-half-hour trip across the Amazon jungle to Brasilia, the newly established capital of Brazil. The city was founded only six years prior in order to move the capital from Rio de Janeiro to this, more central location. The impression was of wide-open spaces and modern architecture and artwork. The city was still bustling with new construction, and even the venue for the evening's concert, the Teatro Nacional, was unfinished. More than seven thousand packed the theater that was estimated to hold four thousand. The makeshift seating provided was on backless, wooden benches and concrete slabs but seemed to matter little to the enthusiastic patrons who applauded at the band's entrance and even as they began to tune their instruments. Once again, the big hit of the night was when the Singing Sergeants sang the popular Brazilian song "A Banda" in Portuguese. The president of Brazil watched the performance from his presidential box, likely *not* sitting on a wood bench. The concert was like so many to come as scores of North American audience members approached Arnald and other members of the band to thank them for this small gesture against anti-American sentiment. Once again, Arnald's the-power-of-music seemed to cut through arcane international complexities and touch the soul of a people.

The Force of Destiny

The next morning they flew to Rio de Janeiro for one evening concert that allowed little time for sightseeing. The performance was attended by a disappointing crowd of about eight or nine thousand, at least half of whom were military, and their tepid response to the music stood in stark contrast to the clapping and whistling of the previous concerts. After a mere fifteen hours in Rio, the exhausted men boarded the plane for the short flight to São Paulo.

The largest city in the southern hemisphere was the cultural center of Brazil and housed a diverse and cosmopolitan populous. There was little in the way of slums and poverty evident in the modern city, and the concert that evening at an indoor soccer stadium drew the most enthusiastic crowd to date. Manny Melendez once again wowed the crowd with his version of "A Banda" and had them on their feet when he pulled a local female TV reporter on stage to help him sing the chorus. The short stay ended too quickly as the happy, albeit tired, group departed for Asunción, Paraguay.

The planned three-day stay in the capital of Paraguay held the promise of catching up on much-needed rest and the modern, well-appointed hotel was a pleasant surprise. Their evening concert was for the benefit of the US Immigration Services and was held at their Cultural Center, a venue so small that only about half the band was used to back up the Singing Sergeants. The audience packed the theater, and a literal overflow crowd spilled into the street, straining to hear the music. The next evening could not have been more different as more than twenty thousand patrons crammed into an outdoor basketball stadium and heard a concert that featured Chief M.Sgt. Larry Wiehe performing the beautiful Irish ballad, "Believe Me If All Those Endearing Young Charms," and, of course, "A Banda," this time performed by a local night club singer Arnald had discovered. The inclusion of the popular local talent brought the house to its feet at the conclusion.

The next stop on their tour of the continent was the Argentine capital of Buenos Aires. The evening concert was in the opera house and was filled to its five thousand–seat capacity. The most boisterous crowd to date cheered the band wildly after each selection and absolutely brought the house down with Manny's performance.

Michael A. Gabriel

The band had been met at the airport by members of the Argentine Air Force Band who served as their in-country hosts for the two-day visit. The next day, the Argentine Air Force sent buses and treated the bandsmen to an *Asado*, an Argentine barbeque of ribs, sausages, steaks, and other cuts of beef and pork. Welcoming speeches by Argentine Col. Armando Nalli were followed by those of thanks from Arnald on behalf of the grateful Americans, and after the sumptuous picnic, the men exchanged small gifts. The reverie was fueled by an ample supply of the local wine, and some of the musicians sat in for an impromptu jazz concert with, to the delight of their men, Arnald and Armando playing trombone. The short visit engendered warm feelings between the two commanders, and in a letter Colonel Nalli later wrote to Arnald's superiors in Washington, he said: "I feel as if I have known Colonel Gabriel all my life."

The evening concert at an outdoor park found thousands of people literally surrounding the band during their performance and mobbed the group afterward seeking autographs. The exuberance of the audience buoyed the spirits of the homesick musicians barely a third of the way through the tour and already thinking of home.

The following day a short flight across the bay brought them to Montevideo, Uruguay, where they were welcomed by a twenty-five piece band. Throughout the short stay, the Air Force Band members were accompanied by security personnel and their buses led by motorcades due to the threat of violence by antigovernment guerrilla groups. Twenty thousand people filled one end of a one hundred thousand-seat soccer stadium for the evening concert and was followed by a reception at the American Embassy. It was good to get a taste of *Norte Americano* food and conduct conversations in English for a few hours. The final concert in Montevideo was a Saturday matinee held in an outdoor amphitheater. The crowd filled the provided seating and spilled over along the hills and cliffs above the stage area. Despite sitting in the blazing sun for more than two hours, the cheering patrons wouldn't let the band leave until they ran out of encores. The bandsmen were mobbed and, with the help of the mounted security forces, pushed through the surging crowd to their buses. A review the next day in the Montevideo *Primera Hara* reported, "The warmth of the people put a final flourish on the concert with their sincere ovation to the performance of this outstanding ambassador of good will through a medium as expressive as music, which creates brotherhood which other media cannot achieve."

Sunday morning they rose before dawn and readied themselves for the longest flight of their trip, almost twelve hours of flying that would have them cross the Andes Mountains to Lima, Peru. Those who stayed awake were able to see some of the isolated countryside and beautiful snowcapped mountains of western Argentina, southern Bolivia, and northern Chile. The hotel in Lima overlooked a seedy section of the city and left them little to do except rest and recover from the flight.

Monday morning they reboarded the C-118 for a flight up the coast to the small town of Trujillo where they played a concert in an outdoor basketball stadium still under construction. Concertgoers swarmed the stadium, apparently unfazed by the scaffolding and half-finished accommodations. It is doubtful many in the audience spoke a word of English or had heard a band of this caliber before (especially dressed in military uniforms), yet none of it seemed to matter. They responded with the same enthusiasm that greeted most of the performances on this trip. Back in Lima, the next couple of days had only an evening concert in a different part of the city each night and left plenty of time to rest and sightsee. The days began to drag with only one concert a day and the realization that there were nearly two weeks of the tour left.

The next few days would prove to be an exhausting experience of travel and political strife. Quito, Ecuador, sits at an elevation of almost ninety-four hundred feet above sea level and is ringed by mountains that rise to higher than sixteen thousand feet. The arrival into the airport is a hair-raising spiral descent between the mountains, and after checking into the modern, new Hotel Quito, Arnald learned that the only concert planned for the capital city had been canceled due to a local situation (the specific event is lost to memory). The following day their destination was another high-altitude capital city, Bogotá, Colombia. Both concerts continued the success of the previous ones on the trip, but the eighty-five hundred-foot elevation (just slightly lower than Quito) caused difficulty in nearly every activity. A couple of oxygen bottles were brought to each concert to allay concerns about performing at those altitudes (neither was ever used), and even sleeping was difficult, obviously adding to the overall fatigue of the trip.

The men had been looking forward to the next destination, yet at the same time, they were unsure whether they would be allowed to stop in Panama. The upcoming election in May caused a great deal of tension, and the threat of violence prevented its inclusion on the tour until just a couple of days prior to their March 31 arrival. It was decided the band would stay and perform only within the American-controlled Canal Zone, a ten-mile-wide corridor that stretched across the isthmus and encompassed the Panama Canal.

For the first time in nearly three weeks, the men of the Air Force Band stepped off the airplane onto American soil. The sight of uniformed Americans, Air Force–blue vehicles, and, of course, the American flag buoyed the spirits of each one. They were able to send packages home, dine at the mess hall, and even go to the base theater to catch a movie. One concert was held at the baseball diamond at the air base and another, after a forty-mile train trip, at an army post on the Atlantic side of the canal. The appreciative audiences spontaneously joined the Singing Sergeants and sang "America the Beautiful" to end the concerts. The hot, humid weather was a big change from the cool mountain air of Bogotá and Quito, but even sleeping in the barracks without air conditioning brought few complaints.

The three-night stay ended too quickly as the men next flew to Managua, Nicaragua, and Tegucigalpa, Honduras. Each concert was performed at large soccer stadiums to enthusiastic crowds, but travel through the two poorest countries to date meant no hot water, no cold water, or sometimes, no water, questionable transportation and a hotel without air conditioning. All the above paled in comparison to the news the men learned after the performance in Tegucigalpa.

When they returned to the hotel, they were told of the assassination of Martin Luther King Jr. that evening in Memphis, Tennessee. The next day, Friday, April 5, they flew to San Salvador, El Salvador, and began hearing reports of the aftermath of the shooting. Riots flared in dozens of cities across the United States, and in Washington, DC, where many of the band members lived, the National Guard was called in to quell the violence, ultimately shutting the city down by literally sealing access in or out. It would be several days before worried band members learned of the safety of their families through the efforts of air force personnel at Bolling, the Pentagon, and the State Department. Real news was hard to come by. One afternoon a group of them were able to read about the riots in a day-old edition of the *Miami Herald.*

On Sunday the band boarded three buses for an hour-and-a-half ride to the town of Santa Ana and played to the mostly rural residents of the mountain town. Near the end of the concert, a group of eight or ten young men approached the band and began handing out envelopes. Expecting some sort of an invitation or perhaps a formal thank-you, Arnald and the men were instead chided for their imperialistic music, and it was made clear that they were not welcome. It is apparent that not all can be persuaded by finely played music.

The band returned to San Salvador and the next day took off for Mexico City. The decision was made to overfly Guatemala City, their next scheduled stop because of a long-simmering civil war and strong anti-American sentiment. Arnald and the men were met at the Mexico City airport by representatives of the upcoming Summer Olympics and then driven into the heart of the large, modern city. Both evening concerts were attended by the same cheering crowds as before, but their response to Manny was even more effusive. More than just a native son, he is the grandson of the former president of Mexico, Benito Juárez. Just as the final evening concert was to begin, a small group of protesters rose and began to chant at the band in Spanish. The rest of the crowd shouted them down, and the Federal Police quickly swept in to remove them. The armed men remained in the theater in strategic positions throughout the remainder of the performance. Disappointingly, Joan and Arnald's planned rendezvous in the capital city was canceled because of the turmoil and uncertainty in both countries' capital cities.

Finally, on the morning of Tuesday, April 9, Arnald and the exhausted Air Force Band members climbed aboard the C-118 for their return to the United States and San Antonio, Texas. They were to have played their final evening concert that night, but severe weather canceled the outdoor event, and the decision was made to return to Washington, DC, immediately. The early return was a triumphant one, and as the numbers were tallied, it was determined that the traveling ambassadors had performed for a total of more than 170,000 people at twenty-six concerts. Millions more had heard the group through three telecasts and seventeen radio shows that were broadcast throughout the continent. After their return, a letter Arnald received from the Commander, United States Military Group, Peru, was one of many and was typical in its praise. "I extend my sincere appreciation to you and the members of the US Air Force Band for the concerts performed in Peru during your recent tour of Latin America. I personally feel that your tour has contributed immensely toward improving the image of the United States Military forces and it also created good will between our country and Peru."

The Legion of Merit

As word of his accomplishments spread, the occasional request to guest conduct became a steady stream of invitations, and now, Arnald spent most weekends traveling to colleges, high schools, and community music groups lending his expertise as a conductor, clinician, and adjudicator. The air force brass to whom he reported at headquarters on Bolling Air Force Base and at the Pentagon were not only aware of the extracurricular activity, but encouraged it. His ambassadorship extended not just to international destinations but to a wide range of domestic opportunities. Arnald's midsummer OER acknowledged the effort with the following: "he has used most of his ordinary leave for personal guest conductor appearances [and] ... all these activities accrue to the band's prestige and the Air Force's credit." Arnald's dynamic approach to his life's work drew critical acclaim, and his soaring demand by music educators at professional conferences and clinics solidified the stature of the US Air Force Band as the world's finest band.

Arnald's success in transforming and building the group drew the attention of his superiors, and on the morning of June 28, 1968, he was told to report to his commanding officer for an award ceremony. Officially, the Legion of Merit Medal is awarded for "exceptionally meritorious conduct in the performance of outstanding services and achievements," and Arnald's transformation of the floundering organization he had taken charge of nearly four years earlier more than qualified him to, once again, receive the high honor. The citation read, in part: "Under his baton the band was molded into an instrument unmatched by any band in the world. His outstanding rehearsal technique, musicianship, talent, and masterful personality were a source of inspiration to the bandsmen as they responded to his dynamic conducting."

In the US Air Force, the Legion of Merit is primarily reserved for colonels and general officers at the end of their careers as acknowledgement of "service rendered in a clearly exceptional manner." Having earned the award twice, the first time as a captain and clearly in the ascendency of his career, was unprecedented, and he was the only active air force musician to hold the award. The ceremony was held at the Headquarters Command, United States Air Force on Bolling Air Force Base in the midst of the summer concert series at the Watergate complex and Capitol steps.

For the Tuesday and Friday performances, Arnald enlisted the help of the Skylarks, the chorus of the Air Force Wives' Club of Washington, to accompany the Singing Sergeants several times that summer performing selections from *The Sound of Music* as arranged by Sgt. Floyd Werle. Their inclusion added to the depth of an already brilliant array of music, playing everything from Sousa marches, a Vivaldi trumpet concerto, Mexican folk songs, to Broadway show tunes, and "Michelle" by John Lennon sung by vocalist Sgt. Cecil Pearce. The concerts drew record crowds, and at the Watergate barge, a flotilla of pleasure boats anchored in the Potomac River expressed their appreciation at the end of each number with a chorus of air horns.

In addition to the workload associated with concerts and rehearsals, both local and away from the Washington, DC, area, Arnald was tasked with the administrative responsibilities of commanding almost 250 personnel. Probably the most difficult of the myriad of decisions was the planning of the national and now international tours. Music was

Michael A. Gabriel

selected for each concert with an eye toward adding some local flavor; rehearsals were scheduled; transportation and lodging was secured at agreed upon tour cities; and dates and times of the performances were set. The final approval of each detail rested with Arnald, and as commander, he coordinated the logistics with the Pentagon, air force personnel in the local area, and in the case of international tours, the State Department and officials in each country. Once the tour launched, he was responsible for personally dealing with each and every detail and the problems associated with about a hundred traveling men and their equipment. Illness, mechanical breakdowns, problems with the concert venue or hotel, or even the weather were daily concerns. Added to this staggering load, Arnald was the face of the organization and became adept at the smooth and articulate public relations that was the core of his job. In meeting with the press, mixing with audience members after a concert, or visiting with public officials at dinner, he exhibited a professional's poise leavened with a sparkling personality. He was the epitome of a career military man and, at the same time, personable and approachable.

The fall tour of 1968 began in Minneapolis, Minnesota, and for the next three and a half weeks wound through North and South Dakota, Montana, Wyoming, Nebraska, and ending in Council Bluffs, Iowa. The trip was filled with capacity crowds who heard a varied selection of music, and despite campus unrest across much of the country, the high school and college venues were among the most enthusiastically received. A couple of weeks after their return home, the band played a concert in Gettysburg, Pennsylvania, to commemorate the 150th anniversary of Abraham Lincoln's Gettysburg Address. The bus ride to the historic battlefield is less than two hours from Washington, and they were able to complete the trip without an overnight stay.

After the busy holiday season, Arnald readied the band for the upcoming Departmental Auditorium series of concerts. Not content to repeat music, his challenge was to search out and present new music and ways to play established hits and orchestral pieces scored for band. Working with his team of talented arrangers, Chief M.Sgt. Floyd Werle, Sgt. Lawrence Odom, Sgt. Greg Sauter, and Sgt. Serge de

The Force of Destiny

Gastyne, Arnald assembled a slate of music that not only held wide appeal locally but was designed with the upcoming fall tour in mind.

Each week, beginning with the February 2, 1969, concert, they showcased the music of a different European nation and ended the final concert that season with American music. The student artists selected from the Washington, DC, area played selections appropriate to that week's theme, and the Singing Sergeants did a medley of popular songs beginning with Italy and, each subsequent week, Germany, Spain, France, England, Austria, and Ireland. The concerts also featured a prestigious lineup of guest conductors, including Charles Minelli, director of bands at the University of Ohio in Athens; Frederick Fennell, band director at the University of Miami in Coral Gables and former conductor of the Eastman Wind Ensemble; and once again, the number-one radio personalities in the DC area, Frank Harden and Jackson Weaver were scheduled to appear for the final concert of the year.

The selection of the seven countries' music served several purposes: in an effort to broaden goodwill, it allowed the air force to extend a personal invitation to the embassy dignitaries whose nation was featured, it appealed to the diverse and unique population of the Washington area where many different ethnicities resided, and it set the stage for the fall tour, honing the music selection that they would play.

Each concert garnered rave reviews, standing ovations, and overflow crowds, and clearly, the most popular was the final performance on March 23. More than nineteen hundred squeezed into the concert hall with a stated 1,325-seat capacity, and from the opening John Philip Sousa's march "The Stars and Stripes Forever" and Henry Fillmore's "Americans We," the audience responded with unrestrained cheers and standing ovations. Harden and Weaver delighted the crowd with their mostly off-the-cuff rendition of Don Gillis' *The Man Who Invented Music*, apparently unfazed by the composers' attendance that afternoon. Arnald conducted the Singing Sergeants in a Floyd Werle arrangement titled *The Sounds of '68*, which featured popular songs from the previous year. In his introduction of the piece, Arnald acknowledged the younger generation's claim to a new genre of music and his own salute to it.

The afternoon's arc of success led to the final item on the program and, arguably, the highlight of the day. Chief M.Sgt. Floyd Werle's First Trumpet Concerto had been premiered by Doc Severinsen with the Air Force Band at the Watergate barge on August 27, 1965. Doc had since performed it with top high school bands and colleges and at the American School Band Directors Association in Milwaukee. After Floyd transcribed the piece for orchestra, Doc played it with the Minneapolis, Memphis, Pittsburgh, and San Antonio Symphonies led by Arnold and with the Oklahoma City and Baltimore Symphony Orchestras. He also performed it with the American Symphony Orchestra in New York conducted by Skitch Henderson. Following these triumphs, Arnold asked Floyd to write another, more challenging piece for the virtuoso trumpet player.

Doc had given Arnold several of his latest albums, recorded on the Command Label, and Arnold lent them to Floyd. Arnold wanted the new piece written in the third stream, a relatively new concept in music consisting of the fusion of classical and jazz styles, and the result that debuted that afternoon was a technically complex twenty-three-minute masterpiece. After laboring for eight months on rewrites and orchestrations (both band and orchestra arrangements were written), Chief M.Sgt. Werle admitted, "This was the hardest thing I have ever written." He expressed complete joy at the result, praising both conductor and soloist, "Doc and Colonel Gabriel grasped everything I was trying to do." Hard work was the order of the day as Arnold admitted after the concert that "this performance was certainly one of the most challenging I have faced as a conductor." Hearing the premier of the Second Trumpet Concerto, the audience responded with a standing ovation and were treated to three encores, one of which Arnold had Doc conduct.

There were many VIPs in attendance that afternoon, including the legendary Merle Evans who stopped by between his two performances for the Ringling Bros. and Barnum & Bailey Circus. It was a unique gathering of music professionals mixing backstage after the concert. Joining Merle Evens were composer Don Gillis, who was a professor

The Force of Destiny

at the University of North Texas; Forrest McAllister, publisher of the *School Musician Director and Teacher* magazine; Nels Vogel of the Nels Vogel Music Company; Howard "Sandy" Sandberg of the Getzen Company; M. Robert Rodgers, managing director of the National Symphony Orchestra; Mrs. Joan Gaines, public relations director of the Music Educators National Conference; John Wakefield, director of bands at the University of Maryland; and Fritz Velke, an award-winning composer from Northern Virginia.

Before the South and Central American spring tour ended the prior year, Arnald was already thinking about proposing a European tour. Having spent five years living in and traveling the continent, he was intimately familiar with the top destinations and popular venues. Logistically, it promised to be a simpler planning exercise with regard to the host countries' politics, distance between cities, and other travel concerns. Despite the apparent relative ease in planning (compared to South America), military and diplomatic channels are long and slow. Arnald had hoped to establish a tour schedule that featured an international tour in the spring and a section of the United States in the fall, but a slow-moving bureaucracy pushed their planning for the Europe tour into the fall of 1969.

The spring tour of that year was a triumphant West Coast trip playing thirty-two concerts through Washington, Idaho, Oregon, California, and Nevada. Audiences were treated to the band's interpretation of Lawrence Odom's brilliant transcription of Respighi's *Pines of The Apian Way* and Bach's *Toccata and Fugue in D Minor* and responded with sixty-four encores over the twenty-four day tour. Demand was so great that, for example, in Portland, Oregon, a matinee scheduled with a two-day notice attracted more than fifteen-hundred people. The evening performance was attended by more than thirty-four hundred packing the three thousand–seat Civic Auditorium. In its review, the *Portland Journal* enthused: "Lt. Colonel Arnald D. Gabriel not only makes a dashing figure, but he has a verve in programming that produces some beautiful and spectacular effects. An example of the latter was Respighi's *Pines of the Appian Way* and, of course, the crowning glory of the evening was the appearance of the Singing Sergeants."

For the Air Force Band's first-ever appearance in San Diego, Arnald selected music from Spain, Mexico, and the United States, acknowledging the city's past and helping to celebrate its two hundred-year anniversary. Arnald received the key to the city of Riverside, California; April 28 became Air Force Band Day in Bakersfield; and, in response to a last-minute request by their conductor, Arnald graciously gave up an afternoon off to hold an hour-long clinic for a high school band in Pendleton, Oregon. The success of the tour was as much a part of the professionalism of the band as the vitality of their dynamic leader.

Returning to Washington, DC, Arnald was involved not only in selecting music for the summer concert series at the Capitol steps and Watergate, but also preparing himself for a weeklong summer band camp in Kirksville, Missouri, and an historic concert with the Pittsburgh Symphony Orchestra. Although press reports and news articles at the time reported that he'd been invited by the orchestra's management, Arnald had actually gotten a phone call from his old friend Doc Severinsen. Doc had been invited to perform a concert at the popular summertime Promenade Series held in the city's Civic Arena, and he asked that Arnald guest conduct. Arnald accepted immediately. He had a prior commitment in Kirksville but recognized that the public relations coup (and personal prestige) gained by his attendance dovetailed nicely with the desire to help a friend. Scheduling the two events became a delicate balancing act that relied on timing and fortunate airline schedules.

On Monday, June 9, Arnald flew to Kirksville and completed his schedule of activities for the high school summer band camp held at Northeast Missouri State College,[52] including a first rehearsal for the band that evening. Tuesday morning he flew to Pittsburg for an afternoon rehearsal and evening concert. With his June 10 appearance at Pittsburgh's Civic Arena, Arnald became the first US military conductor to guest conduct a major American symphony orchestra. Thirty-two hundred patrons attended the popular Promenade Series concert to hear Arnald lead Doc in Floyd Werle's First Trumpet

---

52 Now called Truman State University.

Concerto and the world premiere of *Rhapsody for Now*, a piece that Chief M.Sgt. Werle had written at Doc's request specifically for the evening's performance.

Arnald chose two orchestral numbers by American composers, *Overture to the School for Scandal* by Samuel Barber and Morton Gould's *American Salute*. Doc concluded the all-American concert by conducting Carmen Dragon's orchestral arrangement of Samuel Ward's "America the Beautiful" that had the audience on its feet praising their excellence and the unabashedly patriotic music selection. During the introduction of his friend and colleague, Doc said of Arnald, "Colonel Gabriel has raised the artistic level of [the US Air Force Band and Symphony Orchestra] to a level far above any other military organization." He was no less heartfelt in his praise of Sergeant Werle, saying, "There is no doubt in my mind that he is one of the greatest composers and arrangers in the world."

The polished performance hid the fact that both Arnald and Doc had climbed a steep learning curve in working with the orchestra. Doc had brought along a few of his band members from *The Tonight Show* to accompany him, including Ross Thompson on piano, Bucky Pizzarelli on guitar, and Ed Shaughnessy on drums. Arnald's experience over the years in many facets of music, and especially with the Air Force Symphony, didn't prepare him for the Pittsburgh Symphony. At the rehearsal, as he began the downbeat, *The Tonight Show* musicians joined in on the beat, and the symphony musicians followed about a half a beat behind. "I sweated through the entire first movement of the concerto," remembers Arnald. He struggled through the piece, making the group stay together until about two or three measures from the end when, without warning, the orchestra members stopped playing and walked off the stage. Strict union rules and conductor William Steinberg's penchant for going over their limit had resulted in the installation of a clock mounted high enough that each musician could see. When they returned after the allotted break, Doc insisted Arnald take a break, saying, "Gabe, you've been working too hard. I'll take over and conduct 'America the Beautiful.'" After painfully dragging the orchestra through the piece, Doc came off the stage rubbing his arm and admitted, "I see what you've been going through!"

The professional relationship between Doc and Arnald was a unique one based on trust and mutual admiration. This concert would be the first of many symphony orchestras Doc would invite his friend to guest conduct over the coming years, including Minneapolis, Memphis, York, and others. Each gig would be scheduled with a simple phone call; no contract was signed or fee discussed. Arnald would show up, conduct the rehearsal and concert, and Doc would hand him a check afterward. They drew equally from each other's talent and enthusiasm, and it sustained a collaboration that would continue for many decades.

The following morning, Arnald flew back to the band camp in Kirksville and picked up where he left off, having missed only a day's work. Because their first rehearsal on Monday had not gone particularly well, and because Arnald had left the following morning, the camp director had told the student musicians that Arnald wouldn't be returning. Return he did and completed the week before heading back to Washington for the summer Capitol steps and Watergate concert series.

Each concert series brought a new level of innovation and performance that was reflected in the increasing attendance figures. Throughout the summer, letters of appreciation flooded in from those above in his chain of command, including Gen. William C. Garland, Air Force Director of Information; Gen. J. P. McConnell, Air Force Chief of Staff; Robert Seamans, Secretary of the Air Force; and Melvin Laird, Secretary of Defense. Arnald's commanding officer acknowledged his efforts in his upcoming OER (report card), saying, "His conducting and planning of the summer series of concerts at the East Capitol Plaza and Watergate set new standards for musical performance and increased his already large audiences to the bursting point. In a region where critics are relentless, his units and the people under his control inspired some of the finest musical reviews published in the Washington newspapers in years." The report also listed his other accomplishments over the past year, including the appearances at Carnegie Hall, the White House, the Pittsburgh Symphony, two of the most successful tours in the band's history—the spring and fall tours—and his by-name request both nationally and internationally

The Force of Destiny

as a guest conductor. Col. Arthur C. Rush concluded the glowing praise with: "Lt. Colonel Gabriel is the epitome of the caliber of Air Force officer desired by any commander. His professional ability is flawless. He and Mrs. Gabriel are outstanding representatives of the United States Air Force and their country and are active in the surrounding community life where they live and travel. Lt. Colonel Gabriel should be promoted to Colonel below the zone."[53] The following year, effective October 1, 1970, Arnald would receive the elevation in rank to full colonel.

That summer marked Arnald's fifth year working with the Air Force Band in Washington, and his success and the support from his superiors spurred him to continue to innovate. His work schedule filled with guest conducting jobs as word of his talent spread throughout music education, and as his friendships grew, he established many contacts that would become long-term relationships; in mid-July he was hired to teach at a summer band camp at the University of Kansas that would continue each summer for the next forty years.

After the band camp in Lawrence, Kansas, Arnald flew home and prepared for a much-looked-forward-to and rare event: vacation. The band was given their annual leave for the two weeks in the middle of July, and either the Airmen of Note or Symphony Orchestra took over the programs at Watergate and the Capitol steps. For a couple of years now, we had been escaping to the solitude and bliss of upstate New York on the shores of pristine Lake Skaneateles. It is one of the longest, deepest, and least spoiled of New York's Finger Lakes, and at our location at the south end of the lake, it was a quiet respite. The time was filled with fishing, swimming, boating, and learning to water ski. One evening found the family all gathered around the small black-and-white television watching, with rapt attention, as Neil Armstrong stepped off the lunar module and set foot on the moon, fulfilling President Kennedy's bold initiative launched more than eight years earlier. Our home for that week was a cabin that cascaded down the steep, rocky shoreline and ended at a boathouse on the water's edge. It was owned by John Tucci who still ran Tucci Bakery, the same bakery

---

53 "Below the zone" refers to a promotion based on merit that occurs well before the "normal" expectation based on his time in the current rank.

at which Arnald worked throughout high school. It was provided to us through his remarkable generosity and allowed Arnald a rare time of rest and visiting with family and childhood friends.

Upon his return to Washington, Arnald fell, once again, into his nonstop work schedule, including the final summer concerts and overseeing the last stages of planning for the band's fall tour. The last concert prior to their departure was held at the Capitol steps and featured an event that caught Arnald completely unaware. The twelve thousand-member (at the time) National Band Association (NBA) is the largest band directors' professional organization in the world and is composed of members across the spectrum of band music, including beginning students, high school, college, community groups, military, and symphonic bands. That evening, Lt. Cmdr. Donald Stauffer, conductor of the US Navy Band and a personal friend, presented Arnald the Citation of Excellence from the NBA. The prestigious award was created to recognize "outstanding individual contributions to the field of band music," and Arnald was further honored by being the first ever recipient. His staff had learned only the evening prior that he was to be honored and, without his knowledge, hastily arranged for Lieutenant Commander Stauffer to present the award. At the start of the concert, M.Sgt. Harry Gleeson introduced the distinguished presenter and remembers, "Colonel Gabriel was completely surprised, and the look on his face when I introduced Commander Stauffer to the audience made the presentation doubly enjoyable." A photographer pressed into service at the last minute captured the moment that was seen in newspapers and press releases in the following days.

European Tour

The next week was spent in final preparation for the band's European tour. It had been more than seven years since Arnald had left the continent, and fond memories of his time there had him looking forward to his return and to some of his favorite places to perform. His memory of the European audiences and their exuberance and love of music would not be disappointed over the nineteen-concert,

The Force of Destiny

eleven-nation tour as they shouted for eighty-three encores and stuffed the venues with more than 103 percent of seating capacity. The tour was officially billed as the Goodwill Concert Tour and became a part of the celebration of the twentieth anniversary of the North Atlantic Treaty Organization (NATO).

The tour began as they boarded their airplane on the morning of September 3 at Andrews Air Force Base, and after a painfully long ten hours of flying, they touched down at Lajes Field in the Azores. Aside from the inclusion of local or regional music at each concert, the matinee and evening performance the following day would be typical over the next four weeks. They played a Lawrence Odom's transcription for band of both Ibert's *Escalles* and Respighi's *Pines of Rome*, two selections normally not heard from European bands. They also played contemporary American wind music, and the Singing Sergeants finished with a Floyd Werle arrangement featuring a medley called "The Gershwin Years" or the more current "The Sounds of Now."

The Air Force Band made their first ever appearance in three cities, including Lisbon, Portugal, Madrid, Spain, and Bern, Switzerland. The National Television Network of Portugal taped the concert in front of a capacity crowd in Lisbon where time constraints limited the band to three encores; the final and most enthusiastically cheered was "The Stars and Stripes Forever" by John Philip Sousa, America's march king, who was of Portuguese decent on his father's side. The rebroadcast in future days would reach more than 4 million television viewers. Leaving Lisbon, the balance of their travel around the continent would be aboard three C-130s or by bus. The C-130 is a four-engine turboprop airplane whose strength is in hauling cargo in and out of short airfields. The use as a troop transport consists of a conversion to nylon-strap seating and, due to the lack of soundproofing, the issuance of hearing protection for each passenger. Their discomfort was exacerbated by their inability to see outside when airborne; the porthole-style windows were far above their heads when seated.

In Madrid, the late (for Americans) start time of 10:30 p.m. did little to dampen the spirits of the concertgoers. The packed house demanded six encores before allowing the band to leave the stage at close to one o'clock in the morning. The scene was repeated the next day in Rome where the concert site was at a beautiful outdoor amphitheater near the Roman Forum and surrounded by antiquity. The audiences were taken by the unique sounds they were hearing, beginning with the pipe band's opening, Arnald's interpretation of *The Pines of Rome* and *Escalles* and finishing with the Singing Sergeants' *The Gershwin Years* and encores of Italian songs. Another late ending was a little easier to take with the following day designated as a day off. Most of the air force musicians used their time resting and attempting to soak up nearly three thousand years of Roman history.

After a short flight to the beautiful city of Venice, the band members boarded water taxis at the edge of the airport for the forty-five-minute ride to their hotel. Disappointingly, a light rain canceled the outdoor concert, the only one scheduled, and the visit became little more than a sightseeing tour of the unique, canal-laced city. The following day they played a single concert in Bern, Switzerland (with another six-encore finish!), and flew to their sixth country in a week by landing in Kaiserslautern, Germany. The city of Kaiserslautern hosts an annual three-day NATO Music Festival, and in 1969 the Air Force Band was honored by being selected to perform the opening concert. It is a distinction worth noting because of the festival participation of more than five hundred military musicians from England, Germany, Portugal, France, and the United States. As was the case for most of the concerts, the attendees included high-ranking military officials from NATO and heads of state from around the continent.

Beginning on Friday, September 12, until the end of the tour, the itinerary was less logically organized and became a zigzag pattern of bus rides and airplane side trips. The band would visit, in order: Denmark, Germany, Holland, England, Luxembourg, Belgium, and back to Germany before passing through Scotland on the way home. The haphazard routing was the result of scheduling issues with regard to the NATO anniversary celebrations, concert hall availability, and coordination with each individual sponsor.[54] Regardless of the travel pattern, the band would see their largest crowds and, in the smallest venues, the most enthusiastic response of the tour.

---

54 A local sponsor in each city was retained to defray costs, and on this tour, most were air force base commanders and NATO generals.

The Force of Destiny

Another massive logistical issue was the billeting of nearly a hundred musicians and support staff in each city. In about half the cities, the group was split between two, to as many as six, hotels, and each city brought its own set of unique problems. In Wiesbaden, a European auto show filled hotels across the city, and band members were spread out across four hotels, three of which were out of town on the Rhine River. Coordinating the transportation of men scattered across the city added another layer of concern to an already-complex operation.

Leaving Kaiserslautern, the two-hour flight in the C-130 brought them to Copenhagen, Denmark. The scheduled concert in the Tivoli Gardens Concert Hall was canceled due to a bomb threat, a stark reminder of the Cold War; however, local authorities recommended that the performance be moved to a safe outdoor location. In order to belay any rumors, band members were told that demand for tickets outstripped the concert hall's nineteen hundred–seat capacity, and the venue was switched to an outdoor amphitheater in Tivoli Gardens. Tivoli Gardens is one of the most popular amusement parks in the world and offers a wide range of entertainment, including pavilions with ballet, rock-and-roll, country-and-western music, acrobatic acts; and a dizzying array of food vendors on beautifully landscaped grounds. On the evening of September 12, it is estimated that more than ten thousand people flooded the amphitheater's stated seventy-five hundred–seat capacity to cheer the Air Force Band. After the highly successful concert, the men boarded the C-130s and flew to Wiesbaden, Germany.

Nearly six years prior, Arnald had performed his farewell concert at Wiesbaden's Kurhaus and now returned in a triumphant concert heralded by the cheering, overcapacity crowd. The mayor at the time had bestowed honorary citizenship upon the departing major, and that evening the city warmly welcomed back their adopted native son. The too-short visit ended quickly as the band climbed aboard buses that would transport them to their next half dozen or so cities.

After a televised concert in the city of Saarbrücken, Germany, on the French border, it was off to Stuttgart for one evening followed by a more than four hundred–mile trip to Breda in the Netherlands. The city in southwest Holland would serve as a base out of which the band would perform two of the most emotional performances to two of the smallest crowds. On September 17, the day following the long travel day, the band traveled an hour east to Veghel.

As they entered the town, many of the band members began to realize that the reason for their appearance that evening was to help conclude the three-day celebration of the town's liberation. Twenty-five years to the day marked the arrival of the US Army's 101st Airborne Division, and all Veghel was draped in decoration. Red candles burned in nearly every window, and American flags blanketed the town. The concert was held in the largest venue in town, the Holy Heart Church, with the band playing in the sanctuary. It was a tight fit with the altar separating Fritz Wyss, the bass player, and the entire trumpet section from the rest of the group. Their placement mattered little to the more than two thousand citizens crammed into the church, which had a seating capacity of just fifteen hundred. The entire band was invited to a reception afterward and were feted with drinks, sandwiches, and cakes made by the grateful Dutch citizens. It was, to Arnold, a vivid reminder of his travels through southern Holland more than twenty-five years prior as a passenger on the 40-and-8 railway with his two buddies Harry and Johnny, all dressed in the uniform of the Army's Twenty-Ninth Infantry. Their hosts' delirious enthusiasm and unbridled love seemed little diminished in the ensuing years. It was a tired but gratified group who returned to Breda and their hotel at 1:15 a.m.

The scene was repeated the following night in Eindhoven but not before Arnold made a side trip to visit old friends. In the nearly twenty-five years since Arnold's first visit to Holland, he had visited the gravesite where his two wartime buddies were buried only once. Because of the serendipitous invitation by the mayor of Margraten in the fall of 1958 when he was conductor of the USAFE Band in Wiesbaden, Arnold was able to fulfill a promise he'd made during the war. Because no matinee was scheduled prior to the evening concert in Eindhoven, and even though it was a two-hour drive, he decided to pay a visit to the Netherlands American Cemetery. Harry Gleeson requisitioned a car and driver and, with an eye toward preserving the moment, grabbed Sgt. Bruce Gilkes, the Air Force Band photographer. From a respectful distance, Sergeant Gilkes captured Arnold as he stood in silent reflection for just a few minutes over each of their final resting places (they are separated by about fifty feet). In the midst of a hectic travel schedule through eleven nations and nineteen concerts, he found a bit of solitude. Arnold is grounded by family, and while standing alone over his two "brothers" for just those few short minutes, he was able to reflect on the improbable arc of his life over the past quarter century. The survivor's guilt of "why not me" still occasionally echoed in the nineteen-year-old machine gunner's mind, but the admonition not to "stare back" pushed him forward. He was gratified and proud of his successes but not content to rest; there were many more things to accomplish.

The evening concert in Eindhoven was, as it was in Veghel, on the twenty-fifth anniversary of the town's liberation. The beautiful, ornate concert hall literally overflowed with between two hundred and three hundred people sitting in the wings backstage perched on empty instrument cases and packing boxes. Somehow, almost fifteen hundred jammed the stated 950-seat theater, and with the knowledge of Arnold's participation in the war, they cheered and clapped in unison as though the Nazis had been driven out last week. Another one o'clock in the morning arrival at the hotel ended the long, emotional day.

The next few days of the trip served as a bit of a break in the packed schedule. The C-130s crossed the English Channel and delivered the musicians to London where, because of a last-minute cancellation, they had only one concert scheduled for their four-day stay. They were able to spend three days sightseeing, relaxing, and enjoying a very modern London before playing a concert that the BBC taped for rebroadcast to the rest of the island nation, reaching millions more.

The following morning, the men reboarded the C-130s and were flown back to the continent, landing in Luxembourg to resume the zigzag pattern of stops. After the evening performance and reception, they were bused to Brussels for one concert and then back to Germany, playing in Bad Godesberg, just south of Bonn. After one day in the city nestled against the Rhine River, they flew to West Berlin.

Michael A. Gabriel

The vibrant western half of the divided city of more than 2 million people was completely surrounded by Communist East Germany and stood in stark contrast to the drab, oppressed eastern side. They landed at Tempelhof Airport, used during the Berlin Airlift twenty years prior, and participated in German-American Friendship Day, a celebration to commemorate the conclusion of the historic event. The evening's concert was held at the unique West Berlin Congress Hall, a sweeping, arched roof structure known locally as "the pregnant oyster." The following day would be their last concert on the continent and would draw the largest crowd of the tour. The festivities were held at the Tempelhof District Race Track, and the band performed between races at the harness track. Almost thirteen thousand cheered the Air Force Band as they concluded with the Singing Sergeants medley of German songs, ending with an emotional *"Auf Wiedersehn."* Their last day was a day off that allowed sightseeing to Brandenburg Gate, the now-abandoned seat of the Nazi Third Reich, the Reichstag, a crumbling Potsdammer Platz with views into the eastern half of the city, and Kaiser Wilhelm Memorial Church. Arnald wandered the city with which he'd become familiar during his visits ten years prior, struck by the differences that existed across the concrete, barbed wire-topped wall. Nowhere in the world were the choices between the world's two dominate ideologies more evident and on more proximate display. That evening he returned to the lively Kurfürstendamm and to some of his favorite haunts, joining in on the celebratory atmosphere of the city.

On September 30 the C-130s delivered the band to a blustery, cold Edinburgh, Scotland. During the tour, the Air Force Pipe Band had opened most of their concerts and with an additional sixteen appearances over the twenty-one days, the unique unit never failed to excite the crowd. Even though their performance during the concert band's intermission in Edinburgh was, in Arnald's words, "bringing coal to Newcastle," the pipe band had the knowledgeable citizens on their feet, demanding encore after encore. After about their third return to play, Arnald reminded pipe bandleader Chief M.Sgt. Sandy Jones, that the concert band had a second-half program to complete that evening, and, "Maybe we should get started." Arnald and the concert band members were surprised by another reaction the audience had. They were singing along to the bagpipe music, joining the pipes and drums by celebrating their music. By the time the second half concluded and the Singing Sergeants finished their medley of music from *The Gershwin Years*, the patrons were on their feet with rhythmic clapping and chants of *bravo* resounding throughout the hall. It was a dramatic end to the tour.

Arnald had deviated from his normal tour strategy of two set programs that alternated and instead employed a completely new concept that guaranteed not only a variety of programing across the nearly monthlong trip, but music specific to each country. He challenged the band by selecting forty-six separate pieces and built programs from them to suit the individual audiences. Among these were seventeen marches, from the American marches familiar to most to the German "*Alte Kameraden*" by Carl Teike and French "*Marche Troyenne*" by Berlioz. The band's most unique offerings were orchestral works transcribed brilliantly for band by M.Sgt. Lawrence Odom that presented familiar works to the European audiences in a new setting. These gems were placed as the centerpiece of the program and were as varied as Puccini's "Intermezzo" from *Manon Lescaut* and Toccata and Fugue in D Minor by J. S. Bach. Modern compositions from Clifton Williams, John Barnes Chance, Charles Griffes, and even Duke Ellington were included, along with Chief M.Sgt. Floyd Werle's arrangements for the Singing Sergeants that never failed to bring the house to their feet. Finally, Arnald was able to showcase the talented members of the Air Force Band by including ten separate vocal and instrumental solos, including the ever popular *Trombone Chronology* performed by Larry Wiehe.

The trip home was always an ordeal, as the stress of travel and fractured sleep patterns combine with the emotional letdown in the aftermath of the final performance to push the weary men to the brink of exhaustion. The next morning's flight to Prestwick on Scotland's west coast positioned them to connect with a civilian-contracted DC-8 for the almost eight-hour flight back to McGuire Air Force Base in New Jersey and, after more than four hours of customs and immigration delays, an additional four-hour bus ride to Bolling Air Force Base and home. Preparation and the performance of the holiday concert season and their annual leave would close out not only the most successful year in the history of the Air Force Band, but a decade of remarkable achievement for Lieutenant Colonel Gabriel; in the 1970s, Arnald would continue to challenge the band to greater heights and renown while elevating his own stature in the music world.

The United States Air Force Pipe Band

CHAPTER SIXTEEN

The 1970s

At the dawn of the new decade and while final preparations were being made for yet another innovative winter season at Departmental Auditorium, orders from Air Force Chief of Staff Gen. John D. Ryan sent shock waves through the makeshift headquarters of the Air Force Band. On January 12, 1970, it was directed that Arnald and his staff deactivate the USAF Pipe Band no later than June 30. The eleven men who made up the heralded unit were to be disbanded. In addition to their popularity domestically on the bands' national tours and locally at concerts in the Washington, DC, area, they were regarded as one of the top bagpipe bands in the world.

In August 1968, the pipe band had embarked on a twenty-one-day tour of England, Scotland, and Wales and played to a combined ninety thousand people across the United Kingdom. The highlight of the trip were their appearances at the famous Edinburgh, Scotland, Music Festival and being honored as the only pipe band invited to the Cardiff Searchlight Tattoo in Wales. With two thousand years of history, and nestled in the heart of the capital city, Cardiff Castle was the site where the USAF Pipe Band joined the Welsh Guards from Windsor Castle, the Cornwell and Somerset Highland Light Infantry Band, and other units from the major British military regiments for an eleven-performance, ten-day tattoo. The evening performances were dramatically illuminated by six ninety-centimeter carbon-arc lights wielded by the 873 Movement Light Squadron. The band's high-caliber and authentic playing of local Welsh music had the cheering throng join in full voice, singing along with the group. The hearty Welsh patrons were not to be deterred by inclement weather, and during one memorable performance, a driving rain filled the snare drum heads and caused sheets of water to rooster tail from the flailing drumsticks but did little to dampen the enthusiasm of the soaked crowd.

At the Edinburgh Music Festival, other pipe bands from regiments across the UK and the USAF Pipe Band performed in the shadow of Edinburgh Castle at the Ross Bandstand in the Princes Street Gardens. For this festival, the pipe band played with the United States Third Air Force Band from London. The Yankee Pipe Band, as they were affectionately referred to by the local musicians, played to more than twelve thousand people over the three-day, five-performance stay. The high praise they garnered was summed up by senior pipe major of the British Army, Lt. John MacLellan, when he said that they were one of the finest military pipe bands he had ever heard. He went on to say that the unit represented the instruments' and uniforms' highest standards.

Pipe major Chief M.Sgt. Noval "Sandy" Jones and lead drummer M.Sgt. John Bosworth were responsible not only for the elite musicianship of the group, but also the authentic uniforms and instruments. The pipe band was as unique a musical group as any in the US military. Originally formed from members of the Air Force Drum and Bugle Corps, they became a separate unit in 1960. When the drum and bugle corps equipment was transferred to the Air Force Academy during the downsizing of the band prior to Arnald's arrival, the pipe band was retained, it was thought, because they were a favorite of President Kennedy. (A couple of years later, Mrs. Kennedy requested they play at his funeral at Arlington Cemetery.) For their early performances, their uniforms were a confusing mix of styles. Some of the musicians chose to wear their own kilts, and although the costume lent authenticity to the performance, no tartan matched another and those without kilts wore their Air Force dress blues. The vice chief of staff of the air force authorized new uniforms, and an authentic highland uniform was designed for the group featuring the Mitchell tartan in honor of Gen. William "Billy" Mitchell. General Mitchell was a World War I veteran and one of the first and probably most vocal proponents of air power and the need for a separate air force service distinct from the army. The uniforms were manufactured in Scotland, and during their tour in England in June 1960, the pipe band proudly accepted delivery of their new garb. With minor improvements, it would be their uniform for the next ten years.

There are scores of bagpipe types from counties scattered across Europe, North Africa, and even Southwest Asia, but the one chosen for the USAF Pipe Band was, naturally, the Great Highland bagpipe, Scotland's national instrument and the type known to most. Sandy Jones began playing the instrument at age eight, and through his life's dedication to its mastery, he came to be recognized as the world's leading virtuoso. He has even written a teaching book called *Beginning the Bagpipe* that is widely considered the standard for bagpipe instruction.

Not only is the style of drumming in a pipe band different from any other, but the construction of the instrument differs as well. The drums, made specifically for the group in London, contain an additional set of snares that lie below the extra-taut top head, and coupled with the custom drumsticks (handmade by lead drummer John Bosworth), they delivered the precise cadence unique to the band. Sandy and John handpicked, hired, and trained each man for the group and molded them into a band easily on par with any other pipe band on the international stage.

The decision to eliminate the only freestanding, full-time pipe band in the US Armed Forces in January 1970 was as baffling today as it was then. The crack unit was at the height of their popularity, and demand for their appearances outstripped their ability to satisfy every request. Their inclusion at the beginning of the Air Force Concert Band performances was a novel and stirring way to open a concert, and it set the tone for the afternoon or evening. Of the eleven members of the pipe band, only three were reassigned to other units of the band; seven left the air force, and one retired. In November 1962, the pipe band played for the grand opening of Dulles International Airport and about a year later had the honor of playing at the funeral of President Kennedy. It is a remarkable indication of their popularity that they were invited to return on the fiftieth anniversary of these historic events to play once again. Four of the original members of the group participated: Sandy Jones, John Bosworth, Leroy Carroll, and Tom Kirkpatrick.

While Arnald began the (ultimately futile) fight to retain the pipe band, he and his staff announced the program for the upcoming winter concert series at the Departmental Auditorium. It would be yet another departure from the norm and would feature some of the world's outstanding guest conductors and performers. Each week showcased music from around the world, beginning on February 1 with Music by Russian Composers. Arnald brought in the brass section from the Air Force Ceremonial Band to augment the concert band for a powerful rendition of Tchaikovsky's *1812 Overture*, and the Singing Sergeants rounded out the performance with a selection of Russian folk songs. To begin the concert, Arnald introduced the pipe band whose appearance that day would begin their final concert series with the Air Force Band.

The series continued the following weeks with Music by Canadian Composers, Music of Eastern Europe, Music of Hollywood, Music by Far Eastern Composers, Music by Latin American Composers, Music by Scandinavian Composers, and the groundbreaking Music by Black American Composers. Since Arnald's assumption of command of the Air Force Band nearly six years prior, he'd rebuilt and grown the organization into one of the finest concert bands in the world. As evidenced by the lineup of guest conductors for each of these concerts, their reputation for excellence was now attracting the interest of the best in the music industry. The emphasis for each concert had evolved to not only innovative programing through the scheduling of new and seldom-heard music mixed with crowd favorites, but the increased use of guest artists. The most well-attended performances had always been those with headlining celebrities, and Arnald expanded the concept to all but the opening concert.

The list of guest conductors that winter included Lt. Cmdr. William J. Gordon, director of music for the National Band of The Canadian Armed Forces; Karel Husa, conductor and recent Pulitzer Prize winner and faculty member of the music department at Cornell University; Carmen Dragon, Academy Award winner and conductor of both the

Glendale and Hollywood Bowl Symphonies; Toshio Akiyama, director of the Sony Concert Band and Assistant Professor at the Musashio Academy of Music in Tokyo, Japan; and Dr. Jester Hairston, composer, arranger, actor, and choral conductor from Hollywood. Each of these men brought a vast wealth of knowledge and experience from around the globe that had each performance a standing-room-only affair.

Karel Husa was a Czech-born composer who, just the year before, had won the Pulitzer Prize for his String Quartet No. 3. Although Mr. Husa was a professor at Cornell, Arnald had met him at Ithaca College (where he was a visiting professor and taught a composition course) a few years prior and invited him to Washington to lead the Air Force Symphony Orchestra in Mr. Husa's new composition, *Music for Prague 1968*. He composed the popular piece upon hearing of the Soviet Union's invasion of his hometown, subsequently transcribed it for band, and conducted the Air Force Band in the new arrangement that Sunday. Arnald's interest in works by contemporary composers went against the grain of many concert band and, to a larger degree, symphony orchestra repertoires. He recognized that a plethora of new works were becoming available and felt that the concert band "is in the enviable position to have at its disposal eager and talented composers who are enriching its repertoire to a greater degree than any other art form."

Later that spring at the convention of the College Band Directors National Association, Arnald introduced Doc Severinsen to Mr. Husa and suggested that he write a concerto for trumpet for Doc. Although the composer was "intrigued by the idea," it would be another three years before he was commissioned by Kappa Psi and Tau Beta Sigma[55] to compose Concerto for Trumpet and Wind Orchestra. As a frequent guest conductor for the group (and honorary member), Arnald was asked to conduct the work for its premiere on August 9, 1974, at the University of Connecticut in Storrs, Connecticut, but a scheduling

---

55 As described by their website, they are "honorary service organizations whose purposes include serving college and university band programs through service projects, fundraisers, social events, and other projects as needed."

Michael A. Gabriel

conflict with his other job at *The Tonight Show* prevented Doc from performing that day.

As director of *The Tonight Show* Band, Doc had a certain amount of scheduling flexibility but when Johnny Carson's sidekick Ed McMahon was absent, Doc took over announcing duties and assumed his position on the interview couch. Arnald was asked who might fill in, and he suggested Raymond Crisara. A Cortland, New York, native, he and Arnald had played together in the Cortland Civic Band when they were in junior and senior high school, and he was currently working as a studio musician in New York City. As one of the premier trumpet players in the country, he had also been consulted during Husa's composition of the concerto.[56]

Mr. Crisara received a photocopy of the original, just-completed manuscript from Mr. Husa only about three weeks before the scheduled premier, and because of further scheduling issues, he was only able to attend one rehearsal with Arnald and the band. It was held in the morning on the day of the performance. Arnald and Ray discussed the complex piece over the phone many times in the few short weeks leading up to the August 9 concert. Innovative concepts such as *aleatory passages*, where the soloist plays a series of notes at his discretion, and *quarter tones*, notes that are between the note and the next half step, join with techniques drawn from traditional trumpet sounds and newer jazz-inspired styles to make Concerto for Trumpet and Wind Orchestra a very technically difficult piece.

The concert was a huge success with the composer remarking sometime later, "I was amazed by Crisara's technique and virtuosity. Both Crisara and Gabriel demonstrated impeccable musicianship and professionalism." Not all were convinced of their success given the short time line and lack of rehearsal opportunity. Ray was on first call for recording sessions in New York for commercials, television shows, etc., and at one of those sessions during a break, he decided to find a quiet corner to practice the concerto. Another trumpet player, hearing

---

[56] Mr. Husa sought the opinion of other trumpet players, including Maurice Stith, Rob Roy McGregor, Frank Cipolla, Michael Ewald, and Fred Sautter. Having never written for trumpet, Mr. Husa was concerned about the concerto being challenging, but not in the extreme.

Ray practicing, peered over his shoulder and asked, "What's that?" Ray explained that he'd only have one rehearsal with Colonel Gabriel and an intercollegiate band before debuting this Karel Husa original work in the span of a few short weeks. "Impossible!" he insisted. "You'd better bring the *Carnival* just in case." It was a reference to *The Carnival of Venice*, a piece that *could* be played with one rehearsal. Obviously, they played the Husa.

The theme of the February 22 concert at Departmental Auditorium was the Music of Hollywood, and Academy Award–winning conductor, composer, and arranger Carmen Dragon stepped in as guest conductor. Arnold had recently met the world-renowned musician through a mutual friend at the Navy Band,[57] Richard Bain, a harmonica player and public relations officer, who had invited him to lunch one day with, "Hey, Gabe, would you like to meet Carmen Dragon?" He leapt at the chance and subsequently invited Mr. Dragon to conduct the Air Force Band; it was to begin a professional and personal relationship that would last for the next fourteen years.

In addition to his many appearances with the Air Force Band, Mr. Dragon invited Arnold to conduct the Glendale Symphony, an orchestra he had formed with Hollywood studio and other freelance musicians in the Los Angeles area. The studio professionals enjoyed the unique treat of being able to play a symphonic piece from start to finish; their studio work was mostly done in small excerpts and snippets that were stitched together for a film. They were being paid more than six figures for the work yet settled for musicians' union scale and the enjoyment of playing in the Glendale Symphony.

Their professionalism and talent was evident one day when Arnold was rehearsing Samuel Barber's *Medea's Meditation and Dance of Vengeance*[58] and noticed an eight-measure phrase that the first violins were not bowing together. His attention to this seemingly minor detail is important because he felt that, "All conductors should pay attention

---

57 Arnold's close association with many of the personnel in the Navy Band stemmed from his acceptance into their band program following his December 1943 audition.

58 Just before his death in 1981, Samuel Barber changed the name of the composition to *Medea's Dance of Vengeance*.

to whether the strings are bowing together. If you see that they are not, stop and ask the concertmaster to clarify the bowings. He will turn to the section and indicate how the passage should be bowed. When they bow together, it will sound together." When he asked Jimmy Getzoff, the Glendale's concertmaster, to correct the bowings, Jimmy turned, spoke quickly to the section, and sat down, ready to play in less than thirty seconds. Studio time is expensive, and their ability to work on the fly is a remarkable attribute and source of pride. Doc Severinsen was part of the rehearsal that day and told Arnald later that the group "ate it up! It was like throwing raw meat to sharks!"

Arnald's close friendship with Carmen Dragon came from their love of music and family and their shared Italian heritage. Carmen Dragon had several brothers who played in a band together (he played piano), his wife Eloise was a classically trained soprano, son Doug was a pianist, son Dennis a drummer and producer, daughter Kathy was a flutist, and daughter Carmen was a harpist. Most notably, son Daryl was Captain from the pop duo Captain and Tennille. During the group's heydays in the 1970s, Mr. Dragon, the Oscar winner (*Cover Girl*, 1940), Emmy winner (*Christmas Television Special*, 1964), music educator and head of a national music program that broadcast into elementary classrooms, film composer in more than thirty films, recording artist with more than forty-six recordings with the Hollywood Bowl Symphony Orchestra, and with a Star on the Hollywood Walk of Fame, jokingly lamented to Arnald one day, "I used to be the conductor of the Glendale Symphony. Now, I'm 'The Captain's' father."

Arnald received a call from his old friend Carmen in February 1984 and was asked to take over the May concert of the Glendale Symphony. He would lead the fine group in *The Roman Carnival Overture,* Grieg's Piano Concerto in A Minor and the Tchaikovsky Symphony Number 4. Arnald agreed but said, "I thought you were going to conduct the concert." He told Arnald that he wanted him to know, before it was made public, that he was dying of cancer and couldn't be there. Carmen Dragon died weeks later on March 28, 1984.

Mr. Toshio Akiyama was the natural choice to conduct the program titled Music by Far Eastern Composers on the first of March. He was an assistant professor at Musashino Academy of Music and director of the

Sony Concert Band in Tokyo. A full slate of Japanese music, including *Divertimento for Band* by Bin Kaneda, tenor soloist Sgt. Howard Hensel singing *Gion-Kouta* by Koka Sasa and arranged by Sgt. Elmer Kudo, and a 1969 Composition Award Winner from the Japanese Bandmasters Association titled *Metamorphosis* by Kenjiro Urata, were followed by a piece penned by the guest conductor: *Three Japanese Songs for Band*. The Singing Sergeants concluded with five selections titled A Holiday in the Far East and music from Indonesia, Korea, Thailand, Japan, and Vietnam. Backstage after the concert, a group dressed in the brightly colored silk dresses of traditional Japanese women were sent over by the Japanese Embassy because of Arnald's effort to reach out; their presence also necessarily attracted high-ranking officials of the US government that resulted in a beneficial exposure for the band.

Some years later, Mr. Akiyama returned the favor and invited Arnald to conduct the Sony Concert Band, a job Mr. Akiyama held for forty-two years before retiring in 2000. The band members were Sony employees and practiced on company time; they had an hour for lunch and an hour for rehearsal. The world-renowned conductor and composer is known as the "father of the wind band movement" in Japan and holds honors from the American Bandmasters Association and the World Association for Symphonic Bands and Ensembles.

Another direct consequence of the rising popularity of the Air Force Band was the increased demand for Arnald as a guest conductor, clinician, and adjudicator. In January, Arnald stepped in front of the Memphis Symphony, and he and Doc Severinsen repeated the success they had enjoyed six months prior in Pittsburgh with the performance of Sergeant Werle's Concerto for Trumpet. Doc returned to play at the March 8 concert, the Latin Sound of Doc Severinsen at the Air Force Band's Departmental Auditorium Series. He again performed Concerto for Trumpet (the third movement is titled "Samba") and *La Virgen de la Macarena*, a traditional Spanish tune played at bullfights and made famous by another talented trumpet player.

Rafael Mendez was a popular trumpet virtuoso who was one of the world's finest players; he had a novel double-tonguing and circular breathing technique that gave the appearance of never having to take a breath while playing. The so-called Heifetz of the Trumpet agreed to appear for the Music by Latin American Composers concert, but his schedule had him in the Southwest United States on the night before the performance. Arnald and his staff exhausted every option to get him to Washington in time for the concert by searching both commercial and military transport schedules. When Arnald called Doc, he expressed mock indignation at being the second choice for the concert, but would soon have the last word.

After the show, Doc, Arnald, and some of his staff went to dinner just over the bridge in Crystal City, Virginia. The restaurant had a group of strolling musicians who, when they recognized Doc, spent most of their time tableside, presumably in an effort to impress the bandleader of *The Tonight Show* Band. Their musical efforts left much to be desired, but not wanting to be rude or to offend the musicians, Arnald and his group allowed them to play throughout the meal. Before Doc left early to catch his flight back to New York, he pulled aside the leader of the musical trio, gave him a folded bill, and asked him to continue his serenade of the remaining dinner guests. With Doc's encouragement and financial incentive, the group stayed for the remainder of the night. When Arnald questioned him about the incident the following day, Doc's only response was, "Gotcha!"

The final concert of the Departmental series featured a full slate and a variety of music, including the Air Force Pipe Band (their final public appearance prior to being disbanded), the Skylarks (the Officers' Wives' Club chorus), the Airmen of Note, and guest conductor Dr. Jester Hairston in a program called Music by Black American Composers.

Dr. Hairston was a highly regarded composer and arranger of gospels and Negro spirituals. He was also an actor who appeared in *The Amos 'n' Andy Show* (both the radio and TV versions), the popular eighties television show *Amen*, and more than twenty films. He is best known for his composition "Amen" from the film *Lilies of the Field*, which he performed with the Air Force Band as one of a medley of his own compositions and arrangements. His rapport with the audience was remarkable. In an effort to explain his music to the assembled patrons, he jokingly told them that, "White people clap on beats one and three when you should clap on beats two and four, like black folks!" With his easy manner and obvious passion for the music, Arnald remembers, "He had them in the palm of his hand."

Spring Tour

The spring tour of the Northeast in 1970 began with an SRO concert in Arnald's hometown of Cortland that included two short matinee concerts for students at his alma mater, Cortland Senior High School. The hometown crowd for the evening performance was treated to a program of music compiled using Arnald's formula for concert programming, an area of concert preparation often overlooked in music performance. The evolution of his philosophy was beautifully articulated in an article he wrote for *The Instrumentalist* magazine some years later using the apt analogy of preparing a fine French dinner:

> A program should include an appetizer to tantalize the appetite (a march), hors d'oeuvres to stimulate (an overture), a salad course with a rare tasting dressing (a brilliant soloist), a main course of whatever suits our fancy that day (a contemporary work, a ballet suite), a vegetable that we don't really like but know it's good for us, a fruit or cheese course (a light work to relax, easy to digest), and for dessert, a flambeau to bring sheer joy to the listener. The meal must be accompanied by fine wine to compliment and heighten the total effect. The conductor takes upon himself the musical creation of a total emotional experience in listening to maintain the essences of unity, variety and interest throughout his work.

The concertgoers at the Cortland Senior High School and patrons at the tour's other venues were served a carefully prepared repast beginning with *Il Guarany* by Carlos Gomez, followed by a march, *The New Colonial*, by R. B. Hall. The alto saxophone virtuoso James "Scotty"

Scott was featured playing a Sgt. Lawrence Odom arrangement of Jacques Ibert's *Concertino Da Camera*. The familiar, haunting melody of *Greensleeves* arranged by Carmen Dragon was a crowd favorite and led to the soaring tenor voice of Sgt. Wesley Garrison singing *Winterstürme* (in German) from *Die Valküre* by Wagner. The main course for the spring tour were excerpts of nine movements from *Pictures at an Exhibition* by Modest Mussorgsky. A guest conductor stepped in after the intermission to conduct *Washington Grays March* and the Singing Sergeants wowed the crowd with Three Spirituals, "Elijah Rock," "Swing Low, Sweet Chariot," and "Amen," the last by Jester Hairston and sung by Sgt. George Merritt, baritone soloist. The stirring finale was a Sgt. Harry Gleeson narration of Carmen Dragon's *I Am an American*, which was dedicated to Jim Lovell, Jack Swigert, and Fred Haise, the Apollo 13 astronauts who had aborted their ill-fated mission to land on the moon in their crippled orbiter and had splashed down in the South Pacific only days earlier. The final sentence, "I speak for democracy and the dignity of the individual," brought not only tears to the packed house but a swelling of pride not often found in an increasingly disillusioned and cynical populous.

Fire

Arnald's emphasis on preparation, especially rehearsals, had always been a tightly scripted affair. Scheduling rehearsals was always the biggest headache, because although the Airmen of Note had their own small rehearsal space in one of the band's four buildings above the audio section, each of the other groups shared just one rehearsal hall. Their delicate scheduling operation was thrown into disarray when, on August 24, 1970, a fire destroyed Building 423, which served as the main rehearsal facility. A frantic search across the base turned up only one possible substitute, but because of its small size and distance from their location on base, they were forced to squeeze all the units into the Airmen of Note's rehearsal space, upstairs in Building 425. The barely adequate space was used for almost two years before they were able to requisition the funds, schedule the repair, and upgrade Building 423 into an acoustically improved rehearsal facility and recording studio. Recordings until then were live tapings of public concerts (an imperfect endeavor in the days long before the magic of computer manipulation of digital files) or the high cost of professional civilian recording studios.

The disruption in the rehearsal schedule for the upcoming fall tour was another challenge with which Arnald chose to lead by example. For several years now, he had been memorizing the scores he would conduct; the impressive feat was a natural progression from his intense and thorough study of the music. Arnald insisted that as a conductor, "Before you mount the podium, you should have the score in your head, not your head in the score." While guest conducting an all-state band a few years prior, he realized that he was looking down at the score less and less and thought, "If I don't really need the music that much, maybe I can retain the whole score."

The memorization is not about having a photographic memory (he doesn't), but instead simply hard work. Arnald employs a systematic approach to any score beginning with an overall first impression analogous to an architect perusing a set of blueprints. The general formation of the building will appear in his mind as he flips the pages beginning with the basic design and gathering more detail with the smaller, supporting infrastructure. "It's a little more difficult for a conductor because there are so many pages, but you should be able to see the high points and positions of repose, then block it out in large hunks in your mind." As the study moves from staff to measure to note, he continues, "Every measure says something. Every measure goes somewhere or comes from somewhere, and there is something musical to be brought out from every note in every measure." Arnald insists, "I have a good memory, but I don't think it's unusual. There is a lot of hard work." Hard work indeed. His analysis and memorization takes about an hour of study for every minute of playing time in the composition.

Because rehearsal time became more limited, preparation became more important. The musicians were acutely aware that every minute in the rehearsal hall was precious, and seeing their commander prepared forced an efficient, productive session due to

Michael A. Gabriel

the time constraints; they were rehearsing two separate evening concert programs and one matinee show. Ultimately, each rose to the occasion, and as Arnald acknowledges, "I've never conducted a great concert when they haven't played a great concert."

Little more than two weeks following the devastating fire, the band set out on what would be a record-setting twenty-five-day tour of the Midwest to nine states. More than 102,000 people (96 percent of venue capacity) attended thirty-four concerts and demanded a record 101 encores following a variety of music with works by Ravel, Von Weber, Kabalevsky, Alfven, Gershwin, and Bizet, as well as two original works for wind instruments, Third Suite for Band by Robert Jager and "Jericho Rhapsody" by Morton Gould.

For Arnald, the personal highlight of the tour was the October 1, 1970, matinee concert at the Worthington, Minnesota, Senior High School gymnasium where, before he stepped onto the podium, he traded his silver oak leaves of lieutenant colonel for the silver eagle insignia of full colonel. It was a gratifying acknowledgement from his superiors at Bolling Air Force Base and the Pentagon of his hard work and successes, because the elevation in rank was fully two to three years before it might normally have been expected. He would now join only 6 percent of US Air Force officers who would achieve the rank.

Celebrity Guests

Many of the ideas for programming came from the weekly staff meetings Arnald held when they were in town. The attendees at the one o'clock Monday afternoon meetings were the officers and NCOs in charge of each performing unit in addition to tech support, admin, the audio section, and supply. Their aim was to program concerts with interest and diversity, and Arnald plumbed the depths of his leaders to expand the agenda. The concert series at Departmental Auditorium in 1971 included: Morton Gould, Paul Lavalle, Edward G. Robinson, Ed Shaughnessy, Clark Terry, and Meredith Willson. The theme for these eight concerts was Musical Americana and covered American works from Broadway show tunes to Sousa marches, symphonic band, popular music from the forties and fifties, jazz, and a concert titled the Music of Young America featuring the Ithaca College Brass Quintet performing the Washington, DC, premiere of *60 Miles Young* by the relatively unknown Chuck Mangione. At the same concert, Ed Shaughnessy, the talented drummer for *The Tonight Show* Band, debuted a Floyd Werle composition of contemporary music written for him.[59]

Arnald first met Meredith Willson at the Air Force Academy in 1963 and invited the prolific composer to conduct the An Afternoon with the Music Man concert that featured a collection of hits from his Broadway productions as well as Sousa marches. Mr. Willson was best known for his 1957 Broadway hit *The Music Man* (later made into a hit movie) and *The Unsinkable Molly Brown*, but his musical career began at age fifteen when he was hired to play flute in John Philip Sousa's band (the youngest musician ever). During the concert, he regaled the audience with stories of his early days with the famous band and even surprised most with his introduction of "the greatest march ever written." Instead of the expected "The Stars and Stripes Forever," he introduced a lesser known Sousa march, "The Free Lance March," from the operetta of the same name.

Although much of Mr. Willson's time was spent in Los Angeles and New York writing for Hollywood and Broadway, he was a proud citizen of Iowa and his hometown of Mason City, the mythical River City of *The Music Man*; he was quoted as saying the musical was "an Iowan's attempt to pay tribute to his home state." Many of the characters were drawn from real life, including the Music Man, Prof. Harold Hill, who was patterned after Carlton Stewart.[60] He had one of the great bands in the 1930s, won the national championship several times, and later

---

59 In a June 2013 interview, just months prior to his untimely death, Mr. Shaughnessy was asked about the highlight of his more than sixty-year music career. He remembered this and another appearance in 1982 with the band by saying, "The Air Force Band is one of the greatest bands in the world. I was featured on two or three pieces that I had had written, and I think I was the most proud of my career with my wife and two boys in Washington, DC."

60 Carlton Stewart and Walter Beeler, Arnald's college band director, sponsored him for induction into the prestigious American Bandmasters Association in 1965, and he was voted in for membership the following year.

opened a music store in Mason City. Some years later, Mr. Willson asked Arnold to be the parade marshal for the North Iowa Band Festival, an annual gathering of Iowa high school marching bands held in Mason City, and by tradition, he led the combined bands at Roosevelt Field in a rousing "Seventy-Six Trombones."

Arnold also remembers Meredith Willson as a warm and engaging gentleman, and he was a great storyteller. After the concert, he and his wife, Rosemary, joined Arnold and several staff members for dinner where Mr. Willson held court, telling many amusing stories of his long, successful career. After some time, Arnold noticed him glance at his watch and go quiet. When he later asked the reason for the sudden halt in conversation, Mr. Willson pointed to the face of his watch where he'd taped the initials: LRT. He explained to Arnold that it meant "Let Rosemary Talk," a subtle reminder to himself to allow his wife into the conversation.

The following week, on February 21, another world-renowned conductor and composer took to the stage to lead the Air Force Band. Morton Gould was a giant in the music industry and one of the contemporary composers for concert band in the twentieth century who was, as Arnold has said, "enriching its repertoire to a greater degree than any other art form." The Contemporary American Music for Band concert was largely chosen from Mr. Gould's own voluminous body of work and featured a band transcription of the popular *American Salute*. They also performed his original symphonic band composition "Jericho Rhapsody." Mr. Gould was commissioned to write the piece by George Howard (the former conductor of the Air Force Band) for the Pennsylvania School Music Association[61] in the late 1930s when Mr. Gould was about twenty-five years old. Arnold insists that "conductors have an obligation to probe the depths of a composition beyond the printed page," and in pursuit of that knowledge, he spoke to Mr. Gould several times about the piece and his preparations before writing "Jericho Rhapsody." His reply was simply, "All I did was read the Book of Joshua."

---

61 Now the Pennsylvania Music Educators Association.

Many years later Arnald wrote what he called "An Interpretive Analysis of 'Jericho Rhapsody'" for *The Instrumentalist* magazine that was an in-depth comparison of Mr. Gould's masterpiece and the biblical writings. The brilliant article spoke of the overall ebb and flow of the story of the Lord's exhortation to Joshua to lead his people across the Jordan River and of the smaller nuances and associations that hadn't even occurred to the composer. A passage of three measures that contain twelve beats (relating to the "twelve men from the tribes of Israel") is not so rigid a construct that Mr. Gould remembers writing but admits a supernatural influence. As Arnald explains, "This is a perfect example of the environment in which a composer writes and which ... the subconscious emerged from his pen." Although Arnald discusses key signatures, phrasings, emphases and shadings, and other technical interpretations, he concentrates on the "imagery and emotion in the music." The article resounded within the concert band community for not only the insightful analysis, but the importance of the conductor's need to ascertain the composer's intent. No one, however, was more impressed than the composer himself. In a conversation and, days later, a note he mailed to Arnald, Mr. Gould said:

Dear Gabe,

I read your Jericho analysis and I more than approve—I learned from it! It confirms our phone conversation which I enjoyed so much and I want to "reconfirm" in writing how impressed I am with your "in depth" sensitivity and approach to the sound of my music. In the name of Joshua my thanks and appreciation!

Morton

Arnald continued the popular Music of Black America concert with jazz trumpeter Clark Terry playing with the Airmen of Note. Mr. Terry was a member of *The Tonight Show* Band (he was the first black

Michael A. Gabriel

staff musician at NBC and was hired in 1960), and Arnald contacted him through his friend, Doc Severinsen. A spring snowstorm in the Midwest delayed Mr. Terry's flight from St. Louis (his hometown and where he lived at the time) and caused him to miss the planned one o'clock rehearsal on the day of the concert. As Arnald began the national anthem to begin the concert, Mr. Terry entered the backstage at Departmental Auditorium. After the anthem, Arnald stepped into the wings and asked him what he'd like to do for the afternoon's concert. (They'd discussed and planned the lineup, but a rehearsal is needed to work through personal playing styles, tempos, keys, timing, and other small details that add polish to a performance.) Mr. Terry said, "Follow my lead," and both men walked onstage in front of the SRO house. Mr. Terry told the assembled patrons that he'd just arrived from St. Louis and that he and the Air Force dance band hadn't had time for a rehearsal. "Rehearsals are more fun than concerts," he explained, "so we're going to show you how we rehearse." He talked to the audience about the discussions between the conductor and soloist and what direction was given to the band members. What the delighted patrons were treated to was a rehearsal *and* a concert. The highlight of the concert was his big hit, "Mumbles," which, he further explained, began as a scat tune. In his early performances of the tune, the scat he sang sounded a lot like a pastor he once heard, so he modified the vocalizations to a jumble of unintelligible syllables that sounded, almost, like actual lyrics. His off-the-cuff banter and jokes had them, and the Airmen of Note band members, in stitches as the professional jazz musicians rolled through the afternoon.

Arnald and his buddies from Cortland were among the millions of weekly listeners to tune in to NBC Radio to hear a popular radio show of the 1940s and 1950s that began with, "Forty-eight states, forty-eight stars, forty-eight men marching down the main street of everybody's hometown! Here comes the Cities Service Band of America, conducted by Paul Lavalle!" Arnald was commander of the Air Force Band at Sampson Air Force Base at the time, and one day he, brother Min, Mat Dadamio, and Frank Biviano decided to drive to New York City to see the live broadcast. Their friend Ray Crisara played with the band, and after phoning him to arrange an introduction, they attended the taping and met the conductor. Moving forward nearly twenty years, Arnald decided the perfect guest for the An Old-Fashioned Concert in the Park concert would be Paul Lavalle, and he simply picked up the phone, reminded Mr. Lavalle of their meeting two decades prior, and invited the then conductor of the Radio City Music Hall Orchestra to guest conduct the Air Force Band. It was a nostalgic journey back to a slice of Americana that was becoming a fading memory in most cities and towns—a Sunday afternoon concert at a bandstand in the park. The Singing Sergeants completed the trip with a medley of turn-of-the-century favorites.

The final concert of the winter season was an innovative selection of music from some of the finest arrangers and composers of the day, and Arnald had to look no further than his own staff. The Air Force Band Composing and Arranging Staff[62] was a unit unmatched in any of the area service bands due simply to the fact that none of the others had a staff of arrangers. In the early 1950s the Air Force Band's radio broadcast *Serenade in Blue* soared in popularity due to the unique sound generated by true arranging and composing greats like Sammy Nestico and Floyd Werle. Others, including Henry Gass, Jordon Waggoner, Ralph Rayner, Lawrence Odom, John Caughman, E. Takeo Kudo, Serge de Gastyne, and David Avshalomov (although a Singing Sergeant and not technically on the Arranging and Composing Staff), combined to create and arrange some of the finest concert band, orchestra, and jazz band music of the day.

The concert that March 28 contained only five pieces yet was a powerful showcase of the world-class talent employed by the air force and included two Washington, DC, premieres and "Spring Rondo," a world premier by David Avshalomov. The Washington debuts were "Sinfonia Sacra" by Floyd Werle and Serge de Gastyne's Symphony Number 4 for Band; each was a four-movement, technically demanding

---

62 Senior M.Sgt. Harry Gleeson, who was information director, added *Composing* in press releases and on programs to more accurately reflect the work they did and to "make it unique among the major military bands." He also made the change without consulting anyone and remembers: "It stuck. It's amazing what can be accomplished at a low level when you simply don't bother to ask but just do it!"

challenge for both the instrumentalists and conductor, and they delivered what Senior M.Sgt. Harry Gleeson remembers as "one of the finest musical moments in the history of the United States Air Force Band." "Sinfonia Sacra" is scored for concert band and rock band, and the final movement contains a narration taken from the Bible about the relevance of youth; it was a message, thousands of years old, that was as important then as when it was written.

Serge de Gastyne was a French-born composer whom Arnald had hired at Sampson Air Force Base nearly twenty years prior and had written *Conquest of the Air* for the fiftieth anniversary of powered flight. He collaborated with his wife (she wrote the lyrics) on Symphony Number 4 for Band, which contributed to the memorable afternoon. The two numbers that opened the concert were "Mutual Broadcasting System March" by John Caughman and "Partials" by E. Takeo Kudo featuring trumpet soloist John Maiocco.

Within a few short weeks following the Departmental Auditorium concerts, the Air Force Band would embark on their spring tour of southern states but not before Arnald would be invited to the Mid-East Instrumental Music Conference at Duquesne University School of Music in Pittsburgh. He would guest conduct the All-Star High School Clinic Band and teach a clinic titled Careers in Music. It was the practical side to his emphasis on music education that addressed a very real concern in the field: viable work. Budget cuts in school programs usually target music and other fine arts to a greater degree than other programs and, as a result, squeeze an already tight job market. In addition to civilian options, he naturally talked about a career in the military that provided the opportunity of service to one's country while pursuing, at a high, professional level, a career in music. The power of his message was the obvious fact of his standing in the community of music education and performance and his stature and rank in the US Air Force. Because of his passion and commitment to music and to the air force at similar clinics around the country, Arnald was awarded the Air Force Honorary Recruiter's Certificate in October of that year. It is an honor seldom given to active personnel, and during the presentation, Brig. Gen. Conrad S. Allman, US Air Force recruiting service commander, said, "The unusual dedication and help which Colonel Gabriel has given to Air Force recruiters warranted breaking tradition in awarding the certificate."

The spring tour had the band travel to ten southern states to play thirty concerts over twenty-five days to packed houses and some of the most appreciative crowds in the band's history. Four states' governors (Alabama's George Wallace; Mississippi's John Bell Williams; North Carolina's Robert Scott, and Tennessee's Winfield Dunn) declared Air Force Band Week in their states. In both Knoxville and Memphis, the concert venue was moved to a location that more than doubled the capacity, yet still the band played to an overflow house. The tour also wound through South Carolina, Arkansas, Texas, Louisiana, Virginia, and Georgia. Ninety encores were played as a result of more than seventy standing ovations after performances of one of the two selected programs featuring, respectively, *Divertimento for Band* by Karl Kroeger, paired with the Singing Sergeants performance of Floyd Werle's arrangement of Frank Loesser's *The Most Happy Fella*, or a three-menu selection of: Robert Russell Bennett's *Suite of Old American Dances*, followed by *Aegean Festival Overture* by Andreas Makris as transcribed by Major A Bader, and ending with Floyd Werle's concert band and Singing Sergeants medley, *Transcontinental Tour*.

THE AIR FORCE BAND MUSICIANS

Although the winter concert series featured celebrity guests, the spring and fall tour concerts and summer concert series in Washington, DC, increasingly featured the band's fine musicians. Arnald varied programs that allowed him to showcase the wide range of talent he'd hired for the air force. He expanded on the concept he'd begun when he recognized the world-class talent of trombonist Larry Wiehe and featured him at concerts both locally and on tour. The tour of southern states (surprisingly, the first tour of the area since 1958) allowed soloists Lawrence Odom, harp; James Scott, saxophone; Richard Estes, baritone; and singers John Carpenter and William Stevens, both tenors, to step into the spotlight.

Among the vast pool of talent in the Air Force Band, Lawrence Odom deserves special mention for his contribution to the excellence of the group. After his graduation from the University of Oklahoma's School of Music as an oboe major with a piano minor, he joined the Air Force Band as a pianist with the Strolling Strings. Within a year, he found himself as an overage due to the unexpected reenlistment of another musician and was fortuitously hired by Arnold in 1959 to play oboe in the US Air Force Band in Europe. "Those were the good days," Lawrence remembers. "The USAFE Band toured almost every month and 'Domenico' took us to all the great cities and concert halls ... a fabulous education." In an effort to improve their repertoire from strictly "band stuff," Arnold "let me try my hand at arranging." It would be the beginning of what would help to elevate the Air Force Band (in Washington where he would return) to great heights and label him as, "the finest transcriber of orchestral repertoire in the history of wind band music." He would come to transcribe a total of 259 works for orchestra, band, and harp chamber music.

Lawrence Odom's interest in music is unquenchable. While in Germany, he took harp lessons from Heinz Gunter at the opera house and played trombone in the USAFE marching band (the same band featured in the B movie *The Phony American*). When he returned to Washington a couple of years later and learned Arnold would take over the band, he arranged *Salome's Dance* and *Romeo and Juliet* for him "so that he would have some new pieces that the former conductor had never seen." He continued harp lessons with Jeanne Chalifoux, harpist with the National Symphony Orchestra, and when the Air Force Band's harpist left in 1964, legend has it that Lawrence approached Arnold and said, "Give me three months, and I'll be your harpist." As the principal harpist for the US Air Force Band and Symphony Orchestra, he performed at the White House for fourteen years. After he retired from the air force, he became the principal harpist for the Kennedy Center Opera House Orchestra and performed as soloist for the Paris Opera, Vienna State Opera, Stuttgart Ballet, New York City Ballet, the American Ballet Theater, and the Royal Ballet.

At the dawn of the computer age, and while working at the Kennedy Center, Lawrence enrolled in an IBM computer school and became an analyst in New Orleans (where he also played principal harp for the New Orleans Philharmonic). After two years in New Orleans and then a short stint back in Washington, he moved to his native Oklahoma and earned degrees in mathematics and chemistry and a doctor of pharmacy. He would remain a pharmacist until 1999 but would continue to transcribe music and perform at the Kennedy Center and Lincoln Center. Along the way, he designed and built a home "in the grand manner" in Heavener, Oklahoma, and today, he remains active in music, playing for weddings and recitals. Lawrence credits one man for his success and that of the Air Force Band: "In the end, the US Air Force Band had the best repertoire of all the service bands only because of your father. He changed my life, and I can never thank him enough."

The success of every component of the Air Force Band, including the concert band, ceremonial band, Singing Sergeants, Airmen of Note, symphony orchestra, Strolling Strings, and woodwind quintet continued to soar. The smaller groups were made up of members of the larger performance units and were formed to increase their ability to answer the increasing demand for musical support. The ceremonial band could, on occasion, substitute for the full concert band with, in this time of budget cuts, lower cost and little loss of effect.

Budget cuts notwithstanding, Arnald once again chose to innovate to provide a greater opportunity for his musicians to perform and for the public in the Washington area to hear their music. In the fall of 1971, he tasked George Moquin, the band's Scheduling NCO, with booking A Musical Tour of the Beltway, a concert series that would play in every surrounding county in Maryland and Virginia and would, initially, feature the USAF Symphony Orchestra, the Singing Sergeants, woodwind quintet, and Chamber Players.

The woodwind quintet, originally formed in 1961, was then composed of five of the finest instrumentalists in the US Air Force, if not the world. Prior to their joining the Air Force Band in Washington, their résumés reflected the high-caliber training and achievement that was the backbone of the organization. Sgt. Dave Brown, flute, studied at Omaha University and Alaska University and was principal flute with the Anchorage Symphony Orchestra and the Alaska Chamber

Orchestra. Sgt. Cedric Coleman, bassoon, graduated from the New England Conservatory of Music, played with the Boston Symphony and Boston Pops, and was principal bassoon with the Brockton and New Bedford, Massachusetts, orchestras. Sgt. Richard Dorsey, oboe, was a graduate of Boston University and performed with the Portland (Maine) Orchestra and Brockton Orchestra. Sgt. Johnny Woody, horn, was a member of the University Symphonic Band and Symphony Orchestra at Kansas University and performed in both the student and faculty woodwind quintet before graduating. Sgt. William Hilferty, clarinet, attended Juilliard School of Music as a scholarship student and was principal clarinet with the National Symphony Orchestra Association of New York City.

The Fall Tour of the Beltway was another series that continued to evolve over its history. By the fall of 1974, the symphony orchestra was forced into inactive status due to a lack of violinists. Budgetary constraints simply prevented the hiring of musicians the orchestra needed to replace those both leaving the air force at the end of their commitments and those retiring. Arnald shifted the focus of the concerts by scheduling the concert band and Singing Sergeants (both with the band and as a separate unit) to replace the orchestra. The always popular Airmen of Note played two concerts to round out the series.

Because most of the Beltway concerts were held at area high school auditoriums, Arnald decided to, once again, involve the students. The Student Guest Artist Series at the Departmental Auditorium had evolved into concerts utilizing celebrity performers, and Arnald decided to reengage area students by featuring a local high school's music director conducting one number with his student soloist. One of the most popular concerts of the season was held in Burtonsville, Maryland, at Paint Branch High School where the school's chorus joined the Singing Sergeants to form a joint chorus in front of an enthusiastic SRO crowd that underscored Arnald's success at not only entertaining the civilian public, but presenting the air force, and by extension the rest of the military, in a positive light.

Canadian National Exhibition (or, The Ex) is a popular fair held in a 192-acre park in Toronto, Ontario, and is the largest of its kind in

The Force of Destiny

the country. The annual event features agricultural and technological exhibitions, an entire building of food offerings, a midway filled with rides, and a wide variety of entertainment, including, in 1971, Jerry Lewis, The Carpenters, Fifth Dimension, a Showcase of Champions Drum & Bugle Corps Presentation, and many others. The Air Force Band was invited to represent the US Air Force beginning August 30 for an eight-day run that allowed many thousands of Canadians to hear the top-notch band. Remarkably, the eleven concerts, played within the fine acoustics of the CNE Bandshell, were performed without repeating a piece over the eight days.[63] Among the dozens of performing acts over the eighteen-day event, the Air Force Band was singled out in a review published in the *Toronto Globe and Mail* as, simply "the finest band in the world."

Because of the band's commitment to the Canadian National Exhibition, the fall tour of 1971 was a shortened, eleven-day trip through Missouri, southern Illinois, and western Kentucky. Although only about a third of the length of time they would normally spend on tour, for the first time in the band's history, they packed the concert halls by filling them to almost 110 percent of their stated capacity. The enthusiastic patrons demanded an astounding fifty-one encores over the eleven concerts with the most popular being the Singing Sergeants rendition of "Put Your Hand in the Hand," a gospel-rock song that would peak at number two on the charts that year. Arnald chose that and other contemporary rock and popular tunes in his continuing attempt to engage young people. Most concerts were held at high school and college auditoriums and naturally helped to draw students, especially to the matinees whose programs were written with a younger audience in mind. The sobering fact was that, as the decade of the seventies wore on, fewer would attend the matinee concerts, and as a result, Arnald began to cut back on afternoons and concentrated on the evening performances.

---

63 The exception, of course, was the popular encore, "The Stars and Stripes Forever."

Jimmy Stewart, Arnald, and
the Singing Sergeants

Jo Anne Worley

Boris Karloff and
Arnald in England

Edward G. Robinson

Shirley Temple Black and Arnald
accept the George Washington Honor
Medal on *The Mike Douglas Show*

CHAPTER SEVENTEEN

Innovation

When they'd begun the winter concert series at Departmental Auditorium just after Arnald's arrival in Washington, they'd quickly filled the hall and turned away hundreds of patrons each week. The inclusion of the high-profile guests only increased the demand for tickets and ultimately forced the decision to look for a larger venue. Arnald initially resisted the move to a larger facility largely because of the latent fear that many performers harbor: "Can we fill the new hall?" In spite of the overwhelming evidence to the contrary, in the form of rave reviews in Washington area periodicals and the overflow crowds at each concert, Arnald worried about drawing enough to justify the change. In September 1971 an opportunity presented itself.

A National Cultural Center had been discussed and planned for Washington, DC, since the 1930s, and both the funding and the evolution of the idea had advanced to the point that in the mid-1960s, ground was finally broken for construction of the Kennedy Center for the Performing Arts. The National Symphony Orchestra (NSO) took up residence in the massive new structure on the Potomac River, and after much discussion with his staff (and much prodding by Sgt. Harry Gleeson), Arnald decided to move the winter concert series to the DAR Constitution Hall, the NSO's former residence. Even though the decision to move wasn't made until January 1972, just a month before the start of the winter season, and provided more than double the seating capacity over Departmental Auditorium, overflow crowds were the rule at every concert for the inaugural 1972 season. The announcement of an astounding *ten* celebrity performers marked the official beginning of the Guest Artist Series for the Air Force Band. In reality, the concept of celebrity guests had been well established over the years leading up to the first year at Constitution Hall, and the Guest Artist Series was the formal acknowledgement of that success.

The kickoff to the new season at the DAR Constitution Hall in 1972 featured one of the most popular entertainers in the country, Arthur Godfrey. Mr. Godfrey was known around the globe for fifty years of radio, television, motion picture, and stage performances, but because of his early beginnings in radio in the Washington area, and his longtime residence in Loudoun County in northern Virginia, he had a special following locally. He was also a colonel in the USAF Reserves and, in addition to his prior service in the naval reserve, was a proud supporter of the military. Arnald decided to repeat a concert Mr. Godfrey and the band had performed in November 1971 at a dedication of the Sousa Stage of the newly opened Kennedy Center[64] with narrations of Aaron Copland's "Lincoln Portrait" and, in celebration of the Air Force's twenty-fifth anniversary, "An Air Force Panorama." The latter was a compilation arranged and scored by Sgt. Floyd Werle, recorded that afternoon and released as an album. Much to Sergeant Werle's chagrin, Mr. Godfrey insisted on changing the written narration during each rehearsal and the subsequent performances. (He performed the piece several times over the ensuing years with the band.) His famously difficult personality came into play another time as well.

Prior to the November 1971 performance at the Kennedy Center, Sgt. Harry Gleeson phoned Mr. Godfrey to go over the details of the upcoming rehearsal and concert. He informed Mr. Godfrey that Arnald had decided to hold the rehearsal at the later-than-normal

---

64 The concert was attended by Pres. Richard M. Nixon, and in a letter sent to Arnald days later, he wrote, "Bands speak a message understood by all, and I am certain that everyone present was deeply moved by the spirit of patriotism and great pride in our country that permeated the Concert Hall. I wish that every American could have witnessed this outstanding musical tribute to one of our most universally famous bandmasters. It was a pleasure to participate with you on that memorable evening."

10:30 a.m. time to allow a smoother drive in from Leesburg, Virginia, thereby avoiding the legendary Washington, DC, drive-time traffic. Mr. Godfrey told him that he didn't want to put up with any traffic and all the driving and added, "I have a helipad here at the farm. Just have a chopper pick me up around 9:30."

"At first I thought he was kidding, but as the conversation went on, he made it very clear that he was serious," Sergeant Gleeson remembers. After promising to look into it, Sergeant Gleeson made his way into Arnald's office, and with assistant conductor Maj. Al Bader in attendance, he "laid the bombshell on them."

Arnald responded simply, "He's going to have to realize that I don't have that kind of power. I can't order a chopper!"

Not wishing to confront the headstrong celebrity, Sergeant Gleeson called a friend for some guidance at Special Air Mission (SAM) at Andrews Air Force Base in neighboring Maryland. SAM is tasked with the transportation of Congressional, Executive Branch, and distinguished visitors. After a short discussion with his friend, and now armed with his private number, he called the commander of SAM. Sergeant Gleeson laid out to the head of the squadron the dilemma he faced with regard to the strong-willed celebrity, retired Air Force Reserve colonel, and personal friend of Gen. Curtis LeMay. After listening patiently to Sergeant Gleeson's story, the colonel in charge told him he'd get back to him in the next twenty minutes. Ten minutes later, Sergeant Gleeson received a call asking who else would be on the helicopter to pick up Mr. Godfrey, and after indicating that both Colonel Gabriel and Major Bader would accompany him, he was told to be ready at 8:30 the next morning. (Although the runways at Bolling Air Force Base had been closed since 1961, a helipad still existed.)

Sergeant Gleeson returned to his boss's office and informed Arnald of the new development. "The look on (his) face was priceless!" Sergeant Gleeson remembers some forty years afterward.

The next morning, the helicopter landed on schedule, the three men boarded, and after donning headsets, the pilot asked, "Do any of you guys know how to get there?"

Sergeant Gleeson had anticipated that he'd be the one designated to drive Mr. Godfrey to rehearsals and the concert, and as a Loudoun County resident himself, he had scouted the route on a Sunday afternoon family drive in the country. He said to the pilot, "I know how to get there by driving. Will that do?"

The pilot responded, "Sure." And Sergeant Gleeson guided them up the Potomac River to Chain Bridge, over Tyson's Corner (where the new mall was), west on Route 7 past Leesburg, and off Route 9 to the farm, arriving right on time at 9:30. They returned to Bolling Air Force Base by the same less-than-direct, but safe and accurate, route. It was the accommodation of a somewhat unreasonable request through quick thinking (and maybe a little desperation) that, because of bureaucratic complexities, would never happen today and was also the first ever helicopter ride for the three veteran Air Force musicians.

THE GUEST ARTISTS

Harvey Phillips was the world's foremost tuba virtuoso and the man most responsible for expanding the repertoire of an instrument normally relegated to the back row of the band or orchestra. He began the now-cherished tradition of TubaChristmas at New York City's Rockefeller Plaza (now expanded to more than 250 cities) and Octubafest (and later, TubaEaster and Summertubafest), which are all celebratory gatherings of tuba enthusiasts held at venues across the country. His first appearance under Arnald's baton was during the Guest Artist Series on February 20 where he played *Helix*, a piece written for him and the Ithaca High School Band by Warren Benson. He also played the iconic *Tubby the Tuba*, narrated by Fred Eden, the morning announcer on WGMS, Washington's classical music station. Arnald conducted Mr. Phillips at several venues over the years, and Mr. Phillips said of their collaboration, "Colonel Gabriel is a most sensitive musician and conductor. He has the uncommon ability to anticipate the soloist's every mood, and under his direction, the large band seems to become one accompanying instrument—a remarkable achievement."

Leroy Anderson was a prolific composer of what are considered light classical music pieces. The popular tunes, including "Sleigh Ride," "Bugler's Holiday," "Syncopated Clock," "The Typewriter," and others, were regularly found at the top of popular music charts throughout the 1950s. He guest conducted the Air Force Band in a concert featuring ten of his most popular pieces. Just prior to beginning the rehearsal, the stern maestro counseled the musicians, "Gentlemen, this is not great art, but play it like it is." Arnald took the admonition as a valuable lesson to all conductors. "If it is worth playing, rehearse and play it as though it were a Mahler Symphony."

The well-known and well-traveled conductor Dr. Frederick Fennell pioneered the concept of the Wind Ensemble that advanced the idea of one instrument playing each part, thereby increasing intonation.[65] His groundbreaking work began with the Eastman Wind Ensemble and later the Dallas Wind Symphony, Minneapolis Symphony Orchestra, the Tokyo Kosei Wind Orchestra, and others. Dr. Fennell was the conductor in residence at the University of Miami (where he founded its wind ensemble) when he stepped onto the stage at Constitution Hall on March 5 to conduct three pieces in the Ports of Call concert. He led the Air Force Band in *Daybreak* and *Siegfried's Rhine Journey* by Wagner, *Fountains of Rome* by Respighi, and *Finlandia* by Sibelius. While Dr. Fennell was in high school, he was selected to play in the National High School Band that was conducted by John Philip Sousa just a year prior to Mr. Sousa's passing. From that perspective, his acclaim of Arnald some years later is especially meaningful: "Yours has been America's most distinguished military music career—one we've been waiting for these many decades."

Shirley Temple's popularity as a child star extended decades past her depression-era debut in the 1930s. Her films lifted millions of fans with an upbeat message and by the brilliant smile framed by her trademark curls. As an adult, she transitioned seamlessly into diplomacy; when she appeared on the March 12, 1972 concert with the Air Force Band, she was a part of the US delegation to the United Nations. She would be appointed as US Ambassador to Ghana and,

---

65 In practice, however, two woodwinds (clarinets, etc.) would often join to better balance the brass section.

later, Ambassador to Czechoslovakia. The idea to invite the talented childhood icon came not from the weekly staff meetings but from a source closer to home.

One day, Arnald and my fourteen-year-old sister Joanne were watching a Shirley Temple movie on television when Joanne asked, "Is she still alive?" The question sparked an idea, and Arnald responded, "Of course she is, and I'm going to ask her to appear with the band!" From that simple beginning, Arnald called her and suggested she do the narration of Don Gillis' *The Man Who Invented Music*, a children's story. She quickly agreed to appear for the Guest Artist Series in March 1972, but asked if there were another piece she could do because she felt it important to separate her adult life from her well-known childhood. Arnald chose the unabashedly patriotic *I Am an American* by Carmen Dragon, and her stirring rendition had the overcapacity audience at Constitution Hall on their feet at its conclusion. As the many VIPs in attendance filed backstage after the performance, Ms. Black patiently and cheerfully signed each program offered, including those from band members and Singing Sergeants. After nearly an hour of signing, Arnald asked if she'd had enough, but she insisted on continuing until each program was signed and each patron was satisfied.

About two months later, she was cohost on the popular daytime television variety show, *The Mike Douglas Show*, and returned the favor by inviting Arnald and a cut-down version of the band and Singing Sergeants (there was just not enough room on stage in the taping studio). She repeated her narration of Carmen Dragon's *I Am an American* in a performance that earned her, Mike Douglas, and the Air Force Band the coveted George Washington Honor Medal from Freedoms Foundation at Valley Forge, Pennsylvania. The medal is awarded: "For the most significant dynamic ... television program which increase(s) the understanding of our American Way of Life." The award ceremony took place a year later, outdoors, adjacent to Independence Hall in another televised appearance for *The Mike Douglas Show*, this time with the full band and Singing Sergeants. Ms. Black's appearance that day came a little more than six months after undergoing a mastectomy due to a diagnosis of breast cancer. She was one of the first celebrities to publicly announce having the operation and did so in an effort to remove the stigma from a widespread and treatable disease.

There are many examples of her thoughtfulness and concern for others. After the concert and award ceremony for the George Washington Gold Medal in Philadelphia, Arnald asked if she had time to meet his brother Min and three of Arnald's childhood best friends, Albert, Tony, and Nick Doloisio. Tony was in a wheelchair, suffering from the effects of Amyotrophic Lateral Sclerosis (ALS, or Lou Gehrig's disease); the four had driven from Cortland, New York, to see the ceremony and concert. She instead suggested that they meet for dinner, and during the course of the evening, after finding out they were staying the night, she asked to meet for breakfast before they left. She graciously posed for a photograph with the three Rinkydinks, "Dub," "Gallagher," and Nick, and the framed photo hung in a prominent place in the Doloisio home for many years.

Later that year, while on the fall 1973 tour, the band was scheduled to appear at a venue near Ms. Black's Thousand Oaks, California, home. Arnald called her to extend a personal invitation to attend the concert in Monterrey as a special guest. Her daughter Susan answered and explained to Arnald that Ms. Black had been somewhat depressed, had withdrawn from public, and had not ventured out of her home for some time. After discussing the plan with Susan, one morning while en route between concerts, Arnald bused the entire chorus to her home. Parking out of view at the bottom of the driveway, the Singing Sergeants set up facing the back wall of her home near the pool and performed a miniconcert for Arnald's old friend, singing the popular Irving Berlin song, "A Pretty Girl Is Like a Melody." Susan had arranged for a catered lunch to be served, and Ms. Black joined Arnald and the Singing Sergeants, socializing with them for several hours. In a phone conversation after they'd returned to Washington, Susan related to Arnald that her mother had brightened considerably and been deeply touched at his thoughtfulness.

Arnald remembers the former child star and diplomat fondly. "I was impressed by the fact that she was so down to earth and genuine and so cooperative in everything that was expected of her." At the end of every concert, Arnald conducted the rousing "The Stars and Stripes

Forever," and after beginning John Philip Sousa's march, he beckoned his guest artist from the off-stage wings to mount the podium and lead the band in its conclusion. "When Shirley conducted, the band really followed her," Arnald remembers. At the end of the piece, as she stepped off the podium, Arnald met her with a kiss on the cheek to which she answered, "Why, thank you, Colonel!" Arnald's response could have come from any of her millions of childhood movie fans when he said honestly, "No. Thank you. I have been waiting forty years to do that!"

Appearing on the same concert with Shirley Temple Black, those unfamiliar with one of the world's foremost jazz trombonist were in for a pleasant surprise. In addition to Leroy Anderson's *The Irish Washerwoman*, *Sunny* by Bobby Hebb and Hoagy Carmichael's *Stardust*, Urbie Green's version of *Flight of the Bumblebee* was an unforgettable rendition. Mr. Green has played with some of the all-time greats in jazz, including Gene Krupa and Woody Herman, but when Arnald initially contacted Mr. Green, he modestly asked, "Why do you want me? You have Dave Steinmeyer." Sergeant Steinmeyer was the leader of the Airman of Note, and because of his recordings with some of the best in the jazz industry, he was gaining a reputation as a world-class trombonist. Arnald remembers, "Urbie did come and gave a superb concert."

The last of the concerts to feature guest artists for the debut series at Constitution Hall were two giants in the field of jazz. Joe Morello was best known as the drummer in the Dave Brubeck Quartet (he would appear on more than sixty albums and countless appearances with them). His ability to play complex time signatures lent a unique complexity to the group. He was born with partial vision and, he told Arnald, was warned by his doctor as an adult that if he continued to play the drums, he would go blind (because of the vibration and noise). Unconcerned with the diagnosis and unwilling to give up his craft, he continued to play, and for his next appearance with the band, he was accompanied by a Seeing Eye dog who led him to the drum set and laid quietly nearby till the performance was over. On that Sunday afternoon, Mr. Morello was featured on *Soundprint 15* by Monty Tubbs.

Joining Joe Morello was Arnald's friend Doc Severinsen performing Floyd Werle's Concerto for Trumpet; with this concert he had appeared with the Air Force Band more than any other guest artist in their history. He had also not only performed the concerto with Arnald in front of the several other symphony orchestras but at a televised concert with the Boston Pops conducted by Arthur Fiedler.

The final concert of the inaugural Constitution Hall series featured no celebrity guest artists but was a special celebration as a result of a request from an old friend. Lt. Gen. Eugene "Ben" LeBailly was now the chairman of the Inter-American Defense Board, an organization formed thirty years prior to advise and coordinate the member states of the Organization of American States (OAS) with respect to military and defense matters. Ben had asked him to program a concert to celebrate the organization's anniversary, and Arnald put together a variety of the hemisphere's music, including a world premiere of *The Inter-American Defense Board Anthem*, composed and conducted by Chilean Air Force Lt. Col. Rodolfo Martinez Ugarte who'd traveled to Washington, DC, from his home country for the performance. The concert was more than the simple fulfillment of an order from a superior officer; it was truly a labor of love and gratitude for a close friend and professional colleague of nearly twenty years. At Langley Air Force Base in 1955, it was Ben who had convinced Arnald, unsure of his future in the air force, to retain his commission rather than give it up to teach high school music. More than good career advice, it was an honest assessment from one friend to another and one that Arnald would never forget.

TOURS

The spring tour that year wound through fourteen cities in Pennsylvania, four in Ohio, and two in New York with the final stop in Cortland, New York. The concert in Arnald's hometown deviated from the alternating two programs that, now, every tour featured and became a special dedication and celebration of his parents' fiftieth wedding anniversary. *La Forza Del Destino* by Giuseppe Verdi opened the Italian American program and thrilled each of the more than three thousand patrons who filled the Moffett Center Gymnasium, but none more than Filomena and Ferdinando, who'd traveled from Miami to be in attendance.

The concert was also an opportunity for Arnald to recognize an old friend and conductor of the Cortland Civic Band, eighty-four-year-old Frank Crisara. As he introduced Mr. Crisara's selection that afternoon, *American Overture for Band* by Joseph Willcox Jenkins, Arnald noted that Raymond Crisara, Frank's son, was "one of the country's leading trumpet players." Patriotic selections such as "American Variations" and "Americans We" led to a Floyd Werle arrangement of a Singing Sergeants medley titled *A Holiday in Italy*. Included were the popular tunes "*Volare*," "*Arrivederci Roma*," and "*Sorrento*" and soloists Sgts. Cecil Pearce, John Carpenter, and Richard Estes singing in Italian. By the time the chorus began "*Funiculi-Funicula*," Ferdinando enthusiastically leapt to his feet and joined in full voice, singing along to one of his favorite songs.[66] It left little doubt to the audience and band members where Arnald inherited his showmanship.

The spring and fall tours continued to be extremely popular, drawing overcapacity crowds throughout the decade while setting other firsts. The fall tour of 1976, which included stops in Alaska, marked the first time a military service band had played in each of the fifty states, and the Air Force Band was the first military band to play at the Grand Ole Opry during their stop in Nashville on the spring tour of 1980. The tours involve the care and feeding of nearly one hundred musicians and support personnel and are necessarily complex. With regard to band tours, the Pentagon split the country into five geographical areas that each of the four service bands in the Washington, DC, area would tour twice a year. Arnald's initial hope of an annual international tour and a domestic one never came to fruition due to a combination of budgetary considerations and the added complexity of clearances from the State Department and from foreign officials.

---

[66] Although he and Filomena spoke to each other and their circle of friends in Italian, retained their thick accents throughout their lives, and were proud of their Italian heritage, they refused a trip to Italy Arnald and his brothers offered for the anniversary, saying, "Why? What's there for us?" They were obviously content in their adopted country.

Planning for a tour began no less than six months prior to its beginning and involved coordination between the Pentagon, the other service bands, and the Air Force Band tour office. The process began with not only the selection of one of the geographical areas, but specific cities and towns within each area. Coordinating the logistics was (and is) a massive undertaking requiring the cooperation of the tour office and the other support sections such as administration, operations, director of tours, public information, and supply. It further involved contact with local officials, air force recruiters, hotels, local sponsors, newspapers (or other organizations that may disseminate information about the concert, such as booster clubs, chambers of commerce, civic music groups, etc.), and finally, a visit by the director of tours. Supply and music support sections ensure, respectively, that uniforms are properly issued (day/evening/summer/winter) and office supplies, musical instruments, and sheet music are purchased, printed, and distributed. The professionalism with which each tour was planned and conducted was a direct result of the leadership of its commander.

Arnald hired, or retained, the right man, or woman, for each job. His direct involvement was only what became necessary; he delegated authority and retained responsibility. He outlined his philosophy of leadership in an article some years later titled, appropriately, "Accountability." "It is the mandate if the commander is to share the praise of successful ideas with those who contributed to them. It is, however, never acceptable to ask that blame be shared in the event of failure. We praise in public but reprimand, if warranted, in private." This delivered a powerful message and provided an equally powerful incentive to his staff and others under his command to strive for excellence. Just a few of his super chiefs include a team of experts who he relied on to get things done, including Harry Gleeson, director of information; George Moquin, operations; Ray Stone, tours; and H. Miracle, supply.

Because the different units of the US Air Force Band continued to evolve through personnel changes (due to attrition) and the band's stature in the music world attracted the interest of the country's top musicians, Arnald had the luxury of choosing among the best to fill the increasingly fewer vacancies. Requests for auditions outstripped the available positions, and a reenlistment rate of more than 50 percent meant only the best would have a shot at playing in the band. This was a trend unseen elsewhere in the military at a time when government service was an increasingly unpopular career choice. One particular musician's audition and eventual addition to the band roster would herald another groundbreaking first.

The debut concert of the 1973 Guest Artist Series featured the world-renowned conductor, composer, and arranger Carmen Dragon. At the conclusion of his conducting the band in the finale to Symphony No. 5 by Dmitri Shostakovich, Mr. Dragon approached the microphone and asked the capacity audience at the DAR Constitution Hall if they had noticed anything different in that day's performance. The patrons, quiet at first, were then introduced to clarinet player Sgt. Karen Riale (Erler), the first female instrumentalist to become a member of any of the Washington-area service bands; the announcement was met with a tumultuous ovation.

The choice to hire Karen was made with little regard to gender. Born in Cedarhurst, New York, she attended Lawrence High School, and after graduating, she enrolled in the Ithaca College School of Music where she played under Arnald's old mentor, Walter Beeler. She rose to principle clarinetist with the orchestra, and after meeting her future husband, Don Riale, and a move to Washington, DC,[67] she finished her bachelor of music degree in Performance at Catholic University. She won a highly competitive audition in 1972 and, later that year, joined the band. A month after her debut performance with the Air Force Band, she became the first woman member of the Inter-Service Symphonic Band, an elite one hundred–piece band made up of twenty-five members of each of Washington's military service bands. The following month, when the US Air Force Band shipped out for their spring tour of California and the Pacific Northwest, Sergeant Riale became the first woman instrumentalist to tour with a major military band.

The addition of Sgt. Karen Riale seemed to open the floodgates to the hiring of women musicians. By the fall of that year, Arnald had

---

[67] Don was hired as a trumpet player for the Air Force Band.

hired two women to join the chorus, and in just a few short years, ten women's voices filled out the Singing Sergeants to a fully operational mixed chorus. The radical change to a mixed-voice chorus was an immediate success with audiences and broadened their repertoire, but the Air Force Band's music library collection, up to that point, was written for an all-male chorus. Arnald directed the arranging staff, led by Sgt. Floyd Werle, to set to work composing and rearranging their nearly two thousand in-house manuscript compositions. With the introduction of women, the Singing Sergeants, the official chorus of the United States Air Force, would expand to twenty-four voices (from twelve when Arnald first took command), and their increased demand would have them performing as a distinct unit, separate from the concert band.

By 1980, the versatile group's repertoire included a wide-ranging collection crossing genres from jazz, popular, operatic, country-and-western, Broadway show tunes, American folk, spirituals and gospel, and finally, the addition of choreography, showcasing the acting and dancing talents of the men and women in air force blue. Their demand soared, and they were increasingly dispatched to functions around the world as a stand-alone unit. By the late 1970s, the Singing Sergeants had traveled more than 1.5 million miles and performed to 35 million people in more than fifty counties. They performed not only for military functions in the Washington, DC, area, but for civic groups and public celebrations. Their appearances on televisions shows such as *The Joey Bishop Show*, *The Mike Douglas Show*, *The Toni Tenille Show*, *The Tonight Show*, and numerous local broadcasts around the country brought them to millions more.

William Conrad, Arnald, and the USAF Honor Guard

Victor Borge

Colonel Gabriel, Carmen Dragon, and Major Al Bader

Mr. Rogers and friends

CHAPTER EIGHTEEN

The Guest Artist Series

Although the decade of the seventies lacked the social upheaval and revolutionary changes that stressed generational ties during the sixties, the times were no less tumultuous. The Watergate trial and eventual resignation of President Nixon, the United States' withdrawal of troops from Southeast Asia, increasing inflation and unemployment, an oil boycott and ensuing energy crisis, and a spike in tensions with the USSR after their invasion of Afghanistan combined to ratchet up the distrust Americans had with regard to their government and its military. At the Air Force Band, the ongoing military budget cuts meant having to do more with less funding even as their popularity remained at an all-time high. All this occurred when the antiwar movement's animus, unfortunately, spilled over to the returning fighting servicemen. It is interesting to note that capacity attendances at concerts was the rule rather than the exception, demand for tickets on tours outstripped their availability, and standing ovations following multiple encores were heard at most concerts by the uniformed musicians.

Along with the professional successes Arnald enjoyed with his music, the seventies brought personal hardships as well. On August 20, 1974, Ferdinando Gabriele suddenly passed away at the hospital in Miami Beach. Although it is not clear how Arnald's eighty-four-year-old father died, he had complained of abdominal discomfort and was prescribed medication to treat the pain for many years. The unspecified affliction became so bad during the war that he'd requested the army send Arnald home to help run the grocery store. They obviously denied the request. After his passing, Ferdinando was flown to his adopted hometown of Cortland, New York, where the family gathered for an emotional service at St. Anthony's Catholic Church and his interment at nearby St. Mary's Cemetery.

A few months later, Arnald and Joan separated. The simple answer to the breakup of the marriage was one that many couples experience and was just that they "grew apart," but Arnald admits, "My many absences due to tours and guest conducting also became a problem." The travel likely exacerbated the rift caused by their increasingly differing lifestyles, and with the eldest three of us having moved out of the house and away to college, the time seemed right. They would divorce within the year and end their twenty-five-year union.

There is little doubt that among the myriad accomplishments, awards, and worldwide acclaim Arnald garnered with the US Air Force Band, his overarching legacy with the organization remains the establishment of the Guest Artist Series. Hundreds of musicians, actors, politicians, and other celebrities have appeared with the band in the popular series and are drawn by not only the chance to appear at the DAR Constitution Hall, the iconic venue located in the middle of Washington, DC, but the opportunity to perform with the Air Force Band. Dutch conductor Jan Molenaar and French composer and pianist Serge Lancen (who appeared on the same program in 1973) both told Arnald that they'd heard the Air Force Band was the best in the world, and after having appeared, they confirmed what they'd heard as true.

Audiences fill the almost four thousand-seat hall anxious to see their favorite personality step out of his/her comfort zone and perform a selection of music they are not known for or narrate a stirring piece backed by a full concert band. The celebrity guests run the gamut of the entertainment field from stage, screen, and television actors (William Conrad, Edward G. Robinson, Shirley Temple); popular entertainers (Jerry Lewis, Art Buchwald, Arthur Godfrey); comedians, (Jo Anne Worley, Victor Borge); and a cross section of musical guests representing nearly every genre, including classical (Leroy Anderson, Arthur Fiedler, Aaron Copland); jazz (Tommy Newsom, Charlie Byrd, Sarah Vaughan); country-and-western (Buck Owens, Larry Gatlin,

The Force of Destiny

Claude Akins); and children's programming (Fred Rogers, Sesame Street's Big Bird, Ringling Bros. and Barnum & Bailey's conductor Merle Evans).

It is a tribute to the professionalism and dedication of these guest artists (the above is not a comprehensive list but a small sampling of the dozens who appeared with the band throughout Arnald's tenure) that their performances were mounted with a minimum of rehearsal time. The Sunday afternoon concerts were scheduled for a three o'clock downbeat with the single rehearsal with the artist just an hour prior to the doors opening at two o'clock. For the narrations, a script was sent ahead of time, and the one o'clock read-through allowed for timing adjustments and the establishment of Arnald's cues to the performer. If the artist was an instrumentalist or a singer, Arnald requested a recording of the piece. A great deal of preparation prior to the Sunday rehearsal obviously mitigated any major problems (Maj. Al Bader was instrumental in helping to prep the band); however, a certain amount of seat-of-the-pants effort was required to pull together the polished performances enjoyed by the mostly SRO crowds each week.

William Conrad, the popular television, motion picture, and former radio actor first appeared with the band in 1974—the first of many collaborations Arnald and he would have. Over the years, their professional relationship would evolve into a close, personal friendship such that booking a gig became, "When the colonel calls, I come!"[68] He appeared with such frequency that programs and press releases billed him as "the Air Force Band's unofficial Guest Artist in residence." Mr. Conrad was at the height of his popularity when he and Arnald first met and was staring in the hit television series *Cannon*. William Conrad arrived a few days early before the Constitution Hall concert to satisfy a special request to perform at the Pentagon. Arnald got their relationship off to a rocky start with his introduction that day. Mr. Conrad was slated to do the narration of Aaron Copland's "Lincoln Portrait," the deep resonance of his voice a perfect vehicle for the powerful piece, and Colonel Gabriel began by introducing him as William *Cannon*. Without missing a beat, the quick-thinking

---

68 In 1974, for example, he agreed to appear with the band and to fill in when Charlton Heston had to cancel.

professional responded, "Thank you, *Major*," at once displaying his lively sense of humor.

Working together over the few days of rehearsals and concerts, Bill (as he insisted Arnald call him) became fascinated by the appearance of power Arnald wielded in leading nearly one hundred musicians (including singers), and asked Arnald if he could teach him to conduct the group. Arnald invited him to return the following year, and he immediately accepted. As he and his staff were puzzling over what Bill would do with the band, Arnald remembered his request to conduct and came up with an ingenious piece of programming he called *1812 Overture with "Cannon."* Arnald had the thunderous Tchaikovsky piece cut down into a smaller arrangement that essentially consisted of the beginning and the end, omitting the developmental sections, and leaving a compact, lively piece. Several years later, while on tour in Ft. Worth, Texas, Arnald invited Bill to conduct the arrangement once again, this time at the Tarrant County Convention Center in front of a capacity crowd of fourteen thousand. Arnald borrowed antiphonal brass from a friend who was the conductor of the University of Texas in nearby Arlington and staged a performance that not only thrilled the audience, but also the popular television star. A recording of the concert was given to Bill and, Arnald remembers, was "played for everyone who visited him at his home." Bill enjoyed the piece so much that he later did it with the San Francisco Symphony and the Honolulu Symphony.

During a fall tour of the West Coast, the band was scheduled to play an afternoon concert at Disneyland, and one day Arnald received a call from Bill asking if he was free the evening of the concert to come to dinner at Bill's home in the Los Angeles area. Arnald asked about bringing his assistant conductor, Al Bader, and Bill insisted that he meant the entire group: band, singers, loading personnel, truck drivers, all come to dinner. They were feted with two hours of cocktails and a catered dinner for one hundred air force bandsmen. What Bill didn't know was that Arnald was aware that that day, September 27, was Bill's birthday, and during dessert, Arnald led the entire group singing "Happy Birthday" to the tune of Handel's "Hallelujah Chorus." His confidence buoyed by having conducted the *1812 Overture* the previous

The Force of Destiny

year, he thanked them but claimed, "I wouldn't have conducted it quite that way!"

Both men were avid crossword enthusiasts, and one Sunday morning, Arnald answered a call from Bill that began, without preamble, "Hey, Gabe, what's the Italian term for *very* in music?"

Arnald said, "*Assai.*"

Bill thanked him and hung up, leaving Arnald chuckling into a dead receiver.

As a child, Percy Faith played violin and piano, but after a terrible fire burned his hands, he concentrated on conducting and composing to become one of the most popular musicians of the twentieth century. He was one of three performers to have two number-one hits in the same year; the other two artists were Elvis Presley and the Beatles. Percy was invited to conduct the Air Force Band in some of the easy-listening compositions he popularized, and as Arnald remembers, "This wonderful, humble man that everyone admired" returned the following year, in 1975, to lead the band in his own arrangement of *Excerpts from the Rock Opera, Jesus Christ, Superstar*. He would tragically die of cancer a year later.

When Arthur Fiedler was invited to Washington, Arnald felt Mr. Fiedler was at first reluctant to conduct a concert band, his lifelong experience being chamber groups and symphony orchestras. When he agreed to the February 1973 appearance, Arnald simply reminded him, when on the podium, that instead of the violins, the clarinets would be on his left. Maestro Fiedler invited Doc Severinsen to perform Floyd Werle's Concerto for Trumpet with the Boston Pops, a piece that Doc and Arnald had done many times, and while studying the score, Fiedler realized there was a section he didn't understand. Mr. Fiedler phoned Arnald and asked about a passage where Doc plays a pure jazz interval that is, naturally, not written; how would he know when Doc was back to the printed music? Arnald explained that Doc fed him a figure that indicated when he was heading back to the score. The exchange between the two conductors was just one of many that occur daily between professional musicians.

Jerry Lewis, the multitalented comedian, actor, producer, director, and humanitarian (he would raise $1.6 *billion* for the Muscular

Dystrophy Association over the years of his Labor Day Telethons) was fondly remembered by the SRO crowd at Constitution Hall where he entertained them with his comedy between conducting the band in *Rogers and Hammerstein Medley, Pea Dance Ballet,* and *Rhapsody in Blue* and the Singing Sergeants in "Danny Boy." Arnald, however, remembers a difficult personality, and during the preconcert rehearsal, Mr. Lewis's complaints about the sound system, the sound of the band, and "several other areas of which he disapproved." Lou Brown, his accompanist at the time, told Arnald, in way of explanation, that they had been in Miami the night before and had taken an overnight flight to Washington. He also explained that Mr. Lewis was taking medication for severe back pain because of injuries sustained over the years performing his very physical comedy act. In recent interviews, Mr. Lewis has described the midseventies (he appeared with the band in 1973) as "a complete blackout" because of his daily use of pain medication.

Over the years, Arnald began a series of themed concerts during the Guest Artist Series, and the Sunday in mid-March celebrated Irish music when it fell on (or near) St. Patrick's Day. The first concert teamed Academy Award–winning actress Mercedes McCambridge and singer/actor Bob McGrath, who was best known for playing Bob Johnson on *Sesame Street*. After singing "Danny Boy," he mentioned to Arnald that no one's musical accompaniment had ever followed him as well. In 1974, famed Irish musicians (and sisters) Geraldine O'Grady, violinist, and Eily O'Grady, harpist, played on a concert that featured *The Irish Suite, Irish Tune From County Derry,* and *Traditional Irish Airs* and a Singing Sergeants medley, *A Holiday in Ireland.*

One group of performers upon which Arnald continued to rely were the area radio personalities. They were a natural choice given their years in broadcasting and were enthusiastic in the donation of their time (no guest artist is paid; each and every performer is compensated with only standard government per diem for expenses). They spanned the gamut of radio genres in the DC area, with the exception of rock-and-roll, representing news/talk, popular music, classical music, and country-and-western stations. They were the top-rated DJs of the time, and their popularity helped attendance remain at capacity. One of the radio personalities even began what would become an offbeat yet popular tradition.

Bill Cerri of radio station WETA began broadcasting Christmas music in August, a month in Washington, DC, that is known for little more than high temperatures and humidity and a time when many residents choose to vacation (Congress adjourns for the month, and the Capitol is largely handed over to the throngs of tourists). Mr. Cerri, who would on occasion appear with the band, suggested to Chief M.Sgt. Harry Gleeson that the Air Force Band do a program of Christmas music sometime in August that would expand his theme. "At first, I thought it was an insane idea!" Arnald remembers. "But as I found out, it was an overwhelming success." The first concert was August 8, 1975, at the Jefferson Memorial,[69] and in a few short years, it became the most popular and successful concert of the summer. Audiences swelled to more than four thousand patrons, many of whom organized gift exchanges and arrived carrying Christmas cookies and wearing Santa hats in the sweltering DC heat.

In addition to the zany antics of WMAL's Harden and Weaver, other radio personalities included Red Shipley (WPIK/WXRA); Johnny Holiday and Tom Gauger (WMAL); and Peter Jamerson, Fred Eden, Renee Cheney, Bob Davis, and Bill Trumbull (WGMS). Most of these professionals were booked in advance to headline a show or to accompany a national celebrity; their enthusiasm to help Arnald and the Air Force Band was most apparent in their willingness step in as a late replacement for a canceling guest artist.

The carefully planned schedule of concerts for the 1975 Guest Artist Series required some last-minute shuffling due to a cancellation by Peter Nero.[70] The original press release for the eight-concert lineup

---

69 It was the first year the Friday night summer concerts were held at the Memorial on the tidal basin. Although visually a picturesque location on the Potomac River, the Watergate Barge still raised questions of safety and the constant noise from arriving and departing aircraft from nearby National Airport became untenable. Additionally, the new location offered a larger, open-air seating capacity.

70 A close friend of Mr. Nero passed away suddenly, and he was asked to fill in for his Las Vegas gig.

Michael A. Gabriel

on Sundays in February and March showed "To Be Announced" for the second performance in March. Arnald's friend Carmen Dragon agreed to come for the third week of February (the week following William Conrad's *1812 Overture with "Cannon"*), which shifted Harden and Weaver to the open date in March. Appearing with Mr. Dragon was a relatively new voice in the Washington area, Renee Cheney. As the afternoon drive-time DJ for WGMS, the area's classical music station, she'd only been with the station for a year but was rapidly gaining a solid following. Ms. Cheney narrated Floyd Werle's arrangement of *The Gershwin Years* and showcased the mellifluous voice that would soon vault her to the number-one rated personality in her time slot for *any* station in the DC Metro area. Shortly afterward, Arnald and she began to see each other socially. Nearly a year and a half later, on September 11, 1976, with Skitch Henderson graciously serving as Arnald's best man, they were married.

In addition to the appearance of Jerry Lewis, several comedians were invited to perform with the band for the Guest Artist Series, including Jo Anne Worley, who was best known as one of the cast members on the popular TV show *Laugh In*, and Art Buchwald, a newspaper columnist with a biting, satiric wit. For his appearance, Arnald asked Mr. Buchwald to narrate a series of verses by Ogden Nash as set to Camille Saint-Saëns's *The Carnival of the Animals*, a popular pairing to the fun, entertaining piece. Mr. Buchwald agreed to appear, but instead, he read from a series of poems that he'd written, treating the assembled patrons to a cleaver and hilarious rendition that displayed his sharp, comedic brilliance.

Victor Borge's comic genius was exceeded only by his world-class talents at the piano and on the podium. He brought his perfect marriage of these endeavors to Constitution Hall during the Guest Artist Series in 1980 and had the audience (and the band members) in unrestrained laughter, regaling them with his wry observations about life. "I don't know what's wrong with the airline people at National Airport," he began, "I asked for a round-trip ticket, and they responded, 'To where?' and I answered, 'To here, of course!'" His routine was delivered in his signature deadpan while he played a few bars of a classical piece on the piano before interrupting the music to

The Force of Destiny

deliver another joke. Nothing illustrates his intelligence and quick wit like the exchange he and Arnald had preparing for a concert at Wolf Trap Farm in suburban Virginia in 1982.

The Filene Center opened in 1971 and is the main stage at the Wolf Trap Farm Park for the Performing Arts National Park, which features an indoor/outdoor amphitheater seating for about sixty-eight hundred. The wooden structure burned in 1982, and a temporary building was constructed to allow the continuation of performances while the Filene Center was rebuilt. The Air Force Band was invited to perform the first concert at the interim stage with Mr. Borge as the guest artist. At the rehearsal, the late flurry of construction work continued and left only a makeshift ladder as the sole access to the stage. As Mr. Borge began his ascent, Arnald asked him, "Victor, is that a major or minor scale you are going up?" He responded immediately, "Why, the latter [*ladder*] of course!" His answer demonstrated not only the depth of his musical knowledge (the word *scale* in music comes from the Italian *scala*, meaning ladder), but his broad, nuanced comedic mind. It is remarkable that he acquired his deft command of the English language *after* he immigrated to the United States from his native Denmark in 1941; he spoke only Danish when he arrived.

The one group of artists that drew a surprising number of ticket requests were country-and-western[71] musicians. Arnald would rely on Mike Bankhead to secure these artists, as Mike was well connected with several country-and-western artists. The first to appear, in 1977, was the incomparable Buck Owens who would later be inducted into the Country Music Hall of Fame. He and his backup musicians, the Buckaroos, began by playing a few of their more popular songs and were then joined by the band showcasing their Bakersfield Sound with "Buckaroo," "Tall Dark Stranger," "Buck Owens Medley," and even the Chuck Berry standard "Johnny B. Goode." Local DJ Red Shipley of WPIX/WXRA, the local country music station, narrated a Floyd Werle arrangement of western songs titled *Westward Ho!* As they ended the preconcert rehearsal, Buck was so taken with the experience that

---

71 The music was beginning to be referred to simply as country music because of the decline of the popularity of western (cowboy) music, but this term was still widely in use throughout the 1970s.

he implored Arnald to, "Go on the road with me and make a million dollars!"

Other country artists included Larry Gatlin, Freddy Fender, the Statler Brothers, Barbara Mandrell, and Tennessee Ernie Ford. After the Statler Brothers appearance in 1978 on Easter Sunday, they wrote, "Words fail to express the fulfillment we felt during the Easter concert. We have been in this business for over fourteen years and worked with many name bands and orchestras. You, sir, are not only the best, but one of the finest men we have ever had the pleasure of knowing or working with." The high demand for tickets[72] for the above artists came not just from the public, but were the most requested tickets by the general staff of the Pentagon and members of Congress.

Jazz musicians have had a long association with the Air Force Band, primarily through their performances with the Airmen of Note, but Arnald expanded the repertoire of the concert band by inviting several notable jazz artists to perform. Charlie Byrd was a Washington, DC, resident when he appeared in March 1973 for the Guest Artist Series (he would move to Annapolis, Maryland, later that year) and performed Joaquín Rodrigo's *Concierto de Aranjuez*, a composition for guitar and scored for concert band. The three-movement piece was a departure from the Brazilian-style jazz guitar Mr. Byrd was known for and was yet another example of Arnald's penchant for showing an audience a different side of an established musician. The concert also included "The Girl from Ipanema" and other popular tunes more familiar to Mr. Byrd's fans.

One of the most popular musicians in the history of jazz appeared for the Guest Artist Series in February 1978 and brought not only his unique offering of original compositions but an unabashed celebration of family. Dave Brubeck performed with the New Brubeck Quartet whose members were three of his sons, Darius, Chris, and Dan. The musical lineup that afternoon was a tour de force beginning with *They All Sang Yankee Doodle*, a piece Mr. Brubeck had originally written for two pianos and presented as a world premier for concert band featuring two soloists from the Singing Sergeants, Tech. Sgt. Janna

---

[72] Although all concerts were free, tickets were required.

The Force of Destiny

Howard and S.Sgt. Barbara Clippinger. The music uses the original "Yankee Doodle" as the theme while layering influences of music from German, Russian, Spanish, Portuguese, and even Native American cultures. It was followed by the beautiful "Theme for June" from *Dialogue* written by Howard Brubeck, Dave's brother. He recorded the piece in 1959 with the New York Philharmonic, and now scored-for-band, he paired his jazz piano stylings with the written melody from the band. The New Brubeck Quartet continued with a tribute to Ellington titled, simply, "The Duke" and, finally, a movement from *The Gates of Justice* called "Out of the Way of the People," a powerful cantata inspired by the civil rights movement using biblical passages and quotes from Dr. Martin Luther King Jr.

As was typical, the rehearsal began on Sunday afternoon at one o'clock, just two hours prior to the beginning of the concert. Near the end, and just minutes before they were to open the doors allowing the patrons into DAR Constitution Hall, Mr. Brubeck said to Arnald, "I'd like to do an encore." Caught off guard, Arnald replied, "But we don't have one planned." Encores, although performed for nearly every concert, were the standard "The Stars and Stripes Forever," "America, the Beautiful," and a few others that the band and conductor knew from memory.

Mr. Brubeck announced, "I'll take care of it!" and proceeded to transpose his top hit "Take Five" for each section of the band. The sheet music was duplicated during the concert and passed out surreptitiously during the final programed number. As Arnald left the podium at the end of the concert and walked into the wings, the freshly written music was thrust into his hands. He skimmed the score, returned to the podium, and led the New Brubeck Quartet and the Air Force Band in the new arrangement for concert band. Later, Mr. Brubeck was effusive in his praise, saying: "I experienced something rare and rewarding with the United States Air Force Band: their dress rehearsal was like a performance, and their performance was a celebration. This is due to the excellent musicianship of Col. Arnald D. Gabriel and the inspiration with which he leads his band. These outstanding qualities combined with a meticulous attention to detail mean that nothing is left to the last moment, and the New Brubeck

Quartet not only enjoyed, but learned much from their performance with the Air Force Band under Colonel Gabriel's leadership."

Each succeeding season of the Winter Concert Series at DAR Constitution Hall introduced a lineup of celebrity guests that was a varied cross section of the entertainment industry matched with other personalities well known to Americans. CBS Evening News broadcaster, and "the most trusted man in America," Walter Cronkite appeared in March 1975 at the height of his popularity and narrated *We Hold These Truths*, a Floyd Werle original that set the writings of Thomas Jefferson to music. The following year Roger Mudd, another CBS broadcaster and reporter, narrated the same piece (as he was first introduced to Arnald, he extended his hand and said, "Hi, my name's 'mud.'"). He was joined on the same concert by Roy Jefferson, a wide receiver for the Washington Redskins. As an avid football fan, Arnald realized that there was a large segment of the Washington area that might not otherwise choose to spend part of a Sunday afternoon listening to a concert band (that he scheduled these concerts in February and March, after the end of the NFL season, is no coincidence). The inclusion of Mr. Jefferson, a three-time all-pro who played in two Super Bowls, drew area football fans eager to see the premier wide receiver for their team. In March 1983 Redskin fans once again packed Constitution Hall to see Mark Moseley, the team kicker, narrate *I Am an American*, Carmen Dragon's stirring, patriotic piece. Mr. Moseley, an NFL MVP (most valuable player), Super Bowl winner, and three-time all-pro, was featured on the same bill as Academy Award winner and television and movie composer Jerry Goldsmith. Mr. Goldsmith conducted the band in selections from some of his motion picture scores, including *Star Trek, Poltergeist, MacArthur, Patton, The Sand Pebbles*, and *Masada*. That any of these diverse talents listed above could have headlined a concert on their own is without question, but whether the guest artist was an actor, politician, musician, broadcaster, or sports superstar, a distinct phenomenon was becoming apparent: patrons came initially to see their favorite celebrity and discovered the US Air Force Band. The band's growing fan base found a professional organization unmatched in their broad range, expansive repertoire, and world-class sound. Through Arnald's careful guidance and leadership, each reflected the other and proudly stood as America's International Musical Ambassadors.

Additionally, the concerts were more than that; they were performances. Many were more variety show than strictly band concerts. In February 1982 the band and Singing Sergeants mounted a production of the three-act operetta *Die Fledermaus* by Johann Strauss. As the full performance of the operetta could easily exceed two hours and because of Arnald's desire to keep the afternoon matinees to about an hour, the work was artfully cut to the desired length. Less important scenes were eliminated, and radio personalities Tom Gauger of WMAL and Renee Cheney of WGMS tied the action together with a brilliantly crafted narrative delivered while dressed in period costume, allowing a seamless blending with the nine actors/vocalists on stage. Per Arnald's approval, Mike Bankhead made costuming another asset in showcasing the band's talent. The production was so well received that Arnald's superiors requested a repeat performance to be staged at the Officers' Club on Bolling AFB, DC.

The children's concerts certainly fell into the performance category as well and were programed with music that held appeal for both the young and old (or, as the programs promised, "the young at heart!"). Even though the concert at the Departmental Auditorium featuring Merle Evans, the conductor of the Ringling Bros. and Barnum & Bailey Band, was an unqualified success in 1967, there would not be another scheduled strictly as a children's concert until 1976 when area radio DJs would, once again, lend their talents. Bill Cerri of WETA, Peter Jamerson of WGMS, and Bill Trumbull of WMAL narrated, respectively, *Pee-Wee the Piccolo; Tubby the Tuba;* and *The Man Who Invented Music*.

The following year Fred Rogers of the PBS children's show *Mr. Roger's Neighborhood* headlined a concert in front of an SRO audience that featured a full slate of children's music, largely written by Mr. Rogers himself. Air Force Band arranger M.Sgt. Michael Davis arranged songs that were chosen from Mr. Rogers' more than one hundred original compositions. He was accompanied by four of the most popular characters from his show, including Betty Aberlin (Lady Aberlin), David Newell (Mr. McFeeley), Francois Clemmons (Officer Clemmons), and Mr. Rogers' musical director and pianist, John Costa, re-creating his popular TV show on the stage at Constitution Hall. Wonderful memories abound from the band's interaction with the guest artists and with the fans.

Chief Gleeson recalls an almost embarrassing incident after the first concert with Mr. Rogers. There was an entourage of children trying to get backstage to see Fred Rogers after his 1977 appearance. Chief Gleeson, in an effort to protect the artist, prevented the children from getting backstage. What he didn't realize was that Pres. Jimmy Carter's daughter, Amy, was in that group. Fortunately, the connection was made, and Amy and friends enjoyed a nice visit with Mr. Rogers. For his subsequent appearances in 1980 and 1983, he presented a different slate of music and built a show chosen from his vast repertoire. He was "a true professional and kind, gentle man," Arnald remembers.

The children's concerts continued in 1979 with a narration of *The Man Who Invented Music* and *The Magic of Disney* narrated by Bob Keeshan, better known as Captain Kangaroo. In subsequent weeks in 1981, Willie Tyler and Lester, the popular ventriloquist act, took the stage, and some of the characters from *Sesame Street*, including Big Bird (who conducted the band!), appeared. A few years later, the Tonsil Klackers, a wild barbershop quartet dressed in zany costumes and singing made-up lyrics were joined by Mickey, Minnie, and Goofy from Walt Disney World in Orlando, Florida. These shows tended to break the fourth wall of performance and engaged the audience, drawing them out of the passive role of observer. Inhibitions were broken down, and crowds fell into rhythmic clapping and singing, a more common trait of European audiences. Arnald's orchestration of the involvement began with his turning to the patrons during the opening "The Star Spangled Banner" and leading them in singing the national anthem and, during the playing of "Armed Forces Medley," instructing members of the audience who had served in the military to stand when his/her branch of service song was played.

Throughout their history, the Air Force Band has presented patriotic concerts in a nonpartisan, apolitical way; they are offered as a celebration of a citizen's love of country and, regardless of the current political climate, have always been well received. The first concert of the 1981 season was called Welcome Back to Freedom and was dedicated to the fifty-two Americans who had just returned from 444 days of captivity in Iran. The concert featured four celebrity artists beginning with Les Brown who, with his Band of Renown, was one of the most popular big band musicians in the world. He conducted the Air Force Band in his composition of the iconic "Sentimental Journey," which he first recorded with Doris Day in 1945. Next, Susan Powell, the current Miss America, sang "Art Is Calling for Me" from "The Enchantress" by Victor Herbert as arranged by Floyd Werle. Fred Travalena was an impressionist, comedian, and actor who stepped in to narrate the powerful *This Is My Country* by Al Jacobs and arranged by M.Sgt. Michael Davis. The star of more than seventy films and TV shows, Peter Graves, narrated *The Story of The Battle Hymn of The Republic* written by Floyd Werle. The concert ended with Carmen Dragon's *I Am an American*, a moving piece that had the full house at Constitution Hall on its feet at the conclusion.

An interesting and heretofore unknown story involving the behind-the-scenes negotiations for the release of the American hostages has been made available by a friend of Arnald's and involved the strategic use of one of its units. The first meeting of Arnald Gabriel and Charley Irions occurred when Arnald was at the beginning his air force career and Charley was a master sergeant at Sampson Air Force Base on the shores of Seneca Lake in upstate New York in 1951. Master Sergeant Irions was the youngest master sergeant in the Air Force at the time and the NCO in charge of training the thousands of new airmen at the base. Along with many other required skills, he taught them to march, and, "We had lots of parades to let them show off their skills." He worked closely with Warrant Officer Junior Grade Gabriel to discuss the music for the parades and "any special things that we could do to impress the senior dignitaries." Each man excelled in his respective position and, Charlie remembers, "We both thought we were pretty good, and I guess that we were." Leaving Sampson, Charlie Irions began his climb up the career ladder by going on to Officers' Candidate School and pilot training, and he recalls, "When we next met, he was a colonel, commanding the very best band in the world, the United States Air Force Band, and I was a brigadier general at the Pentagon."

Arnald remembers General Irions' presence at most of the Air Force Band concerts in the DC area, saying, "If he was in town, he came to the concert. He was a good friend of the band." In late 1979 or early 1980, General Irions was dispatched to Cairo at the behest of President Carter to again meet with Vice President Mubarak (they'd already met several times) in an effort to secure the use of an airfield in southern Egypt. Although he was not able to divulge the United States' intended use of the field, General Irions was sure that both Mubarak and President Sadat knew it had something to do with the return of the hostages. At this latest meeting, Mubarak countered the inquiry with a request of a squadron of six C-130 aircraft. The preposterous appeal for a half dozen of the four-engine, turboprop transports was deftly deflected by General Irions and countered with the United States' willingness to repave the Cairo airport, which was in dire need of improvement. Several days passed with no word, and General Irions called the Egyptian Ambassador to suggest that the Air Force Band Strolling Strings, who were on tour in Europe, could be flown down for an evening soiree at the ambassador's residence, inviting Sadat, Mubarak, and anyone else he chose, in hopes of favorably influencing their decision. The ambassador loved the idea, and after a flurry of secure phone calls over a few short hours, the arrangements were made. General Irions remembers, "Needless to say, the Strings put on an absolutely spectacular performance. President Sadat and Vice President Mubarak were astounded that the United States would provide them with such entertainment."

Acceptance of the deal came the next day. The United States got the use of the airfield in southern Egypt, and the Cairo Airport would be repaved. As further example of the professionalism of the musicians, as they boarded the airplane that would return them to their tour after playing at the ambassador's residence, fully half of them were suffering from food poisoning. Medical personnel met the arriving flight in Germany and treated the sick airmen; they were needed to perform that night.

There are two solid reasons for the story to have been kept a secret for more than thirty years. On April 24, 1980, a rescue attempt was launched. It was to have been a two-day operation involving staging and execution, but due to environmental and many other complex logistical reasons, the mission was canceled. During the extraction of the already deployed aircraft, a helicopter struck a C-130, and tragically, eight Americans and an Iranian civilian were killed. "So," explained General Irions, "you don't tell nice or funny stories following failure." Additionally, to protect the Egyptian leadership, "You don't tell stories out of school about an ally who is a reigning ruler."

THE NEW MUSIC

Arnald has always placed a strong emphasis on reaching young people through music. It has led to his teaching at hundreds of high school and college band camps, seminars, adjudications, all-state music camps, and a myriad of programming efforts with the Air Force Band calculated to spark an interest in and encourage a love of music—specifically, concert band music. The generation growing up in the 1960s and 1970s, maybe for the first time in history, had a new and radically different genre of music, and their interest in it was reflected in the falling attendance at concerts for high school and college-aged kids. Rather than rail against rock-and-roll music, Arnald recognized the musicality of some of the songs and began to incorporate and adapt them for concert band. In 1969 Floyd Werle wrote a medley of hit rock tunes for the Singing Sergeants called *The Sounds of '68* that was not only popular among the younger members of the audience but showed those unfamiliar with the new music that it was certainly worth considering. Over the next few years, Sergeant Werle arranged two medleys of hits from the genius of John Lennon and Paul McCartney, the song-writing duo of the most popular rock group of all time, the Beatles. The first was written for the Singing Sergeants and another he wrote for Doc Severinsen and was scored for symphony orchestra; Doc later performed the piece with the Buffalo, Minneapolis, and Phoenix Symphony Orchestras.

For several years, the rock music the Air Force Band played was adapted for concert band or, in the case of Sergeant Werle's *Sinfonia Sacra* that premiered in 1971, was written and scored for concert band and rock band. In 1975 Arnald took a bold step and formed a stand-alone rock-and-roll band composed of seven members of the concert band and Singing Sergeants. Their sound was an interesting amalgam of rock, funk, and soul music, and they were an immediate success. Mach One[73] played primarily at high schools and colleges, and any doubt the students may have harbored about the quality of the Air Force Airmen and their music were blown away by the tight, professional group. The original members were: Tech. Sgt. Chuck Carthan, bass vocals, backup vocals, and percussion; Tech. Sgt. Mark Hynes, drums; Tech. Sgt. Mike Askew, guitar and backup vocals; M.Sgt. Mike Crotty, leader, sax, flute, trumpet, flugelhorn, and backup vocals; Tech. Sgt. Ken Buckery, organ and synthesizer; Tech. Sgt. David Chab, trombone, percussion, and backup vocals; Tech. Sgt. Vernia Lewis, lead vocals and backup vocals. (The group's first album was dedicated to S.Sgt. Frank Cobb Smith, one of the original members who died in an automobile accident in February 1975, shortly after their formation.)

Arnald also featured several popular artists who, although not necessarily considered rock-and-roll stars, expanded the already wide diversity of music featured on the Guest Artist Series. The versatile quartet Manhattan Transfer appeared in February 1978, showcasing their genre-crossing vocals singing pop, a cappella, jazz, and R&B. On that Sunday afternoon following the intermission, they sang ten of their most popular songs. Marilyn McCoo's appearance in February 1982 displayed her vast talent with a "Medley of Past Hits," a song made famous by Aretha Franklin and written by Otis Redding titled "Respect," a ballad from the musical *Fame* called, "Out Here on My Own," and Peter Allen's "Quiet Please There's a Lady on Stage." Johnny Rivers, one of the early stars of rock-and-roll, appeared with the band in February 1983 and performed some of his best known hits, including "Memphis," "Poor Side of Town," and "Secret Agent Man."

Whether the guest artist was known for popular music, rock-and-roll, jazz, country, or classical music or featured an actor or celebrity performing a narration or was a children's show re-creation, the Sunday afternoon concerts were built on the foundation of the

---

[73] The group is still active today and is now called Max Impact.

Air Force Band. Although primarily the concert band and Singing Sergeants, the Airmen of Note or the Air Force Symphony Orchestra would occasionally take the stage, but in February 1982, Arnald pulled out all the stops and featured every performance unit under his command. As the patrons arrived at Constitution Hall, the Diplomats, a five-piece group formed to play for the many military receptions in the Washington area, greeted them in the foyer. The concert began as the Ceremonial Brass[74] filed out and lined up in front of the stage and along both sides of the audience. They began with "Our Director," a popular march by F. E. Bigelow and, as always to open a concert, "The Star Spangled Banner." After "Eagle Squadron March" by the British March King, Kenneth Alford, they marched to the exit signs as the curtains opened to reveal Chief M.Sgt. David Steinmeyer conducting the Airmen of Note in "St. Louis Blues March," "In the Mood," and "Cottontail." The Strolling Strings entered next led by Chief M.Sgt. Louis Coppola and demonstrated the breadth of their repertoire with "Play," "Gypsies," and "Czardas, a Johann Strauss Medley" and the bluegrass standard, "Orange Blossom Special" by Ervin T. Rouse. Capt. Craig Jessop led the Singing Sergeants in "Mary, Don't You Weep," "The Squadron Song," and "The Air Force Hymn" as a segue to the Air Force Symphony Orchestra's performance of Slavonic Dance, Op. 46, No. 1 and Aaron Copland's "Lincoln Portrait" narrated by Tom Gauger from WMAL radio. The air force rock band, Mach 1, belted out the popular, "The Boy from New York City," and the Concert Band followed with "The Epiphany from Roman Festivals," "High Flight," and, now joined again by the Singing Sergeants, "Songs of America" and "The Air Force March."

This tour de force was a proud display of the talent and professionalism of the musicians and a bold statement attesting to the accomplishments of their leader. Ever since Arnald made the decision in 1956 to continue in the US Air Force as a career (due largely to the persuasive efforts of Ben LeBailly), he was always facing a mandatory

---

[74] Originally, the Ceremonial Band was formed to play for official military funerals and diplomatic functions. Arnald eliminated the woodwinds, left the brass and percussion, and changed the name to reflect their makeup; it was a more practical construct for their mostly outdoor venues.

retirement age. In the air force, retirement comes at age sixty or after thirty years as a commissioned officer. In Arnald's case, these dates coincided. Although he joined the air force in 1951, he didn't receive the direct commission to lieutenant (an officer) until 1955; he would turn sixty years old in 1985 as well. As the official date of March 1, 1985, drew inexorably closer, Arnald readied himself for his retirement from the military and a return to civilian life after thirty-four years of service to the US Air Force.

Retirement Ceremony

Arnald, Dr. Craig Jessop, Donny Osmond
at the Mormon Tabernacle Choir concert

CHAPTER NINETEEN

Retirement

In the fall of 1984 the Air Force Band packed up and departed for their semiannual tour, and for the first time since they'd resumed touring in 1965, Arnald did not join them. In an interview with *Band* magazine at the time, he said, "I'm sitting here in my office while the band is out on tour and it's one of the strangest feelings in my entire life." The administrative work and the day-to-day logistics of managing 219 musicians and support staff remained, but his true passion of performing music was put on hold. Arnald was determined to make the handover to his successor, and his own transition to civilian life, as smooth as possible. He began to step back from the job gradually, allowing Capt. Mike Bankhead, his deputy commander, to step in. He also conducted none of the Winter Concert Series at Constitution Hall or the Guest Artist Series in 1985 because his retirement date of February 1[75] would be just prior to its beginning.

In November Arnald would have one of his final opportunities to lead the band in a celebration that would feature special appearances from entertainers who can only be described as close friends of the band. A concert was held on November 18, and Tom Gauger of WMAL radio served as announcer and master of ceremonies for A Gala Guest Artist Salute at the DAR Constitution Hall. To begin, Arnald chose a selection from one of his favorite composers, the *Overture to La Forza Del Destino* by Giuseppe Verdi, which was followed by the first of four

---

75 His official retirement date was March 1, 1985, but he would leave the position on February 1 due to accrued leave (vacation) and other days due him.

guest artists to appear that afternoon. Lynda Day George, the popular television and movie actress (and daughter of retired US Air Force Col. Claude Day), delivered a moving narration of Carmen Dragon's *I Am an American*. The next piece was the world premiere of *Preludium and March—A Musical Monogram* by Jerry Bilik who has composed, arranged, directed, and conducted music for stage productions, television shows, concert bands, and marching bands. The music was written specifically for and dedicated to Arnald, and the subtitle refers to the musical pitches Mr. Bilik used in its composition—A, D, and G, which are Arnald's initials.

After a more than twenty-year professional relationship and personal friendship, Doc Severinsen returned to the stage with the Air Force Band to play the popular Floyd Werle composition Concerto for Trumpet Number 1. It was written specifically for the flamboyant musician and his unique talents, and following the spirited third and final movement, *Samba*, the packed house leapt to its feet in cheers and unrestrained applause. Another good friend, Bill Conrad, displaced Arnald on the podium conducting, naturally, Tchaikovsky's *1812 Overture*. At its conclusion, and to everyone's surprise, he returned to the stage and approached the microphone carrying a leather portfolio out of which he withdrew an official-looking letter. In his booming, baritone voice, Mr. Conrad read a personal message from Pres. Ronald Reagan:

> Dear Colonel Gabriel:
>
> I am delighted and honored to have this opportunity to join with so many others in saluting you and your long and distinguished career as Commander and Conductor of the United States Air Force Band.
>
> For over twenty years, you have brought the various units of the band to the peak of their performance abilities. Citizens in communities all over this nation and abroad have experienced the mastery of your conducting and organizing abilities. Your effort on behalf of the Air Force and in including within your

command minorities who had once not been a part of it are a tribute to your spirit and foresight. I personally have enjoyed the skill and virtuosity of you band and I know how much you have had to do with its success and the launching of its many new and different concert programs.

Nancy and I join with so many others in paying tribute to you and the United States Air Force Band. Its current excellence and reputation are owed so very much to you.

God bless you.
Sincerely

Ronald Reagan

The emotional concert ended with Peter Graves' narration of Floyd Werle's masterpiece *The Story of The Battle Hymn of the Republic*. Backed by the voices of the Singing Sergeants and soloist Tech. Sgt. Daisy Jackson's soulful soprano voice, the concert ended with one of the most fitting tributes to the man who transformed the US Air Force Band into America's International Musical Ambassadors. No one remained seated at its conclusion, and not a dry eye remained.

Arnald's final two concerts with the Air Force Band as its commander and conductor were the Christmas concerts on December 1 and 2, and he asked Renee, his wife now of ten years, to narrate the heartwarming story of *The Littlest Angel* with original music by Frank Lockwood.

New Leadership

The process for the selection of the next commander and conductor of the Air Force Band would be Arnald's to orchestrate, owing to his unprecedented twenty-one years in the position, his thirty-four-year air force musical career, and unparalleled experience. There was simply no one else more qualified to choose who would lead the organization he built. The two distinct components of the job, commander *and* conductor, required vastly different and high-level skill sets. Administratively, Arnald was responsible for an annual budget of $1.6 million and managed resources of more than $8 million (each figure in 1985 dollars). In addition, he was responsible for the planning, organization, and implementation of "major National Department of Defense and Air Force recruiting, community relations, and troop programs/activities." He also supervised the musical activities of the five touring units for ceremonies, concerts, and official functions.

Because the music the Air Force Band performed fell into three broad categories—band, symphonic, and pop music—Arnald decided to form a committee of three of the top men in their respective fields of music to assess the applicants. John P. Paynter was a Northwestern University graduate who returned to the school to teach band music, conducting, and arranging and was a prolific composer and arranger of more than four hundred band compositions. Arnald's choice to represent symphonic music was the young, thirty-one-year-old, Harvard educated assistant conductor to Mstislav Rostropovich at the National Symphony in Washington, DC, Hugh Wolff. Finally, Arnald made the easy choice to represent popular music and asked his old friend Skitch Henderson to round out the group.

After an initial screening process of senior officers, the rank of major and above, in the air force music field, an invitation to audition for the job was sent to six men. The committee of four structured the audition such that each applicant would conduct a few sections of the John Krance band transcription of Carl Orff's Carmina Burana and would be allowed to select anything from the standard repertoire.[76] Portions of the twenty-five–movement masterpiece have been used in countless movies, commercials, television, and radio programs and has been less than flatteringly described as "the most overused piece of music in film history." The final audition selection would be supplied by the committee on the day of the audition and would serve

---

[76] The standard repertoire refers to a generally accepted list of compositions played by a group. Each of the six applicants would be very familiar with the makeup of the Air Force Band library.

to measure each applicant's ability to sight-read a score. After the thirty- or forty-minute musical audition, the men would then sit for an interview with three US Air Force colonels from the Pentagon who would grill them on the administrative component of the job.

It's not surprising that one of the six finalists was Arnald's deputy commander, Maj. James "Mike" Bankhead, who had held the position since Al Bader's retirement in 1976. Mike had previously served as deputy commander at the Air Force Academy Band and commander of the Air Force Band in Tacoma, Washington, and then transferred to the Bands Branch in the Pentagon, eventually becoming its director. Because he worked closely with Arnald and his senior staff, Arnald asked Captain Bankhead to a meeting to discuss Major Bader's replacement. He diligently prepared files on the most capable senior officers in the Air Force Band field and briefed Arnald on each, including a recommendation on the stronger candidates. Mike remembers, "Colonel Gabriel listened politely, but it didn't seem that he was really engaged in what I was telling him."

After finishing what Mike thought was an "excellent" briefing, Arnald said, "Mike, is that everyone?"

"Yes, sir. That's everyone," he responded with less confidence than he had entering the room.

Arnald then dropped the bomb, "No, it isn't. Would you consider taking the job?"

As a junior captain, it never occurred to him that he might be eligible. A bit flustered by the offer, he managed to say, "Sir, I need to think about this for a little while."

Arnald responded, "Okay, get back to me tomorrow."

Mike's gratitude is apparent many years later, saying, "Colonel Gabriel gave me the greatest opportunity a young officer in the band career field could ever have."

Although Major Bankhead's duties as deputy commander included conducting the Singing Sergeants, the Air Force Strings, Ceremonial Band, and Concert Band and the opportunity to take part in the operational aspects of running the organization, Arnald insisted the audition for his replacement be a fair, unbiased measure of each applicant. To that end, he cut off all nonessential, work-related communication with his second-in-command for almost three months leading up to the audition. Their conversations about music, rehearsals, and techniques all ended.

"He did not want to taint my chances nor give me any advantage over others. He wanted to make sure that no one could say I had an advantage because of my association with him or that he gave me any kind of help with preparing for the audition." It was a wrenching time for Major Bankhead, because, "the distance from my commander and my mentor was very strange and difficult." He was also asked not to be in the Air Force Band area of the base during the others' auditions. His was to be the final audition.

When Mike's day finally came, he selected one of Lawrence Odom's more challenging transcriptions. He then conducted the required sections of *Carmina Burana*. Finally, the committee supplied him with a mixed metered piece to sight-read, asked a few questions, and excused him. Within days, he was informed of his selection as commander and conductor of the United States Air Force Band and, "I was both thrilled and terrified. I knew what the job was and what was expected ... following a true master conductor and outstanding commander was a daunting task."

About the same time, Arnald was approached by the conductor of the Singing Sergeants, Capt. Craig Jessop. Craig expressed to Arnald his misgivings about staying in the air force due to what he felt were his career limitations as a choral director. Arnald countered with, "Nonsense, you're a conductor!" and encouraged him to seek out a position within the Air Force Band field that would expand his horizons. A few years later, he assumed command of the US Air Force Band in Europe[77] and finished his Air Force career as commander and conductor of the Strategic Air Command Band at Offutt Air Force Base near Omaha. Craig was then offered a position that "was the only thing that could have lured me away from the Air Force Band program." He was hired as the choral director for the Mormon Tabernacle Choir.

Dr. Jessop remembers, "I felt so indebted to Colonel Gabriel for the incredible opportunities he gave me that I wanted to have him come

---

77 Although it was the same assignment as Arnald had nearly thirty years prior, it was no longer in Wiesbaden.

The Force of Destiny

to Salt Lake City and appear with the Tabernacle Choir on the weekly broadcast." The natural fit would be the Memorial Day broadcast that also featured Donny Osmond. The performance, although done some weeks in advance, is done in real time following a rehearsal; Arnald led the choir and orchestra while Donny Osmond sang Mike Davis' arrangement of "The Last Full Measure of Devotion" and followed with John Williams' "Hymn to the Fallen." Although the broadcast featured the three hundred-voice, world-famous chorus, a 110-piece symphony orchestra, and superstar Donny Osmond, Dr. Jessop says of Arnald's performance, "He, of course, was the star of the show." Further, "Colonel Gabriel is one of the most important figures in my life. I will always be grateful to him."

As the last couple of months of Arnald's US Air Force career came to a close, his thoughts naturally focused on, "What next?" The calendar was already filled with guest conducting jobs through at least the next year and a half, but the idea of walking away from what he loved never crossed his mind. He was lucky enough to have several job offers to consider, but his desire was fairly specific. As he said to a reporter in the *Band* magazine article at the time, "What I would really like is a university position, not only in an administrative capacity as chairman of the music department or dean, but also to continue conducting at the school and perhaps with a community orchestra." Additionally, when asked to choose the past accomplishments about which he was most proud, he listed three.

The first was what Arnald considered the crown jewel of the Air Force Band: the Guest Artist Series. The popular winter series showcased dozens of celebrities in an intimate environment and allowed thousands of fans access they might never have had. As to the charge that the concerts smacked of commercialism, Arnald responded, "I believe we must stay out of our ivory towers and share our talents with as many people as we can." He also made the point that "it is very significant that those guest artists now have an appreciation for military bands that they never had before." Secondly, he pointed to the forty-five original compositions specifically commissioned by and or written for the US Air Force Band that were now available to other bands throughout the world. Eventually, as a result of his commissioning program, this number would include more than a thousand compositions that had been written for the exclusive use of the band. "I believe we must constantly nourish the repertoire otherwise our art will be relegated to the museum." Finally, he proudly talked about the touring schedules of the various units, saying, "Any American can hear these concerts free of charge, and they can bring the children along too."

The change-of-command ceremony for the longest tenured commander and conductor of the United States Air Force Band was more than a simple handshake and pat on the back from a superior officer. It was held in massive Hangar One on the flight line at nearby Andrews Air Force Base in Maryland. Each unit of the band was arrayed from one end of hangar to the other and faced a reviewing stand and seating for the assembled guests. Prior to the retirement proceedings that would bring to an end his more than thirty-seven-year combined military career (army and air force), Arnald was awarded an unprecedented third Legion of Merit medal. He is one of the few US Air Force musicians to receive the honor and the only one to have earned it three times. It was presented, generally, in recognition of his years of military service and specifically for his tremendous contribution to music education throughout the United States.

After the official remarks and congratulatory comments from the host and retiring official, Lt. Gen. Robert H. Reed, the string orchestra performed the moving Orchestral Suite Number 3 by Johann Sebastian Bach, made even more powerful by the voluminous, enclosed space. For Arnald's final review of the troops, the ceremonial and concert band combined to play a march, and as a motorcade entered the hangar to pick up the now-retired commander and his wife, Reneé, the Singing Sergeants sang "Auld Lang Syne." Finally, the procession motored out of the hangar to the combined units of the band playing the Air Force Song, "Off We Go!" The tear-soaked day ended with a reception attended by close friends and family.

SECTION III
Academia and Guest Conducting

Pope John Paul II
Arnald on left, Dale Underwood on right with saxophone

CHAPTER TWENTY

George Mason University and the McLean Symphony Orchestra

As Arnald continued to mull over his job offers and think about where he might put his efforts in the search of a new position, a promising lead came from an unlikely source. Settling into the dentist chair for his annual checkup, he mentioned to the doctor his hopes for a university position. The dentist indicated that the president of George Mason University (GMU), Dr. George W. Johnson, was a friend and that he knew the young college was searching for a Chairman of Performing Arts. The school had begun as the northern Virginia campus of the University of Virginia and in 1972 became a separate institution. Pres. George Johnson, a powerful and innovative leader, was in the process of transforming the college from a small liberal arts school, an endeavor that meant expanding enrollment. Arnald subsequently met with the president and was immediately offered the position. In his announcement, Dr. Johnson said that his hiring "symbolizes George Mason's commitment to the arts on both a regional and national scale." Arnald would now be responsible for coordinating the activities of three departments: dance, music, and theater.

His appointment was announced on April 22, 1984, and he wouldn't begin until May 15; in his first full month of retirement, Arnald found enough to keep busy. His three guest conducting gigs in February had him traveling to Lancaster, Pennsylvania; Lincoln, Nebraska; and Cookeville, Tennessee, by far the lightest schedule of work since he started at Ithaca College in the fall of 1946. He occupied part of his free time with the study of his infantry unit during World War II. His impetus was a book, published only a few years prior in 1979, called *29 Let's Go!* by Joseph H. Ewing. The well-researched and painstakingly documented book is a history of the Twenty-Ninth Infantry during the war, and with the safe distance and perspective of nearly forty years, Arnald began to cast some light on this little-talked-about period of his life. The study provided him with not only a greater understanding of his and his regiment's role, but also a broader view of the other units in the Twenty-Ninth Infantry and, ultimately, a better understanding of the war in Europe.

One surprising piece of information he uncovered was that of an award to which he was entitled and hadn't received. The *Croix de Guerre* is a French decoration that may be awarded to either an individual or to a military unit, and because of their heroics on June 6, 1944, and the establishment of the beachhead on Omaha Beach, he and the entire Twenty-Ninth Infantry was honored with the medal. Arnald was neither presented with nor notified of the award, because it wasn't authorized by the French government until July 1946, more than two years after the D-day invasion; at that time, there was apparently little need to contact the boss of the cooker gang at the Hallstead Canning Factory in Cortland, New York. Arnald has since proudly added the medal to the Air Force dress uniform he still wears while conducting.

During Arnald's interview at George Mason, Dr. Johnson expressed a desire to elevate and expand the performing arts department. His efforts to that end had already begun with the construction of the Patriot Center, an on-campus arena designed as a sports and entertainment venue, and a three-phase project that would culminate with a state-of-the-art concert hall called the Center for the Arts. He also expressed a desire to more fully involve high schools in northern Virginia and specifically Fairfax County, where the college is located. This outreach would dovetail perfectly with Dr. Johnson's innovative efforts to involve the local business community in the growth of the young university and goes to the heart of the school's mission statement: "To maintain an international reputation for superior education and public service that affirms its role as the intellectual

The Force of Destiny

and cultural nexus among Northern Virginia, the nation, and the world."

The Patriot Center officially opened in the fall of 1985, and Arnald met with Fairfax County Music Coordinator Lynn Arizzi and Moe Turrentine, Fairfax County Curriculum Specialist, Music (whose wife was a member of the US Air Force Band's Singing Sergeants) to pitch his plan to combine their high school musicians into a countywide band, orchestra, and choral group with a concert to be held at the gleaming new arena. Arnald set out to visit every high school in the county to meet each conductor and choir director. His off-campus recruiting trips ultimately required months of travel around Fairfax County but were generally met with enthusiasm at the prospect of their students' involvement in the unique experience.

The visits to each school across the county over the nearly two years in preparation for the concert also prompted invitations to guest conduct, and in late September 1984 he was invited to be one of the judges at the inaugural Oakton Classic, an invitational marching band competition. The annual event (still being held more than thirty years later) brought together seven area high school marching bands and allowed Arnald the opportunity to interact with each at the weekend show. He was also invited to conduct a Christmas concert at the new West Potomac High School in December. The school was in its first year of existence, having been formed from the combined Fort Hunt and Groveton High Schools on the campus of the latter. Because of the size of the student body, the band consisted of nearly eighty student musicians. Arnald's initial exposure to the realities of collegiate academia, however, was less smooth.

Another of Dr. Johnson's goals was to draw together the three departments that Arnald now chaired. None seemed willing to work with the other two, and Arnald set out to remedy the split. At one of his first meetings with the heads of music, dance, and theater, he laid out his plan to mount a stage performance of *The Pirates of Penzance*, the popular Gilbert and Sullivan comic opera, which would involve all three departments. After listening patiently to each man's long list of reasons why coordination with the other two departments was beyond his ability or was logistically impossible due to time constraints and budget considerations, Arnald responded with, "Well, we're going to do it anyway." Dr. Johnson's unquestioned support ultimately broke down any resistance and prodded each department head into accepting the inevitable. A year after the April 1986 performance of *Pirates*, they combined the talents of the three departments to mount the Cole Porter musical *Kiss Me, Kate*. Both were held at the Harris Theatre, part of the new Center for the Arts.

Although extensive, Arnald's work at George Mason University was not limited to the administrative side of the house. The music department has a symphony orchestra, and Arnald stepped in to conduct the group. Beginning with only about eighteen or nineteen musicians, the first challenge was to recruit new members. He drew from the ranks of area string music teachers and the Air Force Band, and he also hired many players from the National Symphony Orchestra. The talented men and women were featured as soloists, and Arnald was also able to assign them positions as adjunct professors, enriching the classroom experience as well. To anchor the talented group, Arnald hired John "Jack" Falkenstrom as concertmaster. Jack had retired as a violinist with the Air Force Band's Symphony Orchestra, and each man held a mutual respect of the other. Arnald also began a program that allowed talented area high school students to join the orchestra through an audition process. As word spread, more GMU students joined the group, and eventually, he was able to achieve a balance of about half GMU students and half professionals from the surrounding community.[78]

In addition to his efforts at elevating the symphony orchestra to national prominence, Arnald decided to expand the music department by creating a concert band program. It required the formation of a new position at the college, Director of Bands, and he initiated a search to fill it. More than two hundred hopeful applicants flooded Arnald's inbox, and he and the others on the music faculty winnowed the list to a handful of musicians whom they invited to the campus for the interview and audition process. At the end, the unanimous choice was Dr. Anthony Maiello, Professor of Music and Chairman of Performance

---

[78] Today the symphony orchestra is totally composed of GMU students.

at the Crane School of Music, Potsdam College of the State University of New York (SUNY). Since they'd met nearly a decade ago, Arnald and Tony's relationship had evolved from a professional one to becoming close friends; they also shared some striking parallels in their lives.

Tony discovered music in his hometown of Saratoga Springs, New York, at a young age and learned to play the accordion, becoming so accomplished by the time he entered high school that he taught about ten fellow students to play the instrument. He also formed a small dance band and performed at area parties and weddings. Thoughts of pursuing a career in music by attending college was out of the question, however, as his mother worked as a waitress and struggled to support the family after his father passed away when Tony was a young boy. The month after he graduated from high school in July, Tony's music theory teacher, Dr. Robert Campbell, called him into his office and, echoing Arnald's high school teacher, Burton Stanley's words to him nearly twenty years prior, insisted he not waste his musical talent. He needed to apply to college. He also told Tony that the accordion was not a legitimate instrument and instructed him to buy a clarinet and take lessons. Dr. Campbell, a graduate of Ithaca College, set up a meeting with the dean of the school of music at Ithaca, Dr. Craig McHenry. Tony practiced the clarinet five to six hours a day, working to learn the instrument, and after their meeting, Dr. McHenry agreed to allow the young man entry to the college for a one-year trial period to prove himself. Tony Maiello graduated in 1965 with a bachelor of music and in 1967 with a master of music.

Tony had now earned both his undergraduate and graduate degrees at Arnald's alma mater, Ithaca College. Tony remembers music professor Walter Beeler (Arnald's former teacher as well) telling his students that, "If you're good enough, you might be able to play with the Air Force Band. They're the best band in the world!" After graduation, Tony taught high school band for seven years and then applied for and was hired as band director for the Crane School of Music, taking over from none other than retiring Prof. Burton Stanley, Arnald's high school teacher. They became good friends over the ensuing years, and Tony learned more about Arnald's career, becoming more intrigued by the man and his growing reputation for excellence in music and in life.

Arnald and Tony finally met, albeit briefly, when Arnald was invited to conduct the New York All-State Band Festival, held in Potsdam in 1976. A couple of years later, the Crane School of Music offered a stipend to allow advanced study during the summer. Tony was awarded the grant and, working through Burton Stanley to establish the contact, secured a one-hour lesson with Col. Arnald D. Gabriel. He drove from upstate New York to Bolling Air Force Base, and the one-hour conducting lesson lasted for three hours. "It was the best lesson I had in my entire life!" Tony enthused some forty years later. He still owns the cassette recording of the session.

Their paths crossed more regularly when Tony was invited by Festivals of Music to join a select group of adjudicators for a series of spring festivals that included Dr. William Revelli, University of Michigan; Dr. Don McGinnis, Ohio State University; Jay Chattaway, US Navy Band; Jay Bocook, Furman University; and Col. Arnald Gabriel. Five years later, Arnald encouraged Tony to apply for the new position of Director of Bands at George Mason University. After Tony was hired, and working with Dr. Johnson at GMU, Arnald was able to offer him a raise in pay, a full professorship, tenure as of his first day of employment, and moving expenses for his family from Potsdam, New York.

Tony and his family's smooth transition to the new job hit a snag when they arrived in the northern Virginia area. They'd purchased a new home in Herndon, Virginia, and expected to move in when they arrived in the summer of 1986. They were shocked to learn the house was barely under roof and was two and a half months behind schedule. Arriving with his wife, two teenage daughters, and two trucks full of furniture, he had nowhere to live. Arnald immediately suggested the family stay with him and Renee at their home in McLean, but although extremely grateful for the generous offer, he declined to subject the couple to what Tony described as "my personal family drama that had taken over our lives since leaving Potsdam." Arnald then offered to house them in a rental property that he and Renee owned after asking the current tenant to agree to a temporary move; she graciously acquiesced. Arnald charged Tony nothing during his stay.

During Tony's first week on the job, he discovered Arnald's powerful leadership style. Tony asked if the two could meet to discuss his duties, expectations, immediate issues, and anything else Arnald wanted him to do. His answer was simple and to the point: "If I have to tell you what to do, I've hired the wrong person for the job." The clear message was that Tony was in charge of forming and developing the band program and would have all the support he needed. Arnald provided financial support as well by allocating more money for the band program than for the orchestra. Arnald gave Tony a generous two years to build the program before requiring him to perform a public concert, but Tony promised one by the end of the first semester—a tough challenge considering that thirteen students showed up for his first rehearsal, only three of them music majors. Quickly filling the ranks, he was able to stage their first concert in November with forty-two musicians. In the ensuing ten years, he'd build a full symphonic band with seventy-five players and a wind ensemble of forty-five. Dr. Anthony J. Maiello has been at the university for more than thirty years, and beyond his work at the university, he is very active in conducting music festivals, adjudicating, and presenting clinics and workshops both nationally and abroad.

At George Mason, Arnald surrounded himself with some of the best minds in music education. Among these were Dr. Stan Engebretson from the University of Minnesota, chorus; Prof. Tony Maiello, band; Prof. Patricia Miller, Boston University and New England Conservatory, voice; Prof. Dale Underwood, saxophone; and Joe Kanyon who, as the former Chairman of Performing Arts, stepped in to assist Arnald with the myriad administrative details of running the department. The two would meet regularly, and Joe's invaluable help allowed Arnald to concentrate more on the music.

Arnald's choice of Dale Underwood as saxophone professor was another example of a professional relationship that had evolved into a personal one over their years together. Dale is from the small upstate New York town of Cortland, Arnald's hometown. Arnald's fame locally was well established on the day Dale attended the Air Force Band concert in 1966, and Dale remembers, "It was the greatest thing I had ever heard." Dale played in the Cortland High School band and was already an accomplished saxophone player, and because of the US Air Force Band's performance, he decided that's what he wanted to do. He approached several members of the saxophone section after the concert and discovered that no openings would become available for many years due to the men's age and tenure. After music studies at Ithaca College and Texas Tech, he auditioned for and was hired by the Navy Band in Washington, DC. Arnald's and Dale's meetings at Washington-area concerts and the Midwest Clinic became more frequent, and their friendship deepened.

Though they'd occasionally worked together in a combined service band in the Washington area, the first concert Arnald conducted with Dale as soloist wasn't until his hiring at George Mason. That concert was the first of many collaborations the two would enjoy over the ensuing years, including several years of performance at the Brazilian Conservatory of Music in Tatui, Brazil (just outside of Sao Paulo). One concert they played together was particularly noteworthy. In the year 2000, each was invited on a cruise with community band members from around the country, and Arnald shared conducting duties with John Bourgeois, retired leader of the US Marine Band. The Cradle of Civilization cruise visited the cities of Ephesus, Turkey; Athens, Greece; and Rome, Italy, among others. In Rome they had an audience with Pope John Paul II and had an opportunity to play for him. During a papal blessing of Catholic newlyweds that would take about twenty minutes, Arnald asked if the band could play. He was told, "Yes, but keep the pieces short." Arnald turned to Dale and said, "Let's do the Gershwin," a reference to the saxophone piece written for Dale called "A Gershwin Fantasy." In its entirety, it was too long, but to shorten it, Arnald said, "Begin at measure 150." As the blessing began, the band played "It Ain't Necessarily So," and the seventy thousand Catholic faithful heard the band finish with "I've Got Rhythm."

Afterward, the Pope invited Arnald, Dale, and a few others of the band to pose for pictures. At one point, the Pope turned to Dale and said something to him. Later, Arnald asked Dale the nature of the question. Dale deadpanned, "He asked me what kind of reed I use." "No, really," he corrected, "he asked me, 'How the hell did you get in here?' I thought Gabe would never stop laughing," Dale remembers.

As with most military service members, a friendly rivalry exists, and Dale's navy career serves as a constant source of ribbing directed toward Arnald's air force. While backstage waiting for their introductions at a long-forgotten concert, Dale turned to Arnald and said, "You never have thanked the navy."

Caught off guard, Arnald asked, "For what?"

"Well, who took you over and dropped you off on D-day?"

Laughing now, Arnald said, "Yeah, and then they left!"

Dale responded, "Well, we're no fools. They were shooting at you!"

Arnald struggled to regain his composure as they strode onstage.

In the late spring of 1986, Arnald heard of a local northern Virginia orchestra that had fallen on hard times and made a few inquiries as to their needs. The McLean Orchestra is a community, all-volunteer organization that had had some disagreements with their music director and conductor; he'd subsequently left his position to form another orchestra in the same town. Arnald was interviewed by the board of directors and stepped in to help rescue the foundering group. Because many of the musicians had joined the new crosstown rival, Arnald's daunting task was to rebuild the McLean Orchestra from what was left: five brass players. He began to recruit immediately and drew from the George Mason Symphony Orchestra in addition to some of the sources he'd used to build that group. By the fall of 1986, less than six months later, they were able to mount their first concert. In about a year, by the spring of 1987, the McLean Orchestra boasted seventy players, and attendance at their concerts was surging.

Arnald employed the same successful philosophy with the George Mason University Orchestra and the McLean Orchestra that he'd used with the Air Force Band with regard to repertoire and guest performers. He generally had a theme for each concert such as American composers, an evening of opera, or the annual Christmas program. He continued to invite guest artists to perform with each group, and they included familiar local radio personalities, popular vocalists, and world-renowned musicians like his old friend Doc Severinsen. Arnald has a long-held philosophy of performing a cross section of music to attract a wide range of audience members and, naturally, larger crowds. In response to the criticism of "that approach lowers the quality of the music," he says. "In any style of music there is good and bad. The programmer's job is to separate the two and then select only the very best and then prepare and perform it with a professional approach."

The ambitious effort to pull together the best student musicians in Fairfax County was dubbed the Music Spectacular and was held on January 17, 1987. It involved the chorus, band, and orchestras from twenty-three high schools and twenty-two intermediate schools (seventh and eighth grade) from across the county. An astounding assemblage of nearly eight hundred student musicians. Arnald invited four distinguished guest conductors, including Allen Crowell, associate professor at Westminster Choir College, Princeton, New Jersey; Joyce Eilers Bacak, a composer of high school–level choral works; Frank Wickes, director of bands at Louisiana State University; and Paul Hill, the founder and conductor of the Paul Hill Chorale, a highly regarded Washington, DC, based choral group.

Arnald began the concert by conducting the combined choruses in Carmen Dragon's "America the Beautiful," and each guest conductor led, respectively, the best musicians from across Fairfax County, including the Intermediate School Chorus, the High School Orchestra, High School Chorus, and the High School Band. The finale was Boito's powerful *Prologue to the Mephistopheles* with the combined high school orchestra and high school choruses. Arnald added immeasurably to the dramatic effect by positioning antiphonal brass in each of the four corners of the Patriot Center to accompany the young bass soloist Russell Penney. The unmatched experience the students garnered by their participation in the event was echoed by Lynn Arizzi and Moe Turrentine in a letter to Dr. Johnson a few days after the concert: "One of the greatest privileges for us was to work side by side with Colonel Gabriel to produce this event. The Colonel is a man of extraordinary talent and vision. He willingly gave us many, many hours of his time to plan and prepare for the Spectacular. Our students were indeed fortunate to work and perform under his direction. They certainly demonstrated their appreciation of Colonel Gabriel with their spontaneous cheers and ovations the night of the performance."

Gabriel Hall Dedication with daughter Joanne

CHAPTER TWENTY-ONE

Legacy

Arnald's chairmanship of the Performing Arts Department was a position whose term was limited to four years, and at the end of his first term, he was asked to take on another. He agreed, and after completing the second term, he continued to serve the college by conducting the George Mason University Orchestra for another two years. He had always planned to retire from the college after ten years—the workload and pressures of running the department were markedly different from that of a professional military organization. The annual auditions, the academic bureaucracy, the occasional obstinacy of tenured professors, and the vagaries of the student population all combined to make the decision an easy one. By the time he left, he had vastly exceeded Dr. Johnson's expectations and had not only expanded the department, but had raised their standing and respect across academia to the extent that the college leadership bestowed upon him the title of Professor of Music Emeritus, the first ever the school had awarded.

Arnald continued to work with the McLean Orchestra for another ten years, but his primary focus was on guest conducting. He was in high demand across the United States and abroad for college band camps, all-state music festivals, adjudications, and guest directing professional symphonies, as well as community bands and orchestras. He established long-lasting relationships with many organizations, including invitations to the University of Kansas for forty years, the University of Miami for thirty-five, and Stephen F. Austin University for more than twenty years, just to name a few.

Michael A. Gabriel

In recognition of his remarkable career, he has been gathering accolades and tributes from across the world of music and music education. In May 1989, Arnald's alma mater Ithaca College bestowed upon him an honorary doctor of music degree. He has since established a scholarship program at the college in honor of his high school music teacher, Burton Stanley.

Among the many professional organizations to which Arnald belongs, two stand out in their prestige and importance. The National Band Association (NBA) is the largest band organization in the world with more than three thousand members. Arnald was elected to their board of directors and wrote several articles over the years that were published in the magazine *The Instrumentalist*. Arnald was inducted into the NBA Hall of Fame of Distinguished Band Conductors at Troy State University for "having made a national impact on the American band movement." Inducted at the age of sixty-five, he is still the youngest member in the hall to have been honored. He is also the first recipient of their Citation of Excellence.

The American Bandmasters Association (ABA) is an elite group of conductors and composers. Founded in 1929 (with John Philip Sousa as Honorary Life President), of the more than sixty-five thousand conductors and composers in the United States, there are only about three hundred members in ABA. Two sponsors (now three are required) nominated Arnald for membership—Walter Beeler, his college music professor, and Carlton Stewart, conductor of the Mason City High School Band in the 1930s. Carleton Stewart and the C. G. Conn Company instrument salesman Lynn Sams were the inspiration for Professor Harold Hill, the title character in Meredith Willson's *The Music Man*. Arnald is past president and honorary life member of the ABA.

Arnald's association with the Air Force Band has continued since his retirement in 1984 with numerous guest conducting appearances with the orchestra, concert band, and Singing Sergeants. More recently, he has also lent his expertise by meeting with the director of public affairs for the US Air Force and other top brass at the Pentagon. His input has been critical in ensuring the long-term viability of air force bands and in defining strategy, vision, long-range focus,

The Force of Destiny

and utilization of air force bands at home and abroad. Arnald was recognized for his volunteer efforts and tenacious support of Air Force Band personnel in 2015 when the Secretary of the Air Force authorized the issuance of the Exceptional Service Award, one of the highest civilian awards the US Air Force may bestow.

Honoring the Colonel

Shortly after his retirement, the US Air Force recognized his contributions to the band and named him conductor emeritus in 1990, the first Air Force Band commander and conductor to have received the honor. During his ongoing years of service to the Air Force Band and watching no fewer than eight conductors follow him to lead the band, a quiet effort was begun to honor Arnald's current efforts and past legacy. Borne from a general discussion about the rich history of air force bands across the country, a list of readily agreed upon names was drawn up that included: Glenn Miller, Alfred Reed, Alfred Burt, Henry Mancini, Sammy Nestico, John Williams, Samuel Barber, Floyd Werle, Mike Crotty, Mike Davis, Lawrence Odom, David Glazer, Robert Marcellus, Art Will, Larry Wiehe, Jim Murphy, Karen Riale Erler, David Steinmeyer, the Bowman Family, Lowell Graham, and Craig Jessop, among others. Despite the embarrassment of riches they were faced with in regard to some truly talented men and women, their primary discussions centered on one man, Col. Arnald D. Gabriel.

About that same time, Arnald donated his professional papers to the band's library. In addition to the band's outgoing historian, Anthony Kirkland, three members of the US Air Force Band were extremely interested in researching the unit's early history and included: Joe Tersero, the band's chief music librarian; Rob Mesite, a copyist on the Music Production Staff and trombonist with the Ceremonial Brass; and Jari Villanueva, a bugler with the Ceremonial Brass. The team of three started to sift through the treasure trove of information, which included historic photographs, newspaper articles, planners, and other paperwork.

They would soon discover a small newspaper clipping detailing Arnald's award of his two Bronze Star Medals. Arnald, like most World War II veterans, rarely talked about his wartime experiences, preferring instead to talk about the present or of future events. Rob already knew a few of the details about Arnald's World War II service. What all of them realized is the story had to be told; after all, in their minds, the greatest commander and conductor the US Air Force Band has ever had was also a true American patriot—a highly decorated member of the greatest generation.

What they realized was the band was so busy with the successful, yet extremely taxing, performance paradigm Colonel Gabriel had championed so many years ago, they had forgotten to look back at their rich heritage. Up until that time, only eighteen pictures were on display throughout the entire building, hard to believe considering the enormous size of Historic Hangar II. Most members of the band didn't know the organization's historical significance, and almost no one knew about the legendary service of PFC Arnald Gabriel.

An effort was begun to plaster the walls with the band's history and, more importantly, name the band's rehearsal hall in Historic Hangar II on Bolling Air Force Base, Gabriel Hall. All this was spearheaded by Joe Tersero. In addition to holding jobs as instrumentalist with the concert band and symphony orchestra, he also worked in the office as chief music librarian, archivist, and historian. Joe also wanted to honor Floyd Werle for his thirty-year career as chief composer and arranger, whose astounding body of work comprised 982 original compositions and arrangements,[79] by naming the library the Werle Library.

In the US Air Force, the act of memorializing a building or structure through naming is a daunting task wrought with reams of paperwork that must permeate multiple layers of a dense and viscous bureaucracy. Forms were hand carried (the Pentagon's digitalization didn't occur until late in the process and was of little help) between offices located in Washington, DC, Virginia, and Maryland. Then there were the inevitable request for more (or less) information, lost forms,

---

79 By contrast, the prolific bandsman and composer John Philip Sousa counts 937 of his writings.

the need to nearly begin anew because of the relocation of an office, and the seemingly insurmountable obstacle of being told that the request could only be approved if the honorees were dead—none of these frustrations deterred Joe. The process resulted in three hard-copy forms referred to as a Staff Summary Sheet (SSS) and a digital version being sent to eighteen different offices across four states (for some reason, Texas joined the three above), chewing through two years, three months, and eleven days.

The final approval was signed by Vice Chief of Staff Gen. Duncan J. McNabb on September 21, 2007, and the coordination and organization of the dedication ceremony took another three and a half months. As the efforts clumsily stumbled toward the scheduling of an official ceremony, the date was moved several times and, finally, set for January 9, 2008. The date could not have been more auspicious or poignant. Sixty-three years prior, in a frozen field in Germany near the banks of the Rohr River, a mortar detonated in the foxhole Arnald shared with his two wartime buddies. John Arrowsmith and Harry Aschoff instantly lost their lives, while Arnald sustained a concussion. More powerful than the carnage of June 6, the day had always been "the saddest day of my life. For sixty-three years I've shed a tear." Arnald's longtime fascination with the correlation of yin and yang, good and evil, tragedy and happiness has been integral to his way of thinking, and this serendipitous confluence of events served to provide a sorely needed closure. At the end of his remarks at the dedication ceremony, he talked about the sentiment behind the final line from *Saving Private Ryan* when an aged James Francis Ryan (Matt Damon) stood over the grave of Capt. John H. Miller (Tom Hanks). Coming from a very deep, emotional place, Arnald says, "And he said something that every combat veteran has thought a thousand, a million times who watched his comrades give their lives in their devotion to duty: 'I hope I have lived my life well.'"

The (then) current commander and conductor of the band, Col. Dennis Layendecker, closed the emotional ceremony with a heartfelt tribute to both men saying, "Floyd Werle ... the brilliance of this man and the humility of this man make for a wonderful combination of an individual who is a shining example of the kind of individual that makes up our Air Force." Of his former commander, Colonel Layendecker said, "My childhood perception of the Air Force consisted of the TV show *12 O'Clock High* and Col. Arnald D. Gabriel and the Air Force Band. To me, that was the Air Force."

After the dedication of Gabriel Hall, Arnald's healing process felt complete. He'd balanced the memory of his terrible loss as a nineteen-year-old soldier with the deep satisfaction of the high honor he'd received from an organization from which he felt the utmost pride and even love. He would still feel a certain melancholy on January 9, but the feeling of "why not me" would be somewhat attenuated by a greater sense of "having lived my life well." He never suspected that a few short months later he would receive news that would once again have him revisit his memories of Johnny and Harry.

THE ASCHOFF AND ARROWSMITH FAMILIES

Back on October 9, 1998, Arnald had become a charter member of the World War II Memorial being planned for construction on the National Mall between the Lincoln Memorial and the Washington Monument. He sponsored memberships for Pvt. Harry Aschoff, Pvt. John Arrowsmith, and Capt. Stephen Channey,[80] Renee's father. An Internet search some years later revealed the information, and on July 7, 2008, Arnald found this e-mail in his inbox:

> Dear Colonel Gabriel,
>
> Hello, my name is Nancy Aschoff-Pardo. I am the granddaughter of Harry E. Aschoff Sr. who served in WWII with the 175th. He was a machine gunner and I believe you may have served alongside him. My sister and I have been desperately trying to help our dad out for years in finding any information we can regarding his father and she came across your name. My dad was

---

[80] Their respective ranks at the end of the war; Capt. Stephen Channey would retire from the army as a colonel.

only two years old when my grandfather was killed in the war and doesn't have memories of him. If you could give me any information or would perhaps have any pictures of Harry Aschoff from the war, I would love to hear from you.

I have sent a picture of what he looked like during the war.

Best regards,

Nancy Aschoff-Pardo

Arnald answered immediately. Owing to yet more serendipitous timing, he would be in the Orlando area in a few days (where Nancy and her family lived), conducting at the Florida Bandmasters Convention. He met the family for a tear-streaked, laughter-filled lunch and later hosted their attendance at the concert. Arnald learned about Harry Jr., her father, and arrangements were made for him to make the trip from his home in New Jersey to Washington, DC, to attend two concerts that Arnald would guest conduct with the Air Force Band at both the Capitol Building and the Air Force Memorial the following month.

The weekend with Harry Jr. was filled with Arnald's war stories of Harry and Johnny, a tour of the new Gabriel Hall, and meals with the different elements of the boisterous Gabriel family that took on more the flavor of a family reunion than a get-to-know-you time. Harry's partner, Janis Blackburn, was a pilot for Spirit Airlines, my wife, Trish[81] and I were pilots with American Airlines and Harry is a retired aircraft mechanic for Pan American. There was no lull in the conversation the afternoon we spent with them.

The final afternoon was a concert at the Air Force Memorial, and at its conclusion, Harry and Janis readied for their drive back to northern New Jersey. For Harry, the weekend had filled a void in his life he'd never been able to reconcile; he'd only been told that his dad had lost his life fighting in Germany. Harry didn't even know the

---

81 As of this writing, Trish is still a pilot with American.

whereabouts of his grave. To have made a connection with the man who had shared the same foxhole on his father's final day made a profound impression on him. Hearing the stories brought to life a man he never knew yet always thought about. Walking to the car to say good-bye, Harry, a large man who towers over Arnald and is generally reticent about showing his emotions, turned to him and in a most beautiful, heartbreaking way asked, "I want to ask you something, but first, I want a hug." Then, after the bear hug, he said, "Would you be my dad?" A tidal wave of emotion choked any words, but Arnald's embrace of Harry Aschoff's son said it all.

Two years later, through nothing more than the dogged persistence of Nancy Aschoff-Pardo, contact was made with the family of Johnny Arrowsmith. Through social media, Nancy made contact with a cousin and after some vetting to assure her veracity, the information was passed along to Frances Arrowsmith, Johnny's daughter. After a few e-mails and phone conversations, Fran called Arnald in 2010 on her father's birthday, July 4. Fran knew little about her father because her mother never spoke of him, and her grandmother was so devastated by the loss she attempted to throw herself into the wringer washing machine. They were aware of his final resting place at the Netherlands American Cemetery in Margraten, Netherlands, and Fran had made an emotional visit to the gravesite while on a trip with her Army Reserve Unit (she is a nurse) several years prior.

Because of the fortunate meetings, Arnald, Harry, and Francis have formed a special bond that closes a broken linkage of nearly seven decades. The promises made on the 40-and-8 railway in the early fall of 1944 between three army buddies included not only to return to the grave of the man who was lost, but also a vow to look up his family. Arnald, however, thought it best not to "resurrect old wounds" and chose not to search out the families. "I was wrong," Arnald says regretfully. "The Aschoff family was thrilled to find someone who knew Harry." The sentiment was echoed by the Arrowsmith family, and Fran was thrilled to have learned more about her father, but throughout her life, she's clung to an idea that had allowed her to cope with the loss: "That my father wasn't dead and that he had survived,

The Force of Destiny

leading another life." The bittersweet meeting with Arnald "confirmed the reality, not the fantasy."

The following May, Arnald invited Harry Jr. and Fran to a concert at the Kennedy Center where he was to guest conduct the Air Force Symphony Orchestra for their Memorial Day Concert. Prior to mounting the podium, Arnald explained to the gathered patrons the special meaning "Hymn to the Fallen" has had for him and offered his dedication of the piece to his two new friends. He turned to the box where his guests of honor sat, introduced them to the audience, and came to attention, snapping a salute that traveled decades into the past, not to a foxhole in Germany but to three wartime friends who, together, found their strength and courage and formed a lasting friendship that endures today.

~FINIS~

Printed in the United States
By Bookmasters